T0322121

TIMELINES OF WORLD HISTORY

TIMELINES OF WORLD HISTORY

Penguin Random House

**Produced for DK by
cobalt id**
www.cobaltid.co.uk

Editors Marek Walisiewicz, Johnny Murray
Designers Paul Tilby, Paul Reid

Senior Editor Hugo Wilkinson
Senior Art Editor Duncan Turner
Managing Editor Angeles Gavira Guerrero
Managing Art Editor Michael Duffy
Production Editor Robert Dunn
Production Controller Meskerem Berhane
Senior Jackets Designer Surabhi Wadhwa-Gandhi

**Jackets Design Development
Manager** Sophia MTT
DTP Designer Ashok Kumar
Art Director Karen Self
Design Director Phil Ormerod
Associate Publishing Director Liz Wheeler
Publishing Director Jonathan Metcalf

First published in Great Britain in 2022 by
Dorling Kindersley Limited
20 Vauxhall Bridge Road,
London SW1V 2SA

The authorised representative in the EEA is
Dorling Kindersley Verlag GmbH. Arnulfstr. 124,
80636 Munich, Germany

Copyright © 2022 Dorling Kindersley Limited
A Penguin Random House Company
10 9 8 7 6 5 4 3
024-325054-May/2022

All rights reserved.
No part of this publication may be reproduced,
stored in or introduced into a retrieval system,
or transmitted, in any form, or by any means
(electronic, mechanical, photocopying, recording,
or otherwise), without the prior written permission
of the copyright owner.

A CIP catalogue record for this book
is available from the British Library.
ISBN: 978-0-2415-1575-4

Printed and bound in India

www.dk.com

MIX
Paper | Supporting
responsible forestry
FSC™ C018179

This book was made with Forest
Stewardship Council™ certified
paper – one small step in DK's
commitment to a sustainable future.
Learn more at www.dk.com/uk/
information/sustainability

CONTRIBUTORS

Tony Allen
Tony Allen has written many works on history for the general reader and was Series Editor for the 24-volume *Time-Life History of the World*.

Dr Kay Celtel
A writer and historian, Kay Celtel has written numerous popular books on subjects ranging from history to architecture, culture, and literature.

R. G. Grant
Historian R. G. Grant is a prolific author of books for adults and children, covering a wide range of topics in cultural, technological, and military history.

Ann Kramer
Having studied history at Sussex University, Ann Kramer has written on topics ranging from women's experiences of war through to black American history.

Philip Parker
Philip Parker is a historian specializing in the medieval world, and has written numerous books including on the Romans, Vikings, and several historical atlases.

Marcus Weeks
Musician and author Marcus Weeks has written and contributed to many books on philosophy, the arts, and the history of the ancient world.

CONSULTANTS

Professor Michael Fisher
Robert S. Danforth Professor of History, Emeritus, Oberlin College, USA

Dr Connor Judge
Postdoctoral Fellow in China Studies, Somaiya Vidyavihar University, India

Professor Tyesha Maddox
Professor of African Diaspora History, Fordham University, USA

Dr Angélica Baena Ramírez
Former professor of History, Acatlan National Autonomous University of Mexico. Guest researcher and lecturer, UNAM UK and UK Mexican Arts Society

CONTENTS

1700–1799

1800–1879

1880–1934

1935–1979

1980–2021

170

202

232

258

288

Commissioned by Mughal emperor Shah Jahan as a mausoleum for his wife Mumtaz Mahal, the white marble Taj Mahal in Agra is considered to be the pinnacle of Indo-Islamic architecture. Begun in 1632, the perfectly symmetrical building took 16 years to complete.

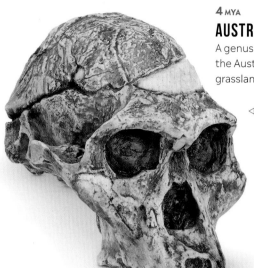

4 MYA
AUSTRALOPITHECINES FLOURISH
A genus of early hominins capable of walking upright, the Australopithecines, began to thrive on the grasslands of Africa.

◁ Replica *Australopithecus africanus* skull, named "Mrs Ples"

1.9 MYA
USE OF SPECIALIZED TOOLS
Homo erectus ("upright man"), a descendant of the Australopithecines, evolved. Recognizably different from the earlier ape-like ancestors of humans, *Homo erectus* developed the skill of chipping stone to make sophisticated cutting and hunting tools, and about one million years ago learned how to make and use fire.

2.5 MYA *Homo habilis* emerges and uses simple stone tools

△ **Stone hand-axe** of the lower Palaeolithic

4 MYA

300 KYA *Homo sapiens,* the first modern humans, appear in Africa

▷ **Fossilized headless** remains of a young Neanderthal man

400 KYA
NEANDERTHALS APPEAR
Neanderthals, named after the Neander Valley in Germany where they were discovered in 1856, first began to appear in Europe and Asia. They were well adapted to the colder climate of the north, and flourished there until about 40 KYA. Contrary to popular belief, the Neanderthals were intelligent and inventive, and as well as being skilled toolmakers, made clothes and footwear, and had a culture that included burial of the dead.

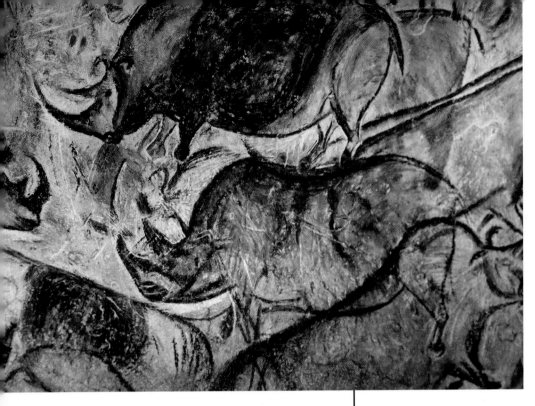

46–40 KYA
PAINTINGS APPEAR ON CAVE WALLS

The earliest known representational art, dating from more than 45,500 years ago, was discovered on the walls of caves in Sulawesi, Indonesia. Although some non-figurative cave decoration predates this, it marks the beginning of a period of cave painting in various locations in Indonesia, France, and the Iberian peninsula. At the same time, the first representational sculptures appeared in Europe, carved in bone, ivory, and stone.

◁ **A painting** from Chauvet Cave in France

200 KYA Human migration from Africa into Europe and Asia begins

62 KYA The bow and arrow replaces the spear for hunting smaller game

10,000 BCE

20 KYA The craft of pottery develops in China

◁ **The polar ice cap** in the Last Glacial Period

113 KYA
100,000 YEAR ICE AGE BEGINS

The climate change that had begun in about 200 KYA accelerated, marking the beginning of the Last Glacial Period, an ice age that lasted for over 100,000 years. As it intensified, the expanding ice sheet forced human populations southwards.

14–12 KYA
FIRST HUMAN SETTLEMENTS

The Last Glacial Period was followed by a rapid warming, bringing major environmental changes. Large animals adapted to the ice age, such as the mammoth, died out, causing a shortage of big game for hunting. The new conditions forced a change in human behaviour: people largely abandoned the nomadic hunter-gatherer existence in favour of a settled lifestyle in small communities, prompting the development of domestic utensils such as pottery.

◁ **Reconstruction of** Jōmon pot, Japan

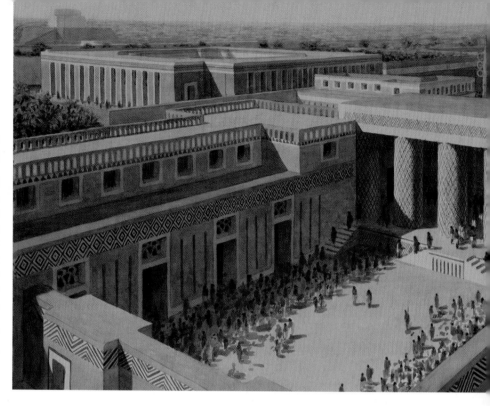

c. 4100–2900 BCE
CITY-STATES APPEAR IN MESOPOTAMIA

One of the earliest civilizations, Sumer, emerged as settlements appeared in the region between the Tigris and Euphrates rivers in present-day Iraq. Many of these villages developed into larger urban centres. The most important of these was Uruk, the first true city, which became the political and cultural centre of the region. At its height, the city-state of Uruk had up to 80,000 inhabitants, about half of whom lived in the city itself.

▷ **White temple at Uruk,** modern visualization

10,000 BCE

c. 5500–2800 BCE Settlements in the Indus Valley mark the beginnings of the early Harappan Civilization

c. 8000 BCE Walled settlements, such as Jericho, arise, offering defence against flood as well as invasion

c. 5000–3520 BCE Small villages are established during the Early Jōmon period in Japan

The first metals to be worked were gold and copper

c. 9500 BCE
TEMPLES OF GOBEKLI TEPE

A complex of circles of stone pillars was constructed in Anatolia, southeastern Turkey, at the site known now as Göbekli Tepe. The intricately carved, T-shaped pillars were set in sockets cut into the rock floor. They were arranged in circular layouts believed to have had a religious or ritual purpose, making them the earliest known religious structures in the world.

◁ **Circular temple** at Göbekli Tepe

3100 BCE
NARMER UNIFIES EGYPT

The two kingdoms of Upper and Lower Egypt were unified by Narmer (also known as Menes), who then became the founder of the First Dynasty, the first pharaoh of the Early Dynastic Period. His momentous achievement was commemorated in the images and hieroglyphics inscribed on artefacts such as the "Narmer Palette", an ornamental tablet for grinding and mixing cosmetics.

▷ The Narmer palette

c. 4500 BCE Metal smelting develops from the extraction of copper from ore in fires

c. 3500 BCE Huaricanga, the first city of the Norte Chico civilization in Peru, is founded

c. 3500 BCE The earliest earthwork complex in North America is constructed at Watson Brake, Louisiana

3000 BCE

c. 3500 BCE
EARLY WHEELED TRANSPORT

As farmers in Mesopotamia domesticated larger animals, such as cattle and donkeys, they realized their potential as draught animals for drawing a plough or pulling a cart. Using solid wooden wheels, the Sumerians built four-wheeled carts for agricultural use. Chariots for military and ceremonial purposes modelled on these carts soon followed.

△ **Sumerian chariot** depicted on the Standard of Ur

c. 9500–3500 BCE
EVOLUTION OF AGRICULTURE

The adoption of agriculture and abandonment of the nomadic lifestyle prepared the ground for the first settled civilizations.

c. 9500 BCE In the "fertile crescent" of Egypt and western Asia, people harvest and later cultivate wild grasses.

c. 8500 BCE Goats and sheep are the first animals to be domesticated as agriculture becomes established in the Middle East.

c. 5000–3000 BCE The Yangshao Culture emerges in China from the Yellow River to parts of Gansu. The people grow mainly millet.

3500 BCE Early forms of plough are invented in several different places; cattle and donkeys are used as draught animals.

△ **The god Anubis** mummifies a corpse, painting at Tomb of Amennakht

c. 2686–2181 BCE

MUMMIFICATION DEVELOPED

In the Egyptian Old Kingdom (c. 2686–2181 BCE), the bodies of the pharaohs, their families and other nobles, were preserved by a process of mummification, embalmed and wrapped in cloth, before being entombed with a wealth of funerary treasures.

c. 3000 BCE The Elam civilization emerges along the eastern side of the Persian Gulf

c. 2560 BCE The Great Pyramid of Giza, tomb of the pharaoh Khufu, is completed

3000 BCE

c. 3000 BCE Construction of Stonehenge begins on Salisbury Plain in the west of England

c. 2600 BCE The first stepped pyramids are built in Caral, the major city of the Norte Chico civilization, Peru

c. 2900 BCE

CUNEIFORM WRITING SYSTEM

The Mesopotamians of Sumer devised a method of recording transactions by making impressions in soft clay with a stick. These simple tally marks developed into a sophisticated writing system using wedge-shaped (cuneiform) symbols to represent words and syllables, rather than the pictograms used in hieroglyphics.

△ **Clay tablet** with cuneiform inscription

2334–2279 BCE

SARGON THE GREAT OF AKKAD

Through his conquests of neighbouring kingdoms, Sargon extended his rule from Akkad (east of the Tigris), becoming the first leader to rule over an empire of subject city-states.

"Only the gods dwell forever in sunlight. As for man, his days are numbered."

EPIC OF GILGAMESH, *MESOPOTAMIAN POEM*, c. 2100 BCE

2112–2095 BCE
GREAT ZIGGURAT BUILT IN UR

After freeing his city from Akkadian and Gutian rule, King Ur-Nammu of Ur founded the neo-Sumerian Third dynasty of Ur. He built a huge ziggurat (step pyramid) in honour of the god Nannar. The monumental structure fell into disrepair after the fall of the Third Dynasty, but was rebuilt in the 6th century BCE by Nabonidus, king of Babylonia.

△ **Ziggurat of Ur,** restored and rebuilt

c. 2334–2279 BCE Sargon the Great conquers Sumer and Mesopotamia and founds the Akkadian Empire

c. 2150 BCE The kingdom of Nubia is established in the region to the south of Egypt

c. 2100–2000 BCE The Epic of Gilgamesh is written on tablets in the Sumerian language

2000 BCE

c. 2200 BCE Iron smelting is developed in Anatolia by the Hittites; they keep the process a closely guarded secret

c. 2134 BCE The Egyptian Middle Kingdom is founded as Mentuhotep II reunifies Egypt

▽ **Mohenjo-Daro,** city ruins

c. 2500 BCE
CONSTRUCTION OF MOHENJO-DARO

The Harappan civilization of the Indus Valley reached its peak between 2600 and 1900 BCE. It contained several cities, including Harappa and Mohenjo-daro, with populations of about 50,000. Mohenjo-daro in particular was notable for its brick buildings, methodical urban planning, and sophisticated irrigation and sewage systems.

2070–1600 BCE
XIA DYNASTY IN CHINA

According to tradition, Yu the Great founded the Xia Dynasty – the first of the Chinese dynasties – when the Mandate of Heaven was bestowed on him by the last of the mythical Five Sovereigns. Yu became legendary not only for instigating dynastic rule in China, but also for his benevolent and wise leadership. Foremost among his achievements was the work he commissioned to control the persistent floods that threatened his homeland in central China.

△ **Yu the Great,** legendary founder of the Xia dynasty

c. 2700–2200 BCE

THE AGE OF THE PYRAMIDS

The Old Kingdom of Egypt is often referred to as "The Age of the Pyramids", because it encompasses the reigns of the great pyramid-building kings of the Third (2686–2613 BCE) to the Sixth (2345–2181 BCE) Dynasties. In the 500-year period from about 2700 BCE, architects developed the techniques to quarry limestone, transport huge quantities of the stone, and assemble the massive monuments that became symbolic of the majesty of ancient Egypt.

The first Egyptian pyramids appeared in the reign of King Djoser, in the Third Dynasty. Djoser moved his royal capital to Memphis, and embarked upon a programme of building works to establish his court. This included the construction of a necropolis complex in nearby Saqqara overseen by his architect Imhotep, who is credited with the design of the first pyramid. The simple step pyramid at Saqqara inspired Djoser's successors in the Fourth Dynasty, such as King Sneferu, to refine the design to create a true pyramid. Pyramid-building reached its high point with the construction of the great pyramids at Meidum and Dashur, and the famous pyramid complex at Giza, built for kings Khufu, Khafre, and Menkaure.

KEY MOMENTS

27th century BCE **Early step pyramids**

The first Egyptian pyramids were tiered structures, built by adding successively smaller storeys of stone blocks onto a square or rectangular base. The model for these was Djoser's Pyramid at Saqqara (*left*), which rose to a height of over 60 m (196 ft) in six steps.

26th century BCE **First true pyramids**

Architects of the Fourth Dynasty used much smaller steps to build a smoother pyramidal shape rising to a point, such as the Bent Pyramid of Dashur (*left*). The effect was further enhanced by cladding the structure with polished white limestone slabs.

26th century BCE **The Sphinx**

Alongside the Giza pyramid complex is another iconic ancient Egyptian structure, the Sphinx (*left*). Carved from the bedrock (but later restored with blocks of limestone), it is a colossal statue of the mythical cat-like sphinx, with the face of the then reigning King Khafre.

The pyramids of Giza were built in the 26th–25th centuries BCE as tombs for kings. The pyramid of Khafre, shown here, is the second tallest of the structures, and was originally 143 m (471 feet) high. It is the only pyramid of the three with part of the original limestone casing still in place.

1900 BCE
STONEHENGE COMPLETED

Built at the centre of circular earthworks dating back to about 3000 BCE, the stone monument now known as Stonehenge was completed some 1,000 years later. Huge standing stones topped with lintels were arranged in a ring around a horseshoe-shape of smaller stones, with an altar stone at the centre. Because the structure, and the avenue leading to it, are aligned with the sunrise at the summer solstice, it is believed to have had a religious or astronomical purpose.

△ **Stonehenge,** stone circle

c. 1900 BCE
THE AMORITE CONQUEST

The Amorites, a Semitic people from the Levant, traded in Akkadian Mesopotamia during the 21st century BCE. They came to occupy much of the southern part of the region, setting up independent city-states. One of these, Babylon, came to particular prominence as the capital of what was to become the First Babylonian Empire.

▽ Old Babylonian relief

2000 BCE

c. 1900 BCE **The Hittites** establish their empire with its capital in Hattusa, Anatolia

1772 BCE **King Hammurabi of Babylon** issues a law code that shifts emphasis from compensation of the victim to punishment of the offender

c. 1900 BCE
MINOAN PALACES

The Minoan civilization became established on the island of Crete in about 3000 BCE. It became a major trading power in the Mediterranean, and its prosperity is apparent in the impressive palaces – mainly administrative buildings – built from around 1900 BCE onwards in cities such as Knossos, Phaistos, and on the island of Thera (Santorini). These were often several storeys high, fitted with plumbing systems, and typically lavishly decorated.

△ **Palace of Knossos,** now partly restored and rebuilt

▽ Ahmose I, limestone statue

1549–1069 BCE
EGYPT NEW KINGDOM

Under Ahmose I – founder of the Eighteenth Dynasty – Egypt was reunified after the expulsion of the Hyksos rulers from the Nile Delta. So began Egypt's most powerful period, the New Kingdom of Egypt, which saw the empire extend into Nubia and western Asia. In keeping with his Theban heritage, Ahmose moved the site of royal tombs from the pyramids to the Valley of the Kings near Thebes.

c. 1650 BCE Northern Egypt is occupied by invaders from the Levant, the Hyksos, the first foreign rulers of Egypt

c. 1600 BCE A catastrophic volcanic eruption on Thera (Santorini) triggers the decline of the Minoan civilization

c. 1600 BCE Global climate begins to cool, possibly as a result of volcanic eruptions around the world

1595–1530 BCE The Hittites and Kassites use iron weapons and horse-drawn chariots in their invasion of Babylon

◁ **Oracle bone** from Shang dynasty

c. 1810–1750 BCE
KING HAMMURABI

Now remembered for introducing his eponymous Babylonian law code, Hammurabi was revered in his own time for expanding the Babylonian Empire across almost all of Mesopotamia.

c. 1600 BCE
SHANG DYNASTY ESTABLISHED

After the semi-mythical Xia Dynasty, the Yellow River valley was ruled by the first Chinese kings for whom there is firm evidence – the Shang Dynasty. It was founded by Chen Tang, victor of the Battle of Mingtiao against the Xia. Artefacts made from bronze, jade, and ceramic, and oracle bones (bones inscribed with characters and used for divination) attest to the cultural sophistication of the Shang.

c. 1500 BCE
NOK CULTURE EMERGES

The Nok culture, named after the village of Nok where its artefacts were first discovered, began to develop in what is today Nigeria. Best known for their stylized terracotta figures, the Nok people also discovered iron-smelting at around the same time as the Iron Age was getting under way in Europe and Asia. Their civilization was very long-lived, lasting until its sudden and mysterious disappearance in about 500 CE.

◁ **Nok** terracotta figure

1500 BCE

c. 1400 BCE Vedic Sanskrit-speaking peoples migrate into India from the northwest and then spread out across north India

1336 BCE Pharaoh Tutankhamun and his queen Nefertiti restore the old Egyptian religion

1348 BCE Religious reforms instituted in Egypt by Pharaoh Akhenaten reject old gods in favour of sun worship

1300 BCE Urnfield culture, named after the practice of storing cremated ashes in urns, emerges in central Europe

△ **Assyrian cylinder seal** with its impression

c. 1400 BCE
ASSYRIANS ASSERT INDEPENDENCE

After centuries of existing as disparate subject states of successive Akkadian and Babylonian empires in Mesopotamia, the Assyrians began to emerge as a single independent power.

1500–500 BCE
THE IRON AGE

Iron smelting was developed in Asia, became widespread in the Middle East in the 12th century BCE, and slowly spread around the world.

c. 1500 BCE The Hittites in Anatolia develop techniques of iron-working (as seen in the axe head, *above*), but closely guard the secrets to maintain their superiority over neighbouring states.

c. 1000 BCE Iron technology spreads into western Asia and Europe, reaching as far north as the Shetland Islands (*above*). It is also discovered by the Nok of West Africa.

c. 500 BCE Chinese metalworkers learn the processes of smelting and working iron and begin producing intricate pieces, such as this gold-inlaid belt hook (*above*).

1264–1244 BCE
RAMESES II EXPANDS EGYPT

Under pharaoh Rameses II, the Egyptian Empire extended southwards into gold-rich Nubia. As well as subjugating the Nubian people, Rameses II instigated a huge construction project in his Nubian territory as a lasting symbol of Egyptian power. This took the form of two massive temples cut into the rock at Abu Simbel, with giant relief figures carved into their facades: the Great Temple dedicated to Rameses himself; and the Small Temple to his chief wife Nefertari.

◁ **Rameses II** depicted in a temple relief

c. 1200 BCE The kingdom of Lydia is established in Asia Minor after the decline of the Hittite empire

c. 1100–800 BCE The Greek Dark Ages begin after the fall of the Mycenaeans

1000 BCE

c. 1200 BCE Chavín culture emerges in the Peruvian Andes

c. 1100 BCE The seagoing Phoenicians rise to become a major Mediterranean power

1046 BCE The Zhou Dynasty conquers the ruling Shang Dynasty in China

c. 1200 BCE
OLMEC CULTURE

The earliest known civilization in Mesoamerica, the Olmec culture, developed from settlements in the Gulf region of Mexico, having its centre first in San Lorenzo and later at La Venta. A prominent feature of the Olmec culture was its stone carving. As well as carved masks and axe heads presumed to be for ritual use, the Olmecs produced a number of massive sculptures in volcanic basalt, known as the "colossal heads".

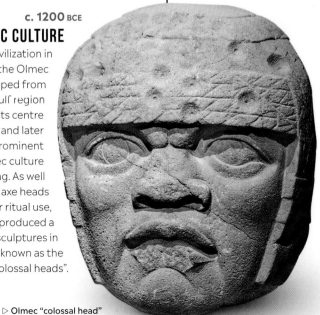

▷ Olmec "colossal head"

The Phoenicians' most important trading commodity was purple dye obtained from the murex sea snail

c. 1000 BCE
KINGDOM OF KUSH

With the collapse of the Egyptian New Kingdom, the Nubians, who had been subjugated by the Egyptians, regained control of their lands. They founded the independent Kingdom of Kush, with its capital at Napata (present-day Karima, Sudan). Within only a couple of centuries, the Nubians controlled Upper Egypt and installed a Kushite dynasty that went on to rule all of Egypt.

▷ **Pottery** from the Kingdom of Kush

c. 969–936 BCE
TYRE PROSPERS UNDER HIRAM I

The city of Tyre was perfectly placed for trade on the coast of what is now Lebanon. Under King Hiram I, Tyre became a hub for much of the region's commerce. A major attraction for merchants was the programme of building works Hiram initiated, providing warehouse facilities in the fortified city.

▷ **Carved head** from Phoenician Tyre

c. 1000 BCE King David unites the Israelite tribes and conquers the city of Jerusalem

1000 BCE

c. 1000 BCE Adena culture starts to develop along the Ohio River in North America

▷ Phoenician merchant ship, relief

c. 1000 BCE
PHOENICIAN PORTS

The Phoenicians were the dominant maritime power in the eastern Mediterranean by the turn of the 10th century BCE. They began founding ports to facilitate the movement of goods around the Middle East: ports such as Tyre, Sidon, and Byblos gradually expanded and became prosperous autonomous city-states.

c. 1035?–970? BCE
KING DAVID

According to Biblical narrative, David was a shepherd and musician who rose to power after killing the Philistine giant Goliath. He succeeded Saul as king of Israel, and led his people into Jerusalem.

c. 950 BCE
NEO-ASSYRIAN EMPIRE

Emerging from a "Dark Age" of decline that had afflicted much of the Middle East for more than a century, Assyria began to re-establish its empire. By the time Adad-nirari II came to the throne in 911 BCE, the foundations for a Neo-Assyrian Empire had been laid, and under his leadership it conquered much of Mesopotamia and beyond. Its expansion made it the largest and most powerful empire the world had yet seen.

△ Assyrian bas-relief

Hiram I supplied Solomon with cedar wood from Lebanon to build the Temple in Jerusalem

c. 930 BCE After Solomon's death, his kingdom divides into Israel in the north, and Judah in the south

901 BCE

c. 910 BCE Scythia, in central Eurasia, becomes home to nomadic people from the steppes of Asia

c. 950 BCE
FIRST TEMPLE BUILT IN JERUSALEM

According to tradition, King David brought the Ark of the Covenant to Jerusalem. However, it was his son Solomon who had a temple built to house it when he succeeded to the throne of Israel. The First Temple, as it became known, was the spiritual and cultural centre of the city, situated on Mount Moriah (the Temple Mount), until it was destroyed by Babylonians in 586 BCE.

▷ Map of Jerusalem

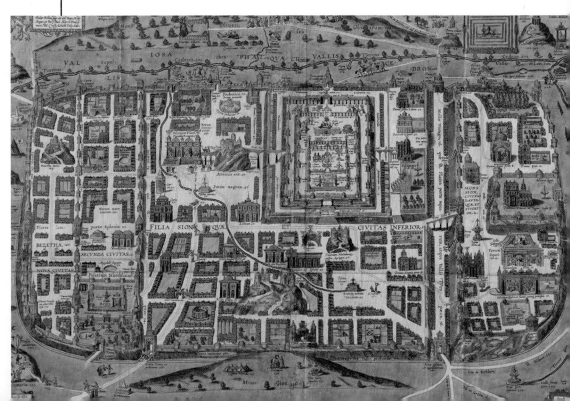

c. 900–400 BCE
ETRUSCAN CIVILIZATION

Several city-states began to flourish in northern Italy in the 9th century BCE, evolving into a civilization with a distinctive Etruscan culture. This prevailed for several centuries before becoming assimilated into the Roman state. Much of what is known about Etruscan society comes from artworks found in family tombs, including wall-paintings, pottery, and bronze sculptures.

c. 890–824 BCE
SHALMANESER III
Throughout his reign from about 859 BCE until his death in 824 BCE, Shalmaneser III waged a relentless campaign to continue the expansion of the Assyrian Empire begun by his father.

▷ **Etruscan** boar-shaped vessel

900 BCE

c. 900 BCE Phoenicians extend their influence across the Mediterranean, establishing colonies in North Africa and Southern Spain

Glyphs found at La Venta suggest that the Olmecs may have been the first New World civilization to devise a system of writing

c. 900 BCE
RISE OF CHAVIN CULTURE
A civilization that emerged in the northern Peruvian Andes established its centre at the location of (modern) Chavín de Huantar. The city built here included a complex of religious and ceremonial buildings adorned with typically Andean stone carvings.

◁ **Chavín gold** pectoral decoration

△ **Decoration** on the Gates of Shalmaneser III, Nimrud

863 BCE
NIMRUD BECOMES ASSYRIAN CAPITAL

The Neo-Assyrian Empire strengthened in the 9th century BCE. When Ashurnasirpal II became king, he embarked on a ruthless campaign of expansion, restoring Assyria to its former glory and power. He moved his capital from Assur to Nimrud (also known as Kalhu) where he built opulent palaces. After his death, his son Shalmaneser III enthusiastically continued in his father's footsteps.

872 BCE The Temple of Luxor, Egypt, is inundated by severe flooding of the Nile

836 BCE Civil war breaks out in Egypt after a power struggle between factions of the royal family

801 BCE

c. 850 BCE The Kingdom of Van (in modern Armenia) asserts its independence from the Assyrian Empire under the reign of King Arame of Urartu

◁ The Great Pyramid, La Venta

c. 900 BCE
OLMEC CULTURE MOVES TO LA VENTA

After the Olmec city at San Lorenzo was badly damaged, perhaps by environmental change, its inhabitants set up a new centre in La Venta, about 75 km (45 miles) to the northeast. The new city was built on a grand scale, with paved roads, and dominated by a massive clay pyramid. Among the numerous artefacts discovered by archaeologists are ceremonial jade axes, sculpture, and pottery.

c. 814 BCE
FOUNDING OF CARTHAGE

Legend surrounds the founding of the city of Carthage by the Phoenicians on the coast of present-day Tunisia. The most enduring account is that of Dido (or Elissa) from Tyre, who purchased the land and became its first queen. What is not in doubt, however, is that it evolved from a Phoenician colony into a thriving city-state, the capital of a powerful Carthaginian Empire.

▷ **Carthaginian** clay protome

c. 800 BCE
VEDIC PERIOD

The composition of Sanskrit texts, the Brahmanas, and the first of the Upanishads, marked the beginning of what is known as the later Vedic period of the Indo-Vedic civilization of northern India. These sacred texts, with others, were arranged into collections, the four Vedas, which were the foundation for Brahmanic religions. The texts were also the cornerstone of the principles of the Kuru regional culture, influencing the development of its hierarchical social structure.

◁ **The sage Vyasa** talks to King Janamejaya of the royal Kuru clan, codifier of the Vedic texts

800 BCE

c. 800 BCE The Hellenic people of city-states such as Sparta, Athens, and Thebes spread from mainland Greece to colonies around the Aegean

776 BCE
FIRST PAN-HELLENIC OLYMPIC GAMES

According to tradition, Olympia hosted the first pan-Hellenic Games in 776 BCE. A religious festival and athletic competition, the games also had a political purpose, both fostering relationships between participating Greek city-states, and rekindling old rivalries. The ancient Olympic Games were held every four years, and continued even under Roman rule until the 4th century CE.

▷ **Naked Greek athletes** depicted on an amphora

771 BCE
EASTERN ZHOU DYNASTY BEGINS IN CHINA

After the invasion of the Zhou capital, Haojing, by barbarians, the royal family were forced to flee eastward, making Luoyi the capital of the Eastern Zhou Dynasty. This heralded the beginning of a period of decline of the power of the Zhou kings, and a fragmentation of the region into more autonomous states. This first half of the Eastern Zhou dynasty became known as the Spring and Autumn Period (722–481 BCE), named after an official chronicle of the state of Lu, the *Spring and Autumn Annals*.

◁ **The sword of Goujian,** king of Yue, one of the hegemons of the period

753 BCE

FOUNDING OF ROME

The enduring foundation myth of the city of Rome tells the story of the twin sons of the god Mars, Romulus and Remus. Left to die on the banks of the Tiber as babies, they were rescued and suckled by a she-wolf. They returned to the site as adults, intent on building a city there. A dispute over where to locate the city led to the death of Remus, after which Romulus founded Rome on the Palatine Hill in 753 BCE and reigned as its first king.

◁ Romulus and Remus suckled by a she-wolf

> "Rome has grown since its humble beginnings that it is now overwhelmed by its own greatness"

LIVY, HISTORY OF ROME, *10 BCE*

745–727 BCE The Assyrian Empire expands across Mesopotamia, out to the Mediterranean, and from Scythia in the north to the Arabian peninsula

701 BCE

c. 750 BCE King Piye of Kush invades Egypt and establishes a Nubian 25th Dynasty

c. 750 BCE The epic poems of Homer are written down for the first time, using a Phoenician-style alphabet

8th century BCE
HOMER
Author of the *The Iliad* and *The Odyssey*, Homer is a legendary figure. As part of an oral tradition, it is possible that poems ascribed to him are in fact the work of several authors over a long period.

▷ Pyramids of Meroë Sudan, Africa

c. 720 BCE

CONSTRUCTION OF THE PYRAMIDS AT MEROE

In the 8th century, the capital of the Kingdom of Kush was at Napata, but several members of the royal family originated from further south, in the city of Meroë. This became the chosen burial site for this side of the family, and a tomb complex was built there in 720 BCE. The pyramids containing the tombs were in the Nubian style, with steep sides.

685–668 BCE
SPARTA EMERGES AS THE DOMINANT POWER IN GREECE

Sparta regarded strength and discipline as ideals, and produced an army of fearless fighting men, conspicuous in the battlefield in their distinctive battle dress and crested helmets. As a result, in the 7th century BCE it emerged as the foremost military power in Greece, valuable as an ally, and dangerous as an enemy.

▷ Spartan warrior, bronze

660 BCE
LEGENDARY FIRST EMPEROR OF JAPAN

According to tradition, Jimmu, a descendant of Amaterasu the sun goddess, became the first Emperor of Japan after conquering the whole country. There is little historical evidence of his existence, and the legend appears to be a conflation of mythology and real events. Nevertheless, the supposed date of his accession, 11 February, is still celebrated in Japan as National Foundation Day.

700 BCE

689 BCE The city of Babylon is destroyed by Assyrian emperor Sennacherib

671 BCE Egyptian capital Memphis is captured by Assyrian king Esarhaddon; it is regained by the Egyptians eight years later

c. 700 BCE
EXPANSION OF NINEVEH

Sennacherib came to the throne of the Neo-Assyrian Empire in 705 BCE. As well as continuing the expansion of the empire, he set about moving the capital to the city of Nineveh. This involved an extensive programme of renovation in the old city, centred around a "Palace without a rival", making it one of the largest and most important cities in the world at that time.

◁ Sennacherib's "Palace without a Rival"

△ **Emperor Jimmu** and the rising sun

7th century BCE

CHINA'S HUNDRED SCHOOLS OF THOUGHT

Philosophy flourished in the Eastern Zhou period in China. The diverse systems that emerged became known as the Hundred Schools of Thought, and included such thinkers as Laozi (founder of Daoism), Kong Fuzi (or Confucius, founder of Confucianism), Mozi (Mohism), and Hang Feizi (Legalism).

△ **Laozi** riding an ox

621 BCE **The so-called "Age of Tyrants"** begins in many Greek city-states

620–600 BCE **True coins** are used as currency for the first time In Lydia (modern Turkey)

601 BCE

620 BCE **Draco sets out the first law** code in Athens (hence "draconian")

612 BCE **The collapse of the Neo-Assyrian Empire** is triggered by the destruction of Nineveh by rebelling Babylonians and Medes

▽ **Stela** of Ashurbanipal

The library of Ashurbanipal contained texts on more than 30,000 clay tablets

668 BCE

ASHURBANIPAL BECOMES ASSYRIAN EMPEROR

Sometimes proclaimed as the "last great king of Assyria", Ashurbanipal came to power when the Assyrian Empire was at its height. During his reign, he established Nineveh as the cultural, political, and commercial centre of the empire, with an extensive library housing texts such as the *Epic of Gilgamesh*, and buildings lavishly decorated with statues and bas-reliefs.

c. 600 BCE
REGENERATION OF BABYLON

Nebuchadnezzar II, ruler of the Neo-Babylonian Empire (r. 605–562 BCE), was an inspirational military leader and became known for his building projects throughout Mesopotamia. He ordered the regeneration of the city of Babylon to restore its fading reputation, including the rebuilding of the ziggurat and – legend has it – the creation of the famous hanging gardens.

◁ **The legendary** hanging gardens of Babylon

600 BCE

590 BCE The Nubian rulers of the Kingdom of Kush move their residence from Napata to Meroë

587 BCE Nebuchadnezzar II destroys the temple in Jerusalem following a Jewish revolt

c. 550 BCE The Temple of Artemis in Ephesus is rebuilt to replace the original destroyed by floods

550 BCE
CYRUS THE GREAT FOUNDS THE ACHAEMENID EMPIRE

Cyrus was a king of Anshan, a subject nation of the Median Empire. He led a revolt, defeating the Medians and then conquering the Lydian Empire to form a new Achaemenid Empire, the First Persian Empire. Subsequently, Babylon also fell under Achaemenid rule, leading Cyrus to declare on an inscribed clay cylinder "I am Cyrus, King of the World".

△ The Cyrus Cylinder

600–322 BCE
GREEK PHILOSOPHY

The foundations of western philosophy were laid by Greek thinkers, beginning in the 6th century BCE and reaching a high point in Classical Athens.

c. 600 BCE Thales of Miletus is one of the first thinkers to speculate about what everything in the universe is made of.

c. 530 BCE Pythagoras founds a school of mathematics and philosophy in a commune in Italy.

399 BCE Socrates, first of the great Athenian philosophers, is accused of corrupting youths and disrespecting the gods; he drinks hemlock rather than renounce his views.

c. 387 BCE Plato, a protégé of Socrates, founds the Academy in Athens, where he presents his ideas to students from all Greece.

508–507 BCE

ATHENIANS OVERTHROW THE TYRANT HIPPIAS

For more than 100 years, the Greek city-states had been ruled by leaders known as "tyrants" (both good and bad). In Athens, this "Age of Tyrants" came to an end when Hippias was overthrown, and his successor Cleisthenes introduced a form of democracy, in which the Athenian assembly met on a hill called the Pnyx. This heralded the beginning of a "Golden Age" of Classical Greece, with Athens at its centre.

△ **The steps** of the Pnyx

◁ Cleisthenes

539 BCE Cyrus the Great conquers Babylon and brings its empire into the Achaemenid Empire

525–402 BCE Egypt comes under Persian control and is ruled by Achaemenid kings

c. 509 BCE The Roman Republic is established following the overthrow of the monarchy

501 BCE

c. 550 BCE Celtic people begin to migrate from their homeland in the northern Alps and settle across Europe

c. 335 BCE Aristotle, an alumnus of the Academy, founds his own school, the Lyceum, offering alternative philosophical theories.

△ **Enthronement of Darius,** bas-relief

518 BCE

DARIUS THE GREAT BUILDS PERSEPOLIS, HIS NEW CAPITAL

Darius I ruled the Achaemenid Empire at its most powerful, and his 36-year reign included reforms that unified the Persians. He oversaw a number of construction projects, improving roads and regenerating cities; the grandest of these projects was the building of a completely new ceremonial capital, Persepolis, with a complex of impressive palaces.

c. 500 BCE
ZAPOTECS ESTABLISH MONTE ALBAN

As the Zapotec civilization flourished, a site in the southern Mexican highlands was chosen as its centre. The Zapotecs began to build Monte Albán – the first great city of Mesoamerica – on a steep hill in the Oaxaca valley.

△ Monte Albán, Zapotec ruins

475 BCE
WARRING STATES PERIOD BEGINS IN CHINA

By the beginning of the 5th century BCE, the Zhou kingdom in China had fragmented into several more or less autonomous states. As they vied with one another for power in the region, the Spring and Autumn Period came to an end and was replaced by a time of political turmoil known as the Warring States Period. The conflict was to continue for a further two and a half centuries until the Qin state, with its strict authoritarian regime and disciplined military, emerged victorious.

▷ **Conference of Six States** in the Warring States Period

496 BCE Greek dramatist Sophocles, author of tragedies featuring Antigone and Oedipus, is born

480 BCE Emperor Xerxes I bridges the Hellespont and the Persian army advances as far as Athens

500 BCE

499–449 BCE In the Greco-Persian Wars, the Greeks defend against Persian invasion in a series of famous battles

c. 490 BCE King Ajatashatru founds Pataliputra (modern Patna) in north-east India, as capital of the Magadha Empire

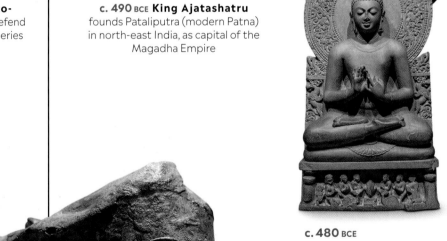

△ The Buddha, seated statue

490 BCE
ATHENIANS DEFEAT PERSIANS AT MARATHON

A decisive battle in the Greco-Persian Wars took place at Marathon, Attica, during the first Persian invasion. Darius I planned to take the whole of Greece, sending his forces by sea to Attica. They were met on the coastal plain at Marathon by Athenian troops who, though outnumbered, outmanoeuvred the Persians and won a crushing victory.

△ **Athenian** battle helmet

c. 480 BCE
TEACHINGS OF THE BUDDHA

Siddhartha Gautama, known later as the Buddha, spent the latter part of his life preaching in northern India. After his death, his disciples collated his teachings and continued to spread his ideas further afield, establishing Buddhism as a major religion.

c. 484–c. 425 BCE
HERODOTUS
Born in Halicarnassus, in the Persian Empire, the Greek writer Herodotus is best known as the author of the *Histories*, an account of the events and leading figures of the Greco-Persian wars.

c. 479 BCE Confucius dies and his disciples begin compiling the *Analects* which record his sayings

c. 440 BCE Herodotus writes the first known history book, the nine-volume *Histories*

401 BCE

449 BCE A law code, *The Twelve Tables of the Laws*, is published in Rome by the governing *decemviri*

431–404 BCE The Peloponnesian War is fought between the Delian League led by Athens and the Peloponnesian League led by Sparta

▽ **The Parthenon** ruins, Athens

447 BCE
BUILDING OF THE PARTHENON BEGINS
After Greek forces had defeated the Persians, Athens began to thrive again. Pericles oversaw the construction of a number of monuments on the Acropolis, most impressive of which was the Parthenon, a temple dedicated to the goddess Athena, patroness of the city, to replace the temple destroyed during the Persian invasion. The building work was finally completed in 432 BCE.

336–323 BCE
ALEXANDER OF MACEDON UNITES GREECE

When Philip II of Macedon was murdered, his son Alexander, aged 20, assumed the throne. He defeated the Thebans, uniting all the Greek peoples under his rulership. Continuing his father's empire-building project, he led Greek forces in a ten-year campaign to conquer the Achaemenid Empire and bring the whole of Persia under Greek control, and went on to expand his empire as far as the Indus valley.

▷ **Alexander** portrayed as a Byzantine emperor

375 BCE Dionysius of Syracuse negotiates a peace treaty with the Carthaginians, ending a series of wars

400 BCE

c. 400–350 BCE The Olmec culture enters a period of rapid decline, possibly caused by environmental changes

356 BCE Shang Yang, a lord of the Chinese state of State of Qin, initiates reforms that boost the state's influence

338 BCE Philip of Macedonia vanquishes the allied Greek forces to take control of almost all of Greece

356–323 BCE
ALEXANDER THE GREAT

Alexander III of Macedon, ruler of the whole of Greece, was a spectacularly successful military leader, who in a series of campaigns spread Greek influence as far as the Indian subcontinent.

c. 350 BCE
CHAVIN CULTURE REACHES ITS PEAK

A rapid increase in the population of the Chavín culture of Peru brought about changes in its social structure around the middle of the century. The major city, Chavín de Huantar, in the Andes, became less important as a political and religious centre as semi-urban settlements and ceremonial centres developed in the lowlands, spreading Chavín cultural influence across the region and along the coast.

△ **Chavín carved** stone panel

305 BCE
FOUNDING OF THE PTOLEMAIC DYNASTY

A former bodyguard and companion of Alexander the Great, Ptolemy was appointed governor of Egypt after Alexander's death in 323 BCE, and in 305 BCE assumed the title of pharaoh. As Ptolemy I he founded the Ptolemaic dynasty, ruling Egypt as a Hellenistic kingdom. He was also a writer and historian, and was instrumental in making his capital, Alexandria, a centre of Greek culture.

▷ **Ptolemy I** inaugurating the Library at Alexandria

332 BCE Alexander conquers Egypt, extending his empire southwards until it reaches the Kingdom of Kush

c. 330 BCE Euclid of Alexandria, author of the mathematical treatise *Elements*, is born

301 BCE

321–185 BCE
THE MAURYA EMPIRE

Chandragupta Maurya established the Maurya Empire by replacing the Nanda dynasty in northern India. When Greek forces began to withdraw from the farther reaches of Alexander the Great's empire after his death, Chandragupta seized the opportunity to invade, bringing all of the north of the subcontinent under Maurya rule.

◁ **Libation cup,** Maurya dynasty

c. 400–51 BCE
THE ROMAN-GALLIC WARS

As Celts began to migrate from the northern Alps to settle in the Po valley in Italy, they triggered a long series of conflicts with Rome.

387 BCE Brennus of the Senones leads Celts in the sacking of the city of Rome; according to legend, geese raise the alarm (*above*).

298–290 BCE An alliance of Samnites (*helmet above*), Gauls, and others engages with Rome for control of central and southern Italy.

125–121 BCE Roman forces defeat the Gauls of the Arverni tribe (*coin above*), claiming their territory as a Roman province.

58–51 BCE Julius Caesar conducts a major military campaign in his determination to conquer the whole of Gaul.

221-206 BCE
THE QIN DYNASTY

The Qin established a unified empire in 221 BCE, marking the end of the Warring States Period in China. Zheng, king of the Qin state, conquered the other six belligerent states and, as Emperor Qin Shi Huang, founded the Qin dynasty, the first Imperial Chinese dynasty.

Qin Shi Huang's success can be attributed to the strict disciplinarian regime he had established in Qin, which he then applied throughout the empire. Among his achievements was the standardization of currency, weights and measures, and writing systems; he also ordered several massive infrastructure projects, including the building of a northern wall which later formed the foundation of the Great Wall

of China, and a major network of roads that helped to encourage trade between China's distant regions. One of his most striking pursuits was a vanity project, the construction of a vast mausoleum, as big as a city, to house his own tomb, defended by an army of terracotta figures.

The Qin dynasty was regarded as tyrannical by many in the conquered states, and the regime came down hard on any dissenting voices. However, Qin Shi Huang and his advisors succeeded in unifying the country after centuries of conflict. The dynasty was not to last: in 206 BCE the second — and final — Qin emperor was overthrown, and the dynasty was brought to an end.

KEY MOMENTS

221 BCE Qin Shi Huang takes power
The founder of the Qin dynasty, Qin Shi Huang (*left*), reigned as king from 247 to 221 BCE, and then proclaimed himself Emperor of a unified China after emerging triumphant over the Warring States. His wide-ranging reforms laid the foundations for subsequent Chinese dynasties to follow for more than 2,000 years. After his death his successor, Qin Ershi, was soon ousted by the Han dynasty.

221-210 BCE Imposition of Legalism
Emperor Qin Shi Huang set about establishing centralized control, ending the political and cultural diversity of the "Hundred Schools of Thought" associated with the Seven Warring States. With the help of his Imperial Chancellor Li Si, he imposed a strict authoritarian form of government known as Legalism, and a brutal purge of the classical scholars of the previous Zhou Dynasty. Books were burned and many scholars were buried alive (*left*).

The Terracotta Army guarding the Mausoleum of the First Emperor is symbolic of the power he wielded. More than 8,000 individually sculpted statues of soldiers, along with hundreds of horses and chariots, were buried with the emperor as his entourage in the afterlife.

268–232 BCE
ASHOKA RULES THE MAURYA EMPIRE

Ashoka began his reign intending to continue the expansion of the empire begun by his grandfather Chandragupta Maurya. Once he had conquered the state of Kalinga in 261 BCE, he ruled over all but the extreme south of the Indian subcontinent. The bloody Kalinga campaign prompted a change of heart, and he devoted the rest of his reign to spreading the doctrine of Buddhism, declaring his moral and social "edicts" by having them inscribed on pillars topped with stone animal capitals around the empire.

▷ **The Lion Capital** of Ashoka

280 BCE The Colossus of Rhodes, a statue at the entrance to the city's harbour, is completed

c. **260 BCE Ashoka converts to Buddhism** and commissions the building of the Great Stupa at Sanchi

300 BCE

285 BCE
THE LIGHTHOUSE AT ALEXANDRIA IS BUILT

Construction of a monumental lighthouse on the small island of Pharos off the coast of Egypt was completed during the reign of Ptolemy II Philadelphus. After 12 years of building work, it stood some 100 m (330 ft) high, the tallest building in the world at that time. The structure, often known as the Pharos of Alexandria, lasted until damaged by earthquakes in the 10th century CE.

◁ **Pharos** of Alexandria

264–241 BCE
THE FIRST PUNIC WAR

The 3rd century BCE saw three long wars between the Romans and the Carthaginians. The two powers fought for supremacy over the western Mediterranean, but the Romans also took the war into Carthaginian territory in North Africa, notably at the massive naval battle of Ecnomus. After the First Punic War, which lasted 23 years, the Romans defeated the Carthaginians and took control of Sicily.

> "I will either find a way, or make one."
> ("*Aut viam inveniam aut faciam.*")

LATIN PROVERB, COMMONLY ATTRIBUTED TO HANNIBAL

247–c. 183 BCE
HANNIBAL
Hannibal was a respected military tactician who led the Carthaginian forces against Rome in the Second Punic War. After the war, he served as a reforming statesman.

▽ Death of Archimedes, mosaic

213–212 BCE
SIEGE OF SYRACUSE
At the height of the Second Punic War (218–201 BCE), the Romans laid siege to the strategically important city of Syracuse in Sicily, then an independent kingdom. In the aftermath, Archimedes, whose ingenious inventions had helped to defend Syracuse, was mistakenly killed by a Roman soldier.

221 BCE The Warring States Period comes to an end after Zheng, King of Qin, unites the kingdoms of China into a single empire

206 BCE The fall of the short-lived Qin dynasty marks the beginning of civil war in China as the Chu and Han kingdoms vie for control

201 BCE

218 BCE Carthaginian general Hannibal crosses the Alps with his army and 37 elephants, and defeats the Romans at the Battle of Cannae

△ Battle of Cape Ecnomus

202 BCE
THE HAN DYNASTY
Discontent with the strict legalist rule of China's Qin dynasty ultimately led to its downfall and four years of conflict, centred around the so-called Chu-Han Contention. The Han dynasty emerged as the victors, and united the empire: they would remain in power for centuries.

△ **Bronze horse**
of the Han Dynasty

181 BCE
SHUNGA DYNASTY ESTABLISHED

Pushyamitra Shunga (r. 185 –149 BCE) –
a general of the Maurya Empire – established
control over northern India after the
assassination of Brihadratha, the last
Mauryan emperor.

▷ **Shunga period** carvings showing scenes from Buddha's life

△ **Hasmonean** dynasty coin

165 BCE
JUDAS MACCABAEUS REVOLTS

After Seleucid ruler Antiochus IV
outlawed Jewish practices in Judea
and Samaria, Judas Maccabaeus
and his brothers led a revolt, taking
Jerusalem in 164 BCE. Judas purified
the Temple, restored Jewish
worship, and established the
Hasmonaean dynasty, which ruled
until overthrown by Herod the
Great in 37 BCE.

▷ *Judas Maccabaeus Praying for the
Dead*, 1635, by Peter Paul Rubens

200 BCE

**171–168 BCE The Romans
defeat Perseus of Macedon**
in the Third Macedonian War

c. 150 BCE
GREAT SERPENT MOUND IS BUILT

The Adena were a people of the
eastern woodlands of North America.
Living in villages of circular houses,
they hunted deer and elk, gathered
edible grasses, and farmed pumpkin
and squash. They built hundreds of
mounds, probably as funerary
monuments, the most spectacular of
which was the Great Serpent Mound in
Ohio. It was fashioned in the shape of a
serpent with sinuous coils.

146 BCE
DESTRUCTION OF CARTHAGE

After the Carthaginians attacked neighbouring Numidia, a Roman army led by the consul Scipio Aemilianus landed in North Africa, blockaded Carthage, and finally took it after a year-long siege. Scipio destroyed the city and sold its people into slavery, ending the 120-year Punic Wars.

▷ Ruins of Carthage, Tunisia

146 BCE The Romans destroy Corinth and annexe Greece to the province of Macedonia

138 BCE China's Han emperor Wu sends out an envoy, Zhang Qian, whose findings usher in an era of westward expansion

101 BCE

▽ Serpent Burial Mound Ohio, USA

104 BCE
GENERAL GAIUS MARIUS REFORMS THE ROMAN ARMY

Marius allowed the landless poor to join the army, organizing it into cohorts (of around 480 men) and legions (of around 5,500). With their regular weapons – the *pilum* (javelin) and *gladius* (short-sword) – the new legions were a formidable force.

▷ Portrait of Gaius Marius, late 1st century CE

"Men who were fond of toil ... without a murmur, were called Marius's mules."

PLUTARCH, LIFE OF MARIUS, C. 110 CE

c. 100 BCE
MONTE ALBAN GROWS

The Zapotec people continued to enlarge the city of Monte Albán in Mexico. They adorned it with stone temples, pyramids, a ball court, and a grand plaza, near which were placed hundreds of "Danzantes", grotesque carvings probably representing prisoners. As the city grew and extended its control throughout Oaxaca, its population reached 17,000.

◁ **Zapotec Danzante relief,** Monte Albán

91 BCE The Social War breaks out, pitting Rome against its Italian allies seeking Roman citizenship

87 BCE Emperor Wu of the Chinese Han dynasty dies after five successful decades in power

100 BCE

△ Coin of Indo-Scythian king Azilises, c. 40 BCE

88 BCE
MITHRIDATES ATTACKS ROMAN ASIA

When Mithridates VI, ruler of the Black Sea kingdom of Pontus, sought to expand his territory southwards, the Romans saw a threat to their province of Asia (modern western Turkey). Ignoring Roman threats, Mithridates marched into Asia and massacred 80,000 Roman citizens. In response, Rome sent an army under Sulla, beginning a bitter four-year war.

▷ **Bust of Mithridates VI**

c. 80 BCE
THE SAKAS CONQUER GANDHARA

In the late 2nd century BCE, the Sakas, a nomadic people of Central Asia, were forced to migrate southwards into Bactria. Under Maues, they invaded and conquered the kingdom of Gandhara around 80 BCE, establishing an Indo-Scythian state that dominated north-western India for over a century before being eclipsed by the Kushanas.

More than 6,000 rebels were crucified following Spartacus's revolt

73 BCE
SLAVE REVOLT AGAINST ROME

In a revolt that began in Capua, Thracian gladiator Spartacus led a band of fighters including his fellow gladiators and escaped slaves. They vanquished several Roman armies, plundered a number of cities, and almost reached Rome itself. In 71 BCE, an army led by Licinius Crassus defeated the rebels in Calabria. Thousands of them were crucified along the Appian Way.

◁ **Gladiator combat,** Roman mosaic

106–48 BCE
POMPEY THE GREAT

One of Rome's greatest generals and a member of the First Triumvirate ruling Rome from 59 BCE, Pompey fell out with his fellow triumvir Julius Caesar, lost the ensuing civil war, and was assassinated.

65 BCE Pompey defeats Mithridates of Pontus to end the Mithridatic Wars

61 BCE

63 BCE
ROMANS ANNEX JUDAEA

The commander of the Roman army in the East, Pompey the Great, had deposed the last Seleucid ruler of Syria in 64 BCE, making his kingdom into a Roman province. He then turned his attention to Judaea, which was riven by a civil war between the rival rulers Hyrcanus and Aristobulus. Hyrcanus opened the gates of Jerusalem to Pompey's forces, which then besieged the Temple Mount for three months before storming it and massacring thousands. Pompey annexed part of Judaea and left the rest under client rulers, including Hyrcanus.

▷ **Desecration** of the Temple of Jerusalem

"I love the name of honour more than I fear death."

WILLIAM SHAKESPEARE, JULIUS CAESAR, 1599

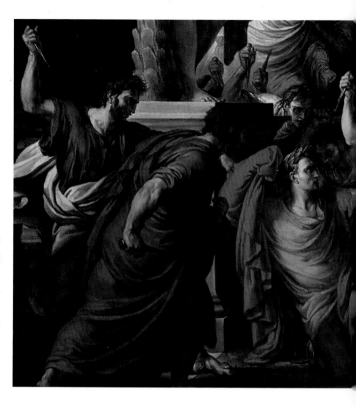

44 BCE

ASSASSINATION OF JULIUS CAESAR

As Julius Caesar made his way to a meeting of the Roman Senate in the spring of 44 BCE, he was already dictator for life and many feared that he intended to make himself king. As Caesar took his seat, a group of senators led by Marcus Brutus and Cassius Longinus struck him down with daggers. The assassination sparked a new civil war.

▷ *Death of Caesar* by Vincenzo Camuccini

60 BCE

60 BCE Establishment of Han protectorate of the Western Regions extends Chinese control northwest into the Tarim Basin

58 BCE Julius Caesar begins the conquest of Gaul, subjugating it within eight years

55 BCE Julius Caesar invades Britain and returns the following year, but ultimately withdraws

46 BCE Roman calendar is reformed, having fallen 80 days out of alignment with the seasons

59 BCE

FIRST TRIUMVIRATE TAKES POWER IN ROME

Weary at the political chaos of the preceding decades, Julius Caesar, ex-governor of Spain, joined with statesman Crassus and fellow general Pompey in a triumvirate to govern Rome, excluding the Senate from power. Crassus's death in battle against the Parthians in 53 BCE and increasing friction between Pompey and Caesar caused the triumvirate's collapse, culminating in Caesar marching an army into Italy in 49 BCE and the outbreak of civil war.

◁ **Lucius Licinius Crassus,** Roman senator

36 BCE
EARLIEST LONG COUNT DATE IN THE MAYAN CALENDAR

Mesoamerican peoples used the Long Count calendar system to record dates over long periods of time. Based on multiples of 20, it counted the time since a start-point in 3114 BCE, expressed in baktuns (roughly 394 years) and their subdivisions. The oldest Long Count inscription found was on a limestone stele of the MIxe-Zoque people at Chiapa de Corzo, Mexico, with a date of 7.15.3.2.13, or 8 December 36 BCE.

◁ A (late) Mayan calendrical stone

31 BCE

31 BCE
CLEOPATRA VII DEFEATED AT ACTIUM

Octavian, Lepidus, and Mark Antony, the victors in the civil war against Caesar's assassins, formed a Second Triumvirate in 43 BCE, but this dissolved and a new conflict began. Mark Antony allied with Egypt's Queen Cleopatra VII, but their fleet was destroyed at Actium off Greece's west coast, leaving Octavian master of the Roman world.

△ **Battle of Actium**, relief

50 BCE–100 CE
ROMAN LITERATURE

Roman literature at first based itself on Greek models, but soon authors were writing epic poetry, drama, fiction, and non-fiction in Latin.

55–43 BCE The Roman statesman Cicero writes works on oratory and politics, including *De Oratore* (*On the Orator*).

42–19 BCE The poet Virgil (*seated, above*) writes the *Aeneid*, an epic poem telling of the flight to Italy of Aeneas, among other works.

c. 70–77 CE Pliny the Younger writes *The Natural History*, a compilation of all Roman scientific knowledge (*15th-century page, above*).

70–100 CE The lawyer Tacitus composes *Annals and Histories*, which is among the finest Latin historical writing.

27 BCE
ROME'S FIRST EMPEROR

Julius Caesar's adoptive son Octavian had defeated his rivals in a civil war by 31 BCE. Rather than restore the Roman Republic, he accepted extensive powers from the Senate, and the titles of *Augustus* ("illustrious") and *princeps* ("the first"), becoming the first emperor. He conquered parts of Central Europe, rebuilt much of Rome, and bequeathed his position to his stepson Tiberius in 14 CE.

▷ **Augustus of Prima Porta,** Roman copy of a bronze original

"He could justly boast that he had found it built of brick and left it in marble."

SUETONIUS, LIVES OF THE TWELVE CAESARS, *121 CE, ON AUGUSTUS'S LEGACY*

30 BCE

23 BCE The Romans
invade Meroë, south-east Egypt, sacking its capital Napata

c. 25 BCE
BUDDHIST CANON IS FIRST WRITTEN DOWN IN SRI LANKA

The teachings of the Buddha, who lived in the 6th century BCE, were passed down orally by his followers for generations. As the religion spread from its north Indian homeland, the need for a written version grew. In around 25 BCE, the scriptures, including theological analysis and rules for monks, were set down in Sri Lanka in a collection known as the Tripitaka or Pali Canon (from the language in which they were written).

▷ **Pages of the Pali Canon**

4 BCE
BIRTH OF JESUS

Jesus was born to Joseph, a humble carpenter, and his wife Mary, in the small town of Bethlehem in Judaea in 4 BCE. His later teachings stressed compassion and forgiveness and attracted many disciples. Claims that he was the Messiah, the long-awaited saviour of the Jewish people, brought him into conflict with the Jewish authorities in Palestine.

▷ **Jesus and Mary**, detail from *Comforter of the Afflicted*

9 CE **German tribes** destroy legions in the Teutoberger Wald, halting Roman expansion into Germany

24 CE

9 CE **The regent Wang Mang** overthrows the infant emperor Ruzi Ying, declaring the Xi dynasty

▷ Herod's Temple model

19 BCE
HEROD REBUILDS THE JEWISH TEMPLE

Appointed King of Judaea by the Romans, Herod maintained his kingdom's independence by balancing Jewish and Roman interests. He commissioned several projects in Jerusalem, most notably, in 19 BCE, a remodelling of the Second Temple (dating from the 6th century BCE), creating a new outer courtyard, levelling part of the Temple Mount to extend the temple platform, and building a new encircling wall, whose remains now form the Western (or Wailing) Wall.

▷ **Han mirror**, 1st century CE

23 CE
DEATH OF WANG MANG AND THE HAN RESTORATION

After seizing power from a weakened Han dynasty in 9 CE, Wang Mang established the Xi dynasty and embarked on a series of hugely unpopular reforms. He was killed in the ensuing rebellion in 23 CE after which Han loyalists under Emperor Guangwu took advantage of the disorder to claim power in 25 CE.

509 BCE–395 CE
ROMAN ENGINEERING AND ARCHITECTURE

The Romans were inventive engineers and relentless builders. Of the buildings that survive from the Republican era (before 27 BCE), many are temples, with high podia and Greek-style columns, but these are complemented by public buildings, such as the rectangular column-aisled basilicas used for law courts and audience chambers. From the Imperial era, Roman architecture developed its own clear identity, relying on new materials such as brick and "Roman concrete" (*opus caementicium*), which incorporated volcanic pozzolana sand for hardness and durability. This allowed the building of domes, huge amphitheatres such as the Colosseum, aqueducts, and great baths, including the Baths of Diocletian in Rome.

The Romans decorated their buildings with carved friezes, portrait busts, and fine statues in marble and bronze, often based on Greek or Hellenistic originals. Roman interiors were painted in stucco and fresco with colourful scenes, both geometric and mythological. Villa floors and walls were adorned with mosaics, often of arena or legendary scenes, made up of thousands of marble and limestone tesserae.

KEY MOMENTS

c. 300 BCE–395 CE **Roman roads**
The Romans built a network of 80,000 km (50,000 miles) of paved roads (*such as the Appian Way, left*) linking major points in the empire. Roads were built straight on levelled earth; layers of gravel were added and topped with a hard concrete surface and blocks of rectangular stone. A pronounced camber and adjacent ditches kept them well drained.

c. 200 BCE–395 CE **Roman grid cities**
Cities founded by the Romans were laid out on a grid pattern based on the plan of a Roman military camp. A main street, the *decumanus maximus*, ran east–west and another, the *cardo maximus*, north–south, with major buildings and the forum, the centre of civic life, placed where they intersected. To lay out the cities, Roman surveyors, or *agrimensores*, used ropes, rods, and the *groma*, a pole with a rotating arm and suspended weights.

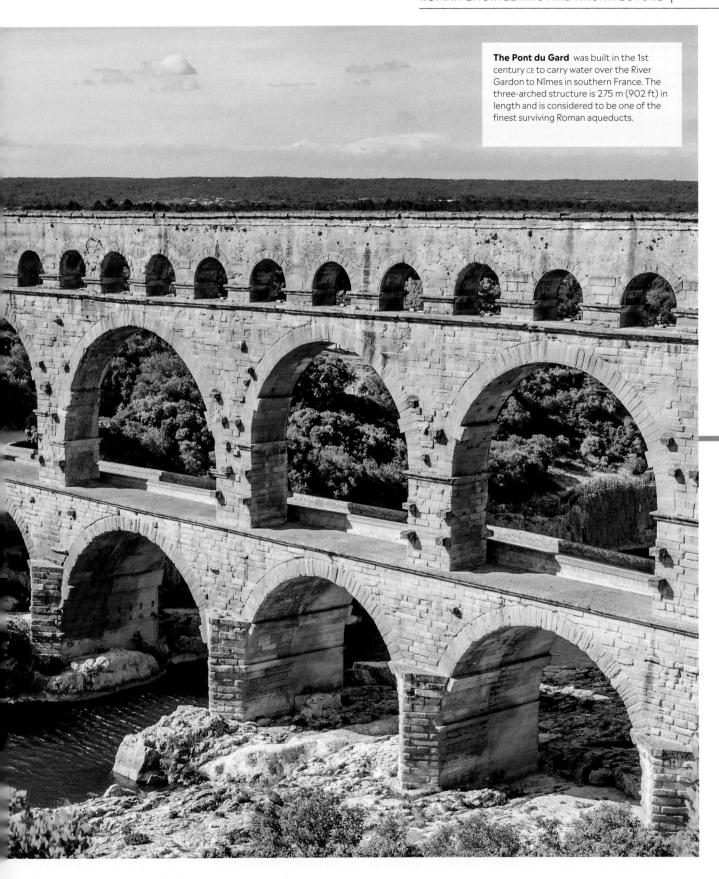

The Pont du Gard was built in the 1st century CE to carry water over the River Gardon to Nîmes in southern France. The three-arched structure is 275 m (902 ft) in length and is considered to be one of the finest surviving Roman aqueducts.

> "All the male heroes bowed their heads in submission;
> Only the two sisters proudly stood up to avenge the country."

15TH-CENTURY VIETNAMESE POEM ABOUT THE TRUNG SISTERS

▷ Page from *De Medicina*

25 CE
CELSUS PUBLISHES DE MEDICINA

Roman author Aulus Cornelius Celsus compiled a general encyclopaedia that included *De Medicina*, a summary of Roman medical knowledge. In its eight volumes he outlined surgical techniques for conditions including hernias, bladder stones, and abscesses, described many types of fever, and was the first to use the term "cancer". His works were lost and only rediscovered in 1426.

25 CE

40–43 CE The Trung sisters revolt against Han Chinese rule, briefly establishing an independent state in Vietnam

△ *The Crucifixion*, Giotto Bondone

33 CE
CRUCIFIXION OF JESUS CHRIST

Having preached for three years, Jesus was arrested by the Jewish authorities and tried by Pontius Pilate, the chief Roman official in Palestine, on the grounds that his alleged claim to be "king of the Jews" was seditious. After his execution by crucifixion, his followers claimed that he had risen from the dead. This belief formed the core of the new religion of Christianity.

43 CE
ROMAN INVASION OF BRITAIN

Emperor Claudius ordered a Roman force of 40,000 men to invade Britain. It landed on the southeast coast and, in bitter fighting, defeated British resistance led by Caractacus, king of the Catuvellauni. The legions soon captured Camulodunon (Colchester), the Catuvellaunian capital, and then advanced to the Midlands, beginning a occupation of Britain that would last over 350 years.

◁ **Caractacus**, king of the Catuvellauni

CARACTACUS

THE ERUPTION OF VESUVIUS

In August 79 CE, Mount Vesuvius in southern Italy erupted, sending a rain of hot ash and pumice down on nearby Pompeii and Herculaneum. A superheated lava flow surged into Herculaneum, destroying it; then, a poisonous cloud of toxic gas suffocated most of the 2,000 or so people who had not fled Pompeii, while a fall of hot rocks and ash killed the rest. The cities remained buried until their excavation began in the 18th century.

▷ *Vesuvius in Eruption*, JMW Turner

c. 65 CE Buddhism first appears in China, having been carried there by monks from India

66–70 CE The Jewish revolt against Roman oppression ends with the capture of Jerusalem

69 CE The Year of Four Emperors: Vespasian wins a civil war between rival Roman emperors

74 CE The Romans capture Masada, ending Jewish Zealot resistance

79 CE

◁ Kushana gold belt buckle

60 CE
KUSHANAS UNITED IN INDIA

The Kushana, descendants of the nomadic Yuezhi, had conquered Bactria in the 2nd century BCE, but remained divided into five kingdoms. Around 60 CE, Kujula Kadphises united the kingdoms, and expanded into northwestern India, conquering Gandhara and founding an empire that would soon dominate northern India and become one of Eurasia's most significant powers.

The lava flow that destroyed Pompeii reached a temperature of over 300 °C (570 °F)

80 CE

ROME'S COLOSSEUM IS INAUGURATED

Commissioned by the Emperor Vespasian in 72 CE, the Colosseum took eight years to build. The amphitheatre's inaugural games, held in 80 CE, lasted over 100 days and featured gladiator fights and beast hunts, including of exotic animals such as rhinoceros. The Colosseum was the empire's largest amphitheatre: it had 80 separate entrances and held over 50,000 spectators.

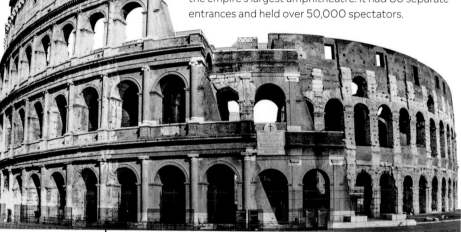

△ **The Colosseum,** Rome

80 CE

100 CE The *Shuowen Jiezi*, the first dictionary to classify Chinese characters, is finished; it lists over 9,000 characters

c. 110 CE Envoys from India reportedly visit Emperor Trajan in Rome

▷ **The Pyramid of the Sun,** Teotihuacán

c. 100 CE

BUILDING OF THE PYRAMID OF THE SUN

The people of the central Mexican city of Teotihuacán constructed a vast pyramid on the eastern side of the Avenue of the Dead, the city's main thoroughfare. Over 70 m (230 ft) high, it was faced in limestone and painted with murals. The great building probably served as a temple; in 2013 a statue of the fire-god Huehueteotl was found near its summit.

101 CE

ROMAN EMPEROR TRAJAN CONQUERS DACIA

Trajan undertook two campaigns (101–102 CE and 105–106 CE) to extend Roman borders beyond the Danube by invading the Dacian kingdom (in modern Romania) of Decebalus. After an initial truce, the legions returned and razed the Dacian capital Sarmizegetusa, capturing Decebalus and reducing Dacia to a Roman province.

◁ **Second Dacian campaign,** detail of Trajan's column relief

76–138 CE
EMPEROR HADRIAN
The adoptive son of Trajan, Hadrian reversed his predecessor's expansionist policy. He consolidated the imperial frontiers, built Hadrian's Wall, and conducted extensive tours of the empire.

c. 130 CE Kushan ruler
Kanishka invades northern India, conquering as far south as Mathura

132 CE Zhang Heng
demonstrates the first seismograph to the Han imperial court

132 CE The Second Jewish revolt against Roman rule is led by Simon Bar Kokhba

139 CE

△ **Hadrian's Wall,** viewed from Hotbank Crags

122 CE

HADRIAN'S WALL BUILT

On a visit to Britain in 122 CE, Emperor Hadrian ordered the erection of a barrier to mark the northern border of the Roman province. When completed, the 5-m (16-ft) high turf and stone wall snaked 80 Roman miles between Wallsend on the River Tyne and the Solway Firth, punctuated by 16 forts and numerous fortlets and turrets for its 9,000-strong garrison.

105–868 CE
PAPER AND THE BOOK

Paper allowed reading material to be produced far more cheaply than papyrus and vellum previously used in Egypt and Greece.

105 CE Chinese official Cai Lun boils rags and tree bark, drying the pulp to create paper, a durable, economical writing surface.

c. 400 CE Codices (books) with stitched-together pages (as *St Cuthbert Gospel, above*) replace older, unwieldy scrolls.

868 CE The *Diamond Sutra,* a Buddhist devotional tract, is the oldest known book printed, produced using a single wooden block per page.

166 CE
BEGINNING OF THE MARCOMANNIC WARS

By the 2nd century CE, Roman frontiers came under increasing pressure from barbarians. In 166 CE, Germanic tribes invaded the province of Pannonia; two years later, the Marcomanni, who had settled near the Danube in Bohemia, surged into Italy. Emperor Marcus Aurelius fought them back and campaigned across the Danube, but it took 14 years of hard fighting before the Marcomannic wars were finally concluded.

▷ **Romans clash with Germanic tribes,** detail from Portonaccio Sarcophagus

169 CE An outbreak of plague in the Roman Empire kills Emperor Lucius Verus

140 CE

143–161 CE The Roman frontier in Britain is temporarily moved north to the Antonine Wall

150 CE
NOK CULTURE FLOURISHES IN WEST AFRICA

Arising in the fertile region around the Benue river in central Nigeria, the Nok culture developed iron-smelting, and produced terracotta figurines of humans and animals of great sophistication. Despite dominating a large region, within 50 years their culture had collapsed, possibly through overpopulation or invasion by neighbouring groups.

▷ **Nok terracotta figurine**

▽ Temple complex at Hatra, Iraq

160 CE
KINGDOM OF HATRA AT ITS PEAK

One of the first Arab states outside the Arabian peninsula, the kingdom of Hatra, in modern northern Iraq, reached its peak in the 160s CE, growing rich from its position astride a major caravan route. It resisted Roman attempts to conquer it in 117 CE and 199 CE, but finally fell to the Sasanian ruler Shapur I in 240 CE.

197 CE
ROMAN CIVIL WAR ENDS

The assassinations of Roman Emperor Commodus and his successor Pertinax led to a scramble between Pescennius Niger, governor of Syria, Clodius Albinus, governor of Britain, and Septimius Severus, governor of Pannonia, to seize power. First allying himself with Albinus, Severus overcame Niger and then in 197 CE defeated Albinus, restoring peace and stabilizing the empire's frontiers.

▷ **Septimius Severus,** marble bust

199 CE

180 CE Emperor Commodus makes a treaty to end the Marcomannic Wars

189 CE Dong Zhuo ends the period of eunuch rule in China and sacks the capital at Luoyang

184 CE Outbreak of Yellow Turban Revolt in China

"The Azure Sky is already dead; the Yellow Sky will soon rise."

ZHANG JUE, YELLOW TURBAN LEADER, HOU HAN SHU, 5TH CENTURY CE

△ **Yaksha** (nature spirit), Champa civilization

c. 192 CE
CHAMPA KINGDOM ESTABLISHED

As internal struggles troubled the Han dynasty, their former dominions in southeast Asia began to break away. In 192 CE, the Cham established four kingdoms around Hue in modern Vietnam. They absorbed Indian and Chinese influences, dominating trade and expanding north towards China and west into the Khmer region of Cambodia.

250-900 CE
THE CLASSIC MAYA CIVILIZATION

A sophisticated civilization of pre-Columbian Mesoamerica developed in the area that today encompasses southern Mexico, Guatemala, Belize, El Salvador, and Honduras. The indigenous peoples, now known as the Maya, began to form complex societies from about 2000 BCE, settling in cities by about 750 BCE. Their distinctive culture continued to flourish in the Classic Period (250–900 CE), which was marked by the introduction of their calendar, known as the Long Count calendar. At this time, the Maya civilization consisted of a network of autonomous city–states linked by trade,

or by rivalry for influence in the region. Urban centres including Tikal, Calakmul, Copán, Palenque, and Yaxchilan were ruled over by dynasties of "divine kings" – spiritual as well as political and military leaders – and an increasingly strong aristocracy. Palaces, monuments, and pyramidal temples were prominent in Classic Maya society; other buildings included observatories and courts for ceremonial ball games. Development of a writing system produced an educated class among which astronomy and mathematics flourished and whose patronage fostered a golden age of arts and crafts.

KEY MOMENTS

250–900 CE Rise of Tikal and Calakmul

The Maya civilization of the Classic Period was marked by the rise of powerful city–states. Foremost among these were the rival cities of Tikal and Calakmul (*left*), which fought for dominance throughout the period.

250 CE Maya script

By around 250 CE, the Maya had developed a writing system that used symbols to represent words and syllables. The symbols, or glyphs, were arranged in blocks to form words and phrases; they were written on a form of paper made from tree bark or inscribed on stone or ceramic artefacts (*left*).

c. 750–900 CE Classic Maya collapse

The Classic Maya city–states of the southern lowlands began to decline for reasons that remain a mystery. By about 900 CE, they were largely abandoned (*left*), and the centre of the Postclassic Maya civilization shifted north to cities including Chichen Itza.

Surrounded by tropical forest, the Temple of the Inscriptions was built on top of the pyramid housing the tomb of K'inich Janaab' Pakal, whose reign (615–683 CE) marked the peak of importance of the Classic Maya city-state of Palenque.

▽ Moche stirrup-spout jar

200-300 CE
MOCHE CULTURE REACHES ITS PEAK IN PERU

Moche, the capital of a people of northern coastal Peru, became a centre for innovation and creativity. Its craftsmen produced beautiful gold- and silver-electroplated jewellery and fine stirrup-spout jars. The Temple of the Sun – a huge stepped pyramid – and the elaborate royal tombs at Dos Cabezas reveal a sophisticated and wealthy culture.

212 CE
ANTONINE CONSTITUTION

Up to the 3rd century CE, Roman citizenship extended to people in Italy, in Roman colonies, and those rewarded for army service. In 212 CE, Emperor Caracalla extended it to all free adults in the empire. He may have done so to raise money, as citizens were liable to inheritance duties, or to counter his unpopularity, but the measure helped knit the empire together in the decades to come.

△ Roman military tablet granting citizenship

c. 200 CE The Bakshali manuscript is the oldest manuscript to contain a sign for zero

200 CE

161-223 CE
LIU BEI

After serving as a Han general, Liu Bei allied with Cao Cao, but later turned on him during the Red Cliffs campaign in 208 CE, becoming the first ruler of the Three Kingdoms state of Shu Han.

220-280 CE
CHINA'S THREE KINGDOMS

By the 190s CE, the Han dynasty had lost most of its territory to contending warlords. One of these, Cao Cao, reunited the north, but he was defeated in 208 CE during his invasion of southern China at the Battle of the Red Cliffs. From 220 CE China dissolved into the Three Kingdoms of Cao Wei, Shu Han, and Sun Wu, in a period of disunity that lasted for 60 years.

▷ **Qing-dynasty illustration** of a battle from the Three Kingdoms era

241 CE
MANI BEGINS PREACHING IN PERSIA

In the chaos caused by the fall of the Persian Parthian dynasty, new religious movements flourished. Mani, who had been raised among one such sect, the Mandaeans, preached a new creed, combining elements of Zoroastrianism and Christianity, with an emphasis on the cosmic battle between good and evil. Manichaeism, which forbade its priests to marry, spread widely, gaining adherents in Persia and the Roman Empire.

▷ **Writings of Mani,** illuminated manuscript

249 CE

235 CE Maximinus Thrax, a lowly soldier, becomes emperor, beginning the Military Anarchy period in the Roman Empire

249 CE The Sima clan seizes power in the Chinese kingdom of Cao Wei

△ Investiture of Ardashir I, stone relief

224 CE
ARDASHIR OVERTHROWS THE PARTHIANS

The Parthian dynasty, rulers of Persia since the mid-3rd century BCE, had been weakened by Roman invasions and a civil war that divided the kingdom. After a Roman invasion in 216 CE, Ardashir, the local king of Pars in the southwest, revolted. Eight years later he defeated the last Parthian king, Artabanus V, to found a new dynasty, the Sasanians, that would rule Persia for the next four centuries.

235 CE
SEVERUS ALEXANDER ASSASSINATED

The stability that Septimius Severus brought to the Roman Empire from 194 CE was short-lived. His great-nephew Elagabalus provoked a revolt by his aberrant behaviour, and was murdered in favour of his cousin, Severus Alexander. But he, too, was assassinated in 235 CE while trying to quell an army mutiny in Germany. Over the next half-century he was followed by over 25 short-lived emperors, many of them army officers.

◁ Severus Alexander

c. 250 CE
YAMATO KINGDOM IN JAPAN

This kingdom arose in the area of the sacred Mount Miwa near Nara. One of its first rulers, Queen Himiko, is mentioned in a Chinese source from 238 CE. An iron-working, agricultural, clan-based culture, it expanded gradually through central Japan. The Yamato maintained links with Korea and China, taking from them cultural influences such as Buddhism, bronze mirrors, writing, and Chinese-style bureaucracy.

◁ **Head of a Warrior,** Yamato period

251 CE Persian Sassanid Roman emperor Decius is killed at Battle of Abrittus against the Goths

250 CE

260 CE Persian Sassanid ruler Shapur I defeats and captures Roman emperor Valerian

260 CE The breakaway Gallic Empire is established by Postumus

275 CE St Anthony establishes a monastery in the Egyptian desert

▽ Ruins of Tiahuanaco, Bolivia

c. 250 CE
CITY OF TIAHUANACO ESTABLISHED

Tiahuanaco, near Lake Titicaca in western Bolivia, began its rise to power. Raised-mound agriculture watered by irrigation channels created food surpluses that enabled the building of a grand ceremonial capital featuring the monolithic Gateway of the Sun and a semi-subterranean temple adorned with images of a Staff God. Tiahuanaco's potters produced distinctive polychrome drinking vessels decorated with human heads, jaguars, and pumas.

269 CE
ZENOBIA OF PALMYRA TAKES SYRIA AND EGYPT

After the assassination of her husband Odaenathus, a strong Roman ally, Zenobia of Palmyra revolted against the Romans. Her armies seized Syria and Egypt before attacking Asia Minor. With the Roman position in the east under threat, Emperor Aurelian marched to meet her, defeating the Palmyrenes at Antioch and then besieging Palmyra, where he captured Zenobia.

◁ *Queen Zenobia Addressing her Soldiers*, Giovanni Battista Tiepolo

"You demand my surrender as though you were not aware that Cleopatra preferred to die a queen rather than remain alive."

ZENOBIA OF PALMYRA, IN RESPONSE TO EMPEROR AURELIAN, FROM HISTORIA AUGUSTA, 4TH CENTURY CE

299 CE

▽ Sima Yan (Emperor Wu of Jin)

280 CE
THE WESTERN JIN REUNITE CHINA

Sima Yan, the grandson of a former imperial general, deposed the last Cao Wei emperor in 265 CE, declaring himself the first ruler of a new dynasty, the Western Jin. He established a new legal code, devolved power to the imperial princes, and then in 280 CE conquered the state of Eastern Wu. However, this reunification of China did not long survive Sima Yan's death a decade later.

△ The Tetrarchs, porphyry sculpture

284 CE
DIOCLETIAN DECLARED ROMAN EMPEROR

Diocletian was of humble birth but rose through the army ranks and was declared emperor after the Emperor Numerian died in mysterious circumstances during a campaign against Persia. Strong, and with a genius for organization, he saw that one man alone could not end the Military Anarchy: in 286 CE he chose another officer, Maximian, to be co-emperor, later extending the system to four emperors (the Tetrarchy).

300 CE

301 CE Diocletian issues
the Edict on Maximum Prices, an attempt to control inflation

303 CE Diocletian orders
Christian persecution, killing many who refuse to renounce their faith

c. 300 CE Start of the Classic Maya period
in Mesoamerica

304 CE

NORTHERN CHINA BREAKS INTO 16 KINGDOMS

The Western Jin dynasty became increasingly reliant on non-Chinese northern nomad soldiers such as the Southern Xiongnu. In 304 CE, Liu Yuan, a commander with Xiongnu origins, overthrew the final Jin emperor and declared his own Han Zhao Dynasty. Northern China dissolved into a chaotic mosaic of small states, known as the Sixteen Kingdoms, ruled by other nomadic groups such as the Xianbei and Jie, until its reunification by the Northern Wei in 439 CE.

◁ **Stoneware** from China's Sixteen Kingdoms Period

320 CE

CHANDRAGUPTA ESTABLISHES THE GUPTA EMPIRE

The grandson of Gupta, founder of a small state in Magadha in north-eastern India, Chandragupta established his dynasty's power by marrying a princess of the neighbouring Licchavi state. He expanded his domains into Ayodhya and southern Bihar, beginning the growth of the Gupta empire that would dominate northern India until the 5th century CE.

△ Gupta dynasty sculpture of Krishna killing the demon Keshi

312 CE
BATTLE OF THE MILVIAN BRIDGE

Diocletian's Tetrarchy (governance of the Roman Empire by four rulers) became destabilized after the death of Constantius I in 306 CE and the declaration of his son, Constantine, as emperor. A struggle ensued with Maxentius, son of Diocletian's former co-emperor Maximian, who claimed rule over the western empire. Allied with Licinius in the east, Constantine marched on Italy, defeating Maxentius in a battle at the Milvian Bridge outside Rome.

◁ Battle of the Milvian Bridge

330 CE
CONSTANTINE FOUNDS A NEW EASTERN ROMAN CAPITAL

After defeating Licinius, his last rival, Constantine I chose the site of the old Greek city of Byzantium to found a new capital to consolidate his rule. Calling it Nova Roma ("New Rome" – though it soon took his own name as Constantinople), he established a new Senate, and had a grand imperial place, baths, a vast Hippodrome and imposing Christian churches built there. The new city, the imperial capital for over 1,000 years, was embellished with statues taken from throughout the empire.

◁ Constantine's Column, Istanbul

320 CE Ezana of the Ethiopian kingdom of Aksum is converted to Christianity

325 CE The Council of Nicaea, a meeting of Christian bishops, agrees the first official Christian doctrine

359 CE

"No one whatsoever should be denied the opportunity to give his heart to the observance of …. that religion which he should think best for himself."

THE EDICT OF MILAN, 313 CE

45–500 CE
THE SPREAD OF CHRISTIANITY

Christianity spreads from its Judaean heartland in the mid-40s CE with missionary journeys by St Paul to Antioch and Asia Minor.

301 CE Armenia becomes first Christian state when its ruler Tiridates III is converted by St Gregory the Illuminator.

313 CE By the Edict of Milan, Constantine I tolerates Christianity and other religions in the Roman Empire.

391 CE Theodosius I bans pagan worship in the Roman Empire. Many temples are attacked and destroyed by Christian mobs.

497 CE The Frankish king Clovis converts to Christianity, accepting baptism into the Roman Catholic Church.

c. 250–476 CE
THE DECLINE AND FALL OF ROME

By the 4th century, the Roman Empire was under increasing pressure from barbarians intent on plundering or settling within the empire. The costs and bureaucracy needed to defend its borders could not be supported, and the empire was unable to cope with attacks on multiple fronts, suffering frequent incursions that devastated its frontier provinces. To manage the threat, the empire was forced to recruit barbarian mercenaries to man its armies, and even its best generals, such as Flavius Stilicho (c. 359–408 CE), were of Germanic origin.

From the 390s CE, Alaric and his Goths devastated the Balkans, even invading Italy; and in 407 CE a large group of Vandals, Alans, and Sueves crossed the Rhine into Gaul, and occupied much of Spain and North Africa. With central control receding, the empire's tax base shrank and it became unable to defend its provinces in the west. Rome was sacked by Vandals and the last Western Emperor, Romulus Augustulus, was deposed by his Germanic army chief Odovacer in 476 CE. In contrast, the Eastern Roman emperors stabilized the Balkans, and their line survived almost 1,000 years.

KEY MOMENTS

c. 250–476 CE Protecting the borders
A weakened Roman Empire responded to the barbarian threat by reinforcing its frontiers. The army became divided into frontier garrisons (*see left*) and elite mobile field armies in a system that was costly to fund.

c. 409–800 CE The Germanic kingdoms
The Germanic barbarians established kingdoms in the Roman provinces they occupied: the Franks in Gaul, the Visigoths (*left*) in Spain, and the Ostrogoths in Italy. Except in Britain, their rulers based themselves in old Roman cities and made use of former Roman officials in their governments.

452 CE Pope Leo I meets Attila the Hun
Attila, king of the Huns, led an army across the Danube into Northern Italy, taking ten cities. An embassy led by Pope Leo I (*left*) met with Attila in an attempt to persuade him not to march on Rome. The Huns withdrew, but probably to avoid harsh winter conditions.

Exquisitely carved in Proconnesian marble, the mid-3rd century Ludovisi sarcophagus shows a battle between Romans and barbarians, possibly Goths. The central mounted figure probably represents the deceased Roman soldier within the sarcophagus.

378 CE
ROMAN ARMY ROUTED

In the 370s CE, the Goths wished to settle in the Eastern Roman Empire. At first denied entry, then mistreated by Roman officials, in 378 CE they surged into the Balkans. The Eastern Roman emperor Valens intercepted them near Adrianople. Finding fewer Goths than expected, he attacked without waiting for reinforcements. The Goth cavalry – returning from a foraging expedition – swelled Goth numbers and destroyed the Romans.

◁ The Battle of Adrianople

360 CE

360 CE Julian becomes Roman emperor, beginning a pagan resurgence

378 CE
SIJAY K'AK' CONQUERS MAYA CITY OF TIKAL

The Maya of Tikal, close to Lake Petén, had expanded their territory slowly throughout the Guatemalan lowlands. However, in 378 CE a new dynasty took power after Sijay K'ak', an outsider from the city of Teotihuacan in central Mexico, overthrew the native dynasty and installed Yax Nuun Ayiin as ruler. Mexican cultural influence in Tikal grew and in this "New Order", Tikal absorbed territory to the north and east, becoming the most powerful of the Maya city-states.

▷ Temple ruins,
Mayan city of Tikal

386 CE
TOBA WEI REUNIFY NORTHERN CHINA

The chaotic 16 Kingdoms period began to resolve itself in 386 CE when the Toba – a non-Han Chinese Turkic people – asserted their independence. Their ruler Toba Gui declared himself first emperor of the Wei dynasty in 399 CE and began an expansion of Toba territory that within 40 years reunified northern China. The Wei adopted Buddhism and were patrons of Buddhist art.

◁ **Buddhist carvings** at Yungang Caves, commissioned by the Wei

> "The renowned city, the capital of the Roman Empire, is swallowed up in one tremendous fire."
>
> *OROSIUS, LETTER TO GAUDENTIUS, ABOUT THE SACK OF ROME IN 410 CE*

404 CE Gwanggaeto, ruler of the Korean state of Silla, defeats an invasion from Yamato Japan

405 CE St Jerome completes the Vulgate translation of the Bible

406 CE Vandals, Sueves, and Alan barbarians cross the Rhine frontier of the Roman Empire in force

419 CE

410 CE
GOTHS UNDER ALARIC SACK ROME

Frustrated at years of broken Roman promises of land for his people, the Gothic chieftain Alaric invaded Italy, aiming to capture Rome itself. A first siege was lifted after the payment of a huge tribute, but Emperor Honorius broke off further negotiations and, after a new siege, the Goths broke into the city in August 410 CE, ransacking many of its buildings.

▷ **The sack of Rome** by Alaric's Goths

400–1700 CE
DEVELOPMENT OF CHINESE PAINTING

From the 5th century CE, Chinese artists developed advanced brushwork techniques and established a tradition of landscape painting that endured for centuries.

c. 400 CE Gui Kaizhi, a leading artist of the Northern Wei, is among the first major advocates of landscape painting.

c. 750 CE Wang Wei introduces ink and wash landscape painting during the Tang artistic revival.

c. 1500 The "Four Masters of the Ming", including Shen Zhou, emphasize individual expression and bring Chinese painting to new heights.

1650–1700 Under the early Qing, individualistic painting styles emerge, notably the fluid brushwork of Shitao (*above*).

c. 450 CE

KINGDOM OF AKSUM AT ITS HEIGHT

The Christian kingdom of Aksum (centred on modern Eritrea and Ethiopia), reached its zenith in the 5th century CE. The first sub-Saharan state to issue coinage, its merchants traded as far as Alexandria, linking into Mediterranean networks, and its rulers erected huge stelae in the capital, Aksum.

▷ **King Ezana's Stela,** Aksum, 4th century CE

439 CE The Vandals capture Carthage, capital of Roman North Africa

△ *The Course of Empire, Destruction* by Thomas Cole imagines the sack of Rome

420 CE

450 CE Execution of Cui Hao, chief architect of the Northern Wei reforms in China

426 CE

ST AUGUSTINE OF HIPPO COMPLETES CITY OF GOD

After a career as a professor in Milan, Augustine converted to Christianity and became first a priest and then a bishop in Hippo in his native North Africa. His writings helped reconcile Classical philosophy and Christian teaching, and in his *City of God* he told the history of the world through divine providence, refuting suggestions that the sack of Rome in 410 CE had been divine punishment for the rejection of paganism.

◁ St Augustine's *City of God,* Spanish translation

> ## "The world is passing away, the world is losing its grip, the world is short of breath."

ST AUGUSTINE OF HIPPO, SERMON 81

455 CE
THE VANDALS SACK ROME

In the 440s, the Roman Emperor Valentinian III strove to keep the peace with the Germanic Vandal barbarians, even betrothing his daughter Eudocia to the Vandal prince Huneric. Valentinian's successor Petronius Maximus broke this agreement. Outraged, Huneric's father, the Vandal King Genseric, landed with a fleet near Ostia and marched on Rome, stripping it of its remaining ancient treasures. Roman fleets sent in 460 CE and 468 CE to exact vengeance on the Vandals were easily destroyed, confirming Rome's terminal weakness.

451 CE Attila the Hun fails to defeat a Roman-Visigothic army at the Catalaunian Fields

467 CE The death of Skandagupta marks the start of the decline of the Indian Gupta Empire

479 CE

455 CE The Anglo-Saxon invasion of England begins (traditional date)

▷ **Romulus,** bust

476 CE
LAST WESTERN EMPEROR

In 475 CE, the Roman official Orestes deposed Emperor Julius Nepos and elevated his own son Romulus to the throne. A revolt broke out among the Germanic mercenaries in the army, who demanded one-third of Italy's land. When Orestes refused, their general, Odoacer, seized the imperial capital Ravenna and deposed Romulus, the very last Western Roman emperor.

▷ The Monkey, Nazca line

c. 450 CE
NAZCA PEOPLE MAKE GEOGLYPHS IN THE DESERT

In the mid-5th century CE, the Nazca people of the southern Peruvian desert created some of the world's most spectacular geoglyphs (massive designs made by using coloured sand and gravel placed into shallow trenches). Some are hundreds of metres in length and depict animals such as monkeys, hummingbirds, and spiders; they can only be clearly seen from the air.

493 CE
THEODORIC, RULER OF THE OSTROGOTHS, DEFEATS ODOACER

In 489 CE, the Ostrogothic king Theodoric invaded Italy, encouraged by the eastern Roman Emperor Zeno to overthrow the Germanic king Odoacer who was threatening the Roman frontier. After a long struggle, Theodoric entered Ravenna in 493 CE and, under cover of a truce, murdered Odoacer. He ruled Italy as a king, respecting Roman rights and laws.

◁ **Theodoric**, ruler of the Ostrogoths

480 CE Hephthalites from Central Asia invade the Gupta empire, hastening its collapse

480 CE

c. 500 CE The Mon state of Dvaravati emerges in Thailand, acting as a conduit for Indian culture

497 CE Clovis, King of the Franks, is baptized, the first major Germanic ruler to accept Catholicism

▷ **Silver-gilt dish** of King Peroz

484 CE
HEPHTHALITE HUNS KILL THE SASANIAN RULER

In 484 CE, Sasanian ruler Peroz marched east to face the Hephthalite Huns who had pressed against Persia's eastern frontier since the 450s CE. He suffered a devastating defeat and was killed near Balkh. Pillaged by the Hephthalites, Persia suffered a period of chaos until the accession of Peroz's grandson Khosrow I nearly 50 years later.

c. 500 CE
RISE OF HUARI CULTURE

The Huari began to flourish in the central Highlands of Peru. They expanded from their capital Huari near Ayacucho, with its monumental stone enclosures and D-shaped temples, to occupy much of the former territory of the Moche. Their bright textiles and ceramics carrying images of the staff god, a rectangular figure with a lavish headdress, spread widely throughout their empire.

△ **Huari** shawl

529 CE
EASTERN ROMAN EMPEROR JUSTINIAN ISSUES HIS LAW CODE

To rationalize the imperial laws that had built up over many centuries, Emperor Justinian appointed a 10-man legal commission to produce a single law code. Two years later, in 529 CE, their work was complete and the Code (together with its later revisions), became the Eastern Roman Empire's sole source of law and a hugely influential legal document for many centuries.

◁ **A later edition of** Justinian's *Body of Civil Law*

482–565 CE
JUSTINIAN I

One of the greatest eastern Roman emperors, Justinian reconquered lost western provinces in North Africa, Italy, and Spain, issued a new law code, and built the church of Hagia Sophia, Constantinople.

c. 535 CE Nubia fragments into three kingdoms – Nobatia, Alwa, and Makuria

536 CE Eastern Roman general Belisarius recaptures Rome from the Ostrogoths

539 CE

507 CE Clovis defeats the Visigoths at Vouillé, driving them into Spain

538 CE
BUDDHISM REACHES JAPAN

Keen to attract allies against China, the ruler of the Korean state of Baekje sent a mission to Japan, which carried with it images of the Buddha and sacred texts. The religion faced fierce opposition from Japanese nobles, but the emperor Kinmei entrusted the Buddhist gifts to Soga no Iname, whose clan became the first Japanese Buddhists and built its first Buddhist temple, the Asuka-Dera.

△ **Asuka-dera temple**, Japan

Average summer temperatures fell by 2 °C (3.6 °F) in summer 536 CE, beginning the coldest decade in Europe for over 2,000 years

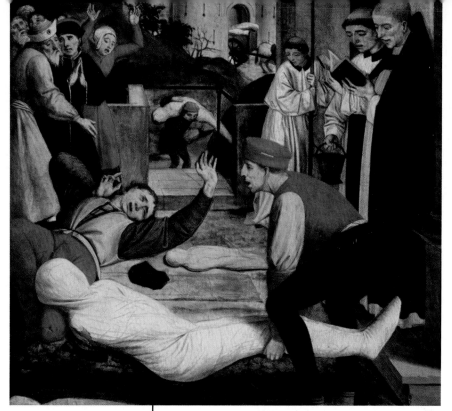

542 CE

PLAGUE OF JUSTINIAN

The first known epidemic of bubonic plague entered the Byzantine empire through the port of Pelusium in Egypt and then spread, reaching the imperial capital Constantinople, where it left streets littered with corpses. Emperor Justinian contracted the disease, but recovered. The plague claimed around 40 per cent of the population of the eastern Mediterranean, caused huge disruption to agriculture, commerce, and military recruitment, and severely weakened the Byzantine empire.

◁ **Prayers for the victims**
of the Justinianic Plague

540 CE

550 CE Kingdom of Ghana founded – the first of the great West African states

c. 570 CE Khan Bayam establishes the Avar kingdom in central Europe

In 542 CE, around 10,000 people died of plague every day in Constantinople

568 CE

LOMBARDS INVADE ITALY

The Lombards, a Germanic people based in Pannonia (modern Hungary) took advantage of the weakness of Byzantine rule following the prolonged war with the Ostrogoths and the Justinianic Plague to cross the Alps into Italy. Their king Audoin rapidly overran the north, capturing Pavia in 572 CE; however, the Lombard kingdom soon fragmented into feuding duchies.

◁ **Detail from helmet**
of Lombard king Agilulf

587 CE
VISIGOTHIC KING OF SPAIN CONVERTS TO CATHOLICISM

The Visigoths, previously adherents of the Arian form of Christianity popular among Germanic groups, adopted Catholicism when their king Reccared converted in 587 CE. The new creed was proclaimed at a Council at Toledo in 589. Despite sporadic uprisings against the new religious policies, it helped integrate Visigoths and Romans and lent the support of the Catholic Church in strengthening the Visigothic monarchy.

◁ Prince Shotoku

593 CE
PRINCE SHOTOKU BECOMES REGENT OF JAPAN

After his aunt Suiko became empress of Japan, Shotoku Taishi was chosen to act as regent by the leader of the powerful Soga clan. He ruled wisely, cementing strong links with China and establishing a Chinese-style bureaucratic system with a hierarchy of ranks. He introduced the Seventeen-Article Constitution – a moral code for the ruling class – and promoted Buddhism, building great temples including the Hōryū-ji in Ikaruga.

◁ **Baptism of the Visigoths** in Spain

599 CE

570 CE Birth of the Prophet Muhammad in the western Arabian town of Mecca

597 CE St Augustine arrives in Kent on a mission sent by Pope Gregory I to convert the Anglo-Saxons

589 CE
CHINA UNIFIED

In 581 CE, a court official, Yang Jian, overthrew the Northern Zhou dynasty and established the Sui. As Emperor Wen, he secured the north, then invaded southern China, defeating the Chen dynasty and capturing its capital Nanjing. With China united in 589 CE after three centuries, he embarked on schemes such as building the Grand Canal, the expense of which contributed to his dynasty's collapse within 30 years.

△ **Emperor Wen and boats** on the Grand Canal

△ **The Battle of Al-Qadisiyyah,** from a Persian manuscript

642 CE
SASANIAN PERSIA CONQUERED

Having swept through Byzantine-controlled Palestine and Syria, Muslim Arab armies invaded the Sasanian Persian empire. They won a series of victories against the Persians at al-Qadisiyyah and elsewhere, before destroying the last major Persian army at Nihavand in 642 CE. With most of his generals dead, the Persian ruler escaped, leaving his empire in the hands of the Islamic caliphate.

600 CE

613 CE The Prophet Muhammad begins preaching in Mecca

622 CE The Hijra, or Hegira, the journey of Muhammad and his followers from Mecca to Medina, begins the Islamic era

618 CE
FOUNDATION OF THE TANG

The failed military campaigns and massive projects undertaken by Yang, the Chinese Sui emperor, caused widespread revolt. To stem the chaos, army general Li Yuan took control, deposed the emperor, and declared his own Tang dynasty. Within six years Li Yuan, now emperor Gaozu, had defeated the rebels and united China under Tang rule, a period that lasted nearly 300 years.

◁ Emperor Gaozu of Tang

"With history as a mirror, one can understand the rise and fall of a nation."

TAIZONG, SECOND TANG EMPEROR, POSTHUMOUSLY PUBLISHED, C. 640 CE

646 CE

TAIKA REFORMS IN JAPAN

The Japanese court had, for half a century, been dominated by the corrupt Soga clan. A coup led by Prince Naka no Ōe and Nakatomi no Kamatari ended Soga influence and a new emperor was installed, his reign referred to as the Taika era. A series of reforms were instituted, based on the model of Tang China. Private ownership of land was abolished, direct control by the emperor over the administration imposed, laws codified, and a fair tax system instituted. These Taika reforms greatly strengthened Japan.

◁ Nakatomi no Kamatari

668 CE

UNIFICATION OF KOREA UNDER THE SILLA

In 660 CE, King Munmu of the Korean state of Silla attacked the rival kingdom of Baekje. Within eight years he overcame both Baekje and the third Korean state, Koguryo, expelled Tang Chinese forces, and united Korea for the first time, establishing a government modelled on that of the Tang.

▷ Silla dynasty stoneware ossuary

699 CE

672 CE Tikal conquers Dos Pilas to become the dominant Maya city-state

650 CE

COMPILATION OF THE QURAN

After the death of the Prophet Muhammad in 632 CE, disputes arose about who should succeed him, and the need grew for an agreed text of the Quran, which had previously been transmitted orally. The process of writing down the sacred book was completed under Caliph Uthman around 650 CE, and the earliest surviving manuscripts date shortly after him.

◁ Birmingham Quran manuscript

711 CE
ARAB-BERBER ARMY INVADES SPAIN

Having conquered North Africa, the forces of the Umayyad caliphate crossed into Visigoth-ruled Spain in 711 CE. This Arab-Berber army led by Tariq ibn Ziyad defeated the Visigothic king Roderic at Guadalete and within six years had overrun the whole of the Iberian peninsula save for small Christian-ruled enclaves in the north.

700 CE

732 CE The Franks defeat an Arab army at Tours, halting the Islamic empire's northward advance

725 CE The Hohokam build settlements with complex irrigation channels in Arizona's Sonora Desert

726 CE
ICONOCLASM IN THE BYZANTINE EMPIRE

The veneration of icons (portraits of Christ and the saints) was popular in the Byzantine Empire, but in 726 CE Emperor Leo III instituted a policy of iconoclasm, banning their worship and ordering their destruction. Leo and his senior clerics blamed Byzantine defeats against the Arabs on divine displeasure at icon veneration, and the policy, although unpopular among many ordinary Byzantines, lasted over 60 years.

◁ Byzantine iconoclasts

◁ The Battle of Guadalete

751 CE

PEPIN III BECOMES KING OF THE FRANKS

The Merovingian dynasty in Francia had become weak, dominated by the mayors of the palace, its most senior officials, drawn from the Carolingian family. In 751, the Carolingian Pepin the Short deposed the last Merovingian ruler Childeric III and, with the blessing of the Pope, had himself crowned king and restored royal authority.

◁ **Pepin III "the Short"**, Carolingian king

751 CE An Arab army of the Abbasid Caliphate defeats the Tang Chinese at the Battle of the Talas River

752 CE The Lombards conquer Ravenna, the last major Byzantine holding in northern Italy

755 CE The An Lushan Rebellion weakens the Tang Chinese empire

759 CE

756 CE Abd al-Rahman I declares the Umayyad caliphate of Cordoba

750 CE

ABBASIDS OVERTHROW THE UMAYYADS

Growing discontent with the Syrian-based Umayyad caliphs led to a revolt by Abu al-Abbas al-Saffah, a descendent of Mohammad's uncle. He defeated the Umayyad caliph and established his Abbasid caliphate in Iraq, where his successor al-Mansur founded Baghdad.

◁ **Baghdad** in the time of al-Mansur

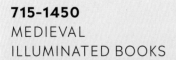    

715–1450
MEDIEVAL ILLUMINATED BOOKS

Lavish hand-painted manuscripts, often of religious or historical works, were produced in the millennium after 500 CE, at first in monasteries but later, as literacy spread, for wealthy patrons.

c. 715 CE The Lindisfarne Gospels, named for the monastery where they were kept, have a jewel-encrusted outer binding.

781 CE The Godescalc Evangelistary is commissioned by the Carolingian ruler Charlemagne.

c. 1113 The Russian Primary Chronicle charts the history of Russia from early times to the accession of Vladimir III.

1405–08 The Book of Hours of Jean, Duke of Berry, and similar prayer collections become popular with rich patrons.

786 CE

HARUN AL-RASHID BECOMES ABBASID CALIPH

Harun's accession on the death of his brother began a golden age for the Abbasid caliphate in which the arts and sciences flourished and embassies were sent as far as Francia and Tang China. Assisted by his viziers, Harun strengthened the caliphal government, which he transferred from Baghdad to Raqqa later in his reign.

▷ Harun al-Rashid

c. 800 CE

BOROBUDUR TEMPLES BUILT

This complex of Buddhist temples was built by the Sailendra rulers of central Java, funded by the wealth of their maritime empire. The largest Buddhist monument in the world, it was built in the form of a three-dimensional mandala that guides pilgrims through three levels symbolizing the soul's journey towards nirvana. It remained an important centre of Buddhist worship until its abandonment in the 11th century.

▷ Borobudur temple

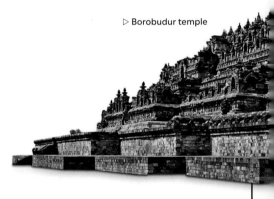

787 CE The Council of Nicaea ends the iconoclast controversy in the Byzantine empire by making the veneration of icons legal again

760 CE

774 CE Frankish ruler Charlemagne conquers the Lombard kingdom of Italy

794 CE The Japanese imperial capital moves to Heian (modern-day Kyoto)

▷ **The Lindisfarne Stone** records a Viking raid

793 CE

FIRST VIKING RAID IN NORTH-WEST EUROPE

A Viking attack on the monastery of Lindisfarne off the north-east coast of England marked the start of two centuries in which raiders from Scandinavia preyed on the coastlines of northern Europe. Their longships, which were able to move swiftly and land in shallow waters, and their ability as warriors, helped the Vikings conquer most of Anglo-Saxon England and bring the Frankish kingdoms close to collapse.

c. 747–814 CE
CHARLEMAGNE

Charlemagne strengthened the Frankish government and legal system, and assumed the title of Emperor of the Romans. He extended Frankish power into Spain, Saxony, Italy, and Central Europe.

The temple complex at Borobudur contains 504 Buddha statues

802 CE

JAYAVARMAN II FOUNDS THE KHMER EMPIRE

Declaring himself *chakravartin* (universal ruler), Jayavarman asserted the independence of the Khmer from the Javanese Sailendra. He established himself in the Angkor region, the first Khmer ruler to do so. His successors would later build the enormous temple complex that includes Angkor Wat.

△ Jayavarman II

800 CE Ibrahim ibn Aghlab establishes the Aghlabid empire, based at Kairouan (in modern Tunisia)

801 CE The Gurjara-Pratihara dynasty becomes powerful under Nagabhata II, later conquering Kannauj in northern India

▽ Coronation of Charlemagne

800 CE

CHARLEMAGNE CROWNED ROMAN EMPEROR

The Frankish ruler Charlemagne was crowned by Pope Leo III in St Peter's Basilica, Rome. The ceremony, on Christmas Day, symbolically established Charlemagne as the heir to the western Roman empire, confirming his power and beginning a line of Holy Roman Emperors that would stretch into the 19th century.

800–1300
ISLAMIC SCIENCE

The five centuries from 800 CE saw science flourish in the Islamic lands as scholars built on a legacy inherited from the classical empires and made advances of their own. The conquest of the eastern provinces of the Roman empire and the Persian Sasanian empire left the Islamic caliphate in control of important libraries and traditions of scholarship. The practical demands of medicine, architecture, and commerce, and the need to understand the geography of a vast empire led Muslim rulers to sponsor the translation of texts such as the Roman astronomer Ptolemy's *Almagest*.

The courts of the Umayyad and Abbasid caliphs at Damascus and Baghdad, and in regional centres such as Córdoba in Spain, became centres of learning, where experimentation and scientific advances outstripped those in Europe. Thinkers such as Al-Khwarizmi (c. 780–850 CE) developed algebra as a distinct discipline and provided solutions to quadratic equations, while in the 11th century, Ibn Sina (Avicenna) devised notions of impetus and inertia that went beyond the work of Aristotle. Al-Biruni (973–1048 CE) calculated the radius of Earth by measuring the height of a mountain.

From the 15th century, as new centralized Islamic empires emerged in India, Turkey, and Persia, Islamic science turned to producing compendia of existing knowledge rather than innovation. Its greatest age began to wane.

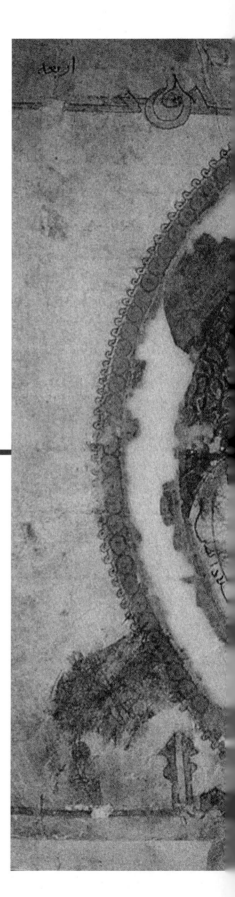

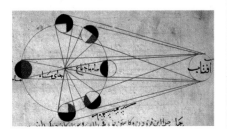

KEY MOMENTS

From c. 770 CE Translating classical works
Abbasid caliphs such as al-Mansur (r. 754–775 CE) established a library in Baghdad. This Bayt al-Hikma ("House of Wisdom") attracted scholars who translated classical manuscripts such as *De Materia Medica* by Dioscorides, (*left*) from Latin, Greek, and Persian into Arabic.

From c. 800 CE Islamic medicine
Physicians such as Persian Al-Razi (854–925 CE) made sophisticated observations (for example, distinguishing measles from smallpox for the first time), while the *Canon of Medicine* by Ibn Sina (980–1037) became a key medical textbook for centuries (*left*).

From c. 800 CE The physical sciences
Islamic scholars made great advances in optics, classified chemical substances for the first time, and produced sophisticated astronomical charts, such as this exposition (*left*) of the phases of the Moon produced by the scholar Abu Rayhan al-Biruni (973–1050).

The Islamic world developed a sophisticated cartographic tradition beginning with the al-Balkhi school in Baghdad in the 9th century CE. This map, compiled by the geographer al-Istakhri around 970 CE, shows the world divided into halves by two great seas.

△ The House of Wisdom

822 CE
BAYT AL-HIKMA (HOUSE OF WISDOM) FOUNDED

A centre for scholarship and, in particular, the translation of Latin and Greek texts into Arabic, the Bayt al-Hikma was established in Baghdad by Caliph al-Mamun. It hosted scholars such as the mathematician al-Khwarizmi, the "father of algebra", and enabled Arab thinkers to have access to classical works of philosophy and science.

△ The House of Wisdom

c. 811 CE The first paper money appears in China, where it is known as "flying money"

810 CE

811 CE The Bulgarian Khan Krum defeats and kills the Byzantine emperor Nicephorus at Pliska, leading to an extension of the First Bulgarian Empire

831 CE
PALERMO FALLS

After the Sicilian city of Palermo was taken by Muslim Aghlabid forces, the Tunisian-based emirate came to dominate the entire island by 902 CE. Palermo prospered under the rule of Ziyadat Allah I (r. 817–38 CE) and his successors, becoming an important trading centre where Islamic, Byzantine, Jewish, and western Christian influences fused to create a rich hybrid culture that thrived until the 13th century.

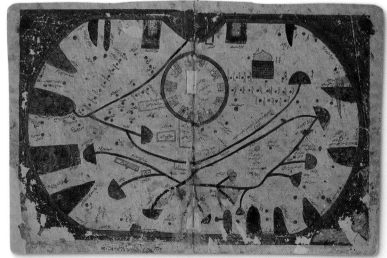

△ Arabic map of Sicily

843 CE

THE TREATY OF VERDUN

On the death of Charlemagne, his great empire was inherited by his son, who ruled as Louis the Pious for 26 years. When Louis died in 840 CE, his sons became embroiled in a civil war. After two years of bitter fighting, a division was agreed at Verdun, which gave France to Charles the Bald, the German lands to Louis, and the area in the middle (Lotharingia) to Lothar.

◁ Treaty of Verdun, miniature

804–872 CE
FUJIWARA NO YOSHIFUSA

In 858 CE, Fujiwara no Yoshifusa was appointed *sessho* (regent) to his nine-year-old grandson Seiwa. He began a line of Fujiwara regents who served as the real rulers of Japan until the mid-12th century.

848 CE The kingdom of Pagan is founded in Myanmar's Irrawaddy Valley by the Mranma

869 CE

850 CE The Chola ruler Vijayala captures the city of Tanjore in south India from the Pandyas

858 CE Fujiwara no Yoshifusa of Japan's influential Fujiwara clan becomes regent, beginning three centuries of Fujiwara domination

841 CE

DUBLIN SETTLED BY VIKINGS

The Irish city was initially settled as a longphort (fortified harbour) for raids inland. However, by the 850s CE it had developed into the Kingdom of Dublin under Olaf the White and his brother Ímar, whose rulers held the area, often in alliance with the Viking kingdom of York, until the 11th century.

◁ Viking war axe

▷ An early Chinese depiction of firearms in use

c. 850 CE

GUNPOWDER IS FORMULATED

Daoist monks in China, searching for the elixir of immortality, produced a formula for gunpowder. It was known that saltpetre had medicinal properties but, when mixed with sulphur and charcoal, it became combustible. In the 11th century it was used to produce the first firearms, such as flame-throwers and explosive arrows.

874 CE
ICELAND SETTLED BY VIKINGS

Led by Ingólfur Arnarson, hundreds of Vikings migrated from Scandinavia to Iceland. Thousands more followed in a time known as the landnám ("land-taking"). They soon established farms across the whole island and developed an Icelandic Commonwealth, governed from 930 CE by the Althing, one of the world's first parliaments.

◁ **Viking bronze** figure of Thor, Iceland, c. 1000

c. 882 CE
OLEG, CHIEFTAIN OF THE RUS VIKINGS, BECOMES RULER OF KIEV

Moving from his base around Novgorod, the chieftan Oleg defeated his rivals Askold and Dir and took their stronghold at Kiev. He transferred his capital there, raiding local Slav tribes such as the Drevlians, who he forced to pay tribute. As Kiev's power grew, it became the nucleus of the Kievan Rus state.

△ **Oleg of Novgorod** in battle

870 CE

896 CE **Tsar Symeon of Bulgaria** defeats a Byzantine army at Bulgarophygon

878 CE
ALFRED THE GREAT DEFEATS THE VIKINGS

At the Battle of Edington, Alfred saved his Kingdom of Wessex from conquest by the Norse raiders of the Great Heathen Army who had defeated the Anglo-Saxon kingdoms one by one since their arrival in England in 865 CE. The Vikings caught Alfred by surprise, forcing him to flee into marshes around Athelney, but he regrouped and was victorious at Edington, forcing the Vikings to sue for peace.

▷ **King Alfred the Great**

> "The heathen, terrified by hunger, cold, fear, and last of all by despair, begged for peace."

ASSER, LIFE OF ALFRED, C. 900 CE

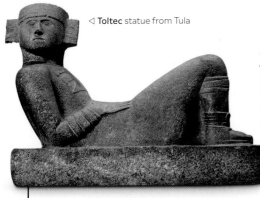

◁ **Toltec** statue from Tula

c. 900 CE
TOLTEC CAPITAL OF TULA FLOURISHES

Located in Hidalgo state, Mexico, Tula was the Toltec capital. Extending over some 8 sq km (3 sq miles), the city contained several temple pyramids (notably the five-stepped pyramid of Quetzalcóatl), ball courts, and many huge anthropomorphic statues of warriors. Tula was the largest city in the region between the fall of Teotihuacan and the rise of Tenochtitlan, although it is unclear whether the Toltecs built an empire or simply exercised cultural influence.

The Japanese Kokinshū anthology contains 1,111 poems

909 CE The Fatimid caliphate begins when Abdullah al-Mahdi overthrows the Aghlabids in North Africa

918 Chola King Parantaka I conquers the Pandya kingdom of southern India

919 CE

905 CE Compilation of the Kokinshū, the first anthology of Japanese poetry

907 CE
FALL OF THE TANG IN CHINA

After a long period of weak rulers, dominance of the court by eunuchs, and a series of rebellions, the last Tang emperor was deposed by Zhu Wen, a former rebel turned general, who established the short-lived Later Liang dynasty. In the following decades – the time of the Five Dynasties and Ten Kingdoms – China dissolved into a mosaic of competing states and was reunited by the Song only in 960 CE.

▷ **Tang soldiers** on horseback, tomb painting

929 CE
UMAYYAD CALIPH IN CORDOBA

The emir Abd ar-Rahman III declared himself Umayyad caliph in Córdoba after the North African Fatimid caliphs threatened to invade Spain. He united Muslim-controlled al-Andalus and reduced the Christian territories in the north to vassalage. Under his rule, Córdoba reached a cultural zenith, with the building of the Madinat al-Zahra palace complex and a university that attracted students from throughout the Muslim world and Christian Europe.

▷ **Abd-ar-Rahman** statue in Córdoba

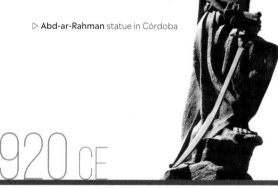

920 CE

c. 950 CE Tihuanaco, the city at the centre of a little-known civilization in Bolivia, is abandoned

946 CE The Persian Shi'ite Buyid dynasty captures Baghdad

935 CE
THE UNIFICATION OF KOREA

Taejo, ruler of Goryeo, unified Korea with his conquest of the state of Later Baekje, which followed his victory over Later Silla the previous year. Taejo and his successors curbed the strength of regional warlords, increased tax revenues, and reformed the bureaucracy. The enhanced royal power helped create a strong centralized state.

▷ King Taejo

960 CE
SONG DYNASTY FOUNDED

Zhao Kuangyin, a general of the Later Zhou dynasty in northern China, seized the capital Kaifeng and declared himself Emperor Taizu of the Song dynasty. Over next 20 years he conquered the rest of China, reunifying it after the chaotic Five Dynasties and Ten Kingdom period. His promotion of education, scientific academies, and a rigorous civil service examination strengthened China's central bureaucracy.

◁ *Along the River During the Qingming Festival,* one of the most famous Chinese paintings, depicts life in the Song capital Kaifeng (Bianjing)

961 CE Nicephorus Phocas, Byzantine emperor, takes Crete from the Arabs

c. 965 CE King Harald Bluetooth of Denmark converts to Christianity

962 CE German king Otto I is crowned Holy Roman Emperor in Rome

969 CE The Fatimids conquer Egypt and transfer their caliphate there

969 CE

▽ Imperial Crown of Otto I

955 CE
OTTO I DEFEATS THE MAGYARS

At the Battle of Lechfeld, the heavy cavalry of the German king Otto I routed a force of Magyar horseman. The death of most of the Magyar leaders ended their raids westward. In 962 CE, Otto was crowned Holy Roman Emperor by Pope John XII.

930–1789
HISTORY OF PARLIAMENTS

The Middle Ages saw the establishment of assemblies of commoners that asserted their rights against monarchs and gradually evolved into today's democratic parliaments.

930 CE The Althing, the world's first parliament, is established in Viking-ruled Iceland, meeting annually to decide on laws.

1188 The Cortes of León, the first parliamentary body in mainland Europe, meets, including nobles, merchants, and townsmen.

1295 The English Model Parliament is called by Edward I: it includes nobles and two representatives from each city and borough.

1789 The First US Congress meets in New York City; representatives from the 13 states are elected by popular vote.

988 CE

BAPTISM OF VLADIMIR OF KIEV

The Grand Prince of Kiev was baptized in a ceremony at Kiev. He had reputedly sent envoys to neighbouring lands to investigate their religions, and found all but Greek Orthodox Christianity disagreeable. His baptism in the faith made possible an alliance with Byzantium through his marriage to Emperor Basil II's sister.

▷ Baptism of Prince Vladimir

> "Drinking is the joy of the Rus. We cannot exist without that pleasure."

VLADIMIR OF KIEV'S REPLY TO BULGAR MUSLIM ENVOYS SUGGESTING HE CONVERT, c. 987 CE

975 CE Byzantine Emperor John Tzimiskes recaptures Damascus after a successful Syrian campaign

987 CE The Capetian dynasty is founded in France by Hugh Capet, elected king after the death of the last Carolingian

970 CE

973 CE Parantaka II defeats the Rashtrakutas, establishing the Chola dynasty's supremacy in south India

982 CE The Dai Viet kingdom destroys the Champa capital of Indrapura

985 CE

VIKINGS COLONIZE GREENLAND

After being exiled from Iceland for his involvement in a fatal brawl, Erik the Red sailed to a land that he named "Greenland" in order to attract more colonists. He was followed by thousands of migrants who established two settlements (the Eastern and Western) on the southern tip of the island; these survived for over 400 years.

▷ Erik the Red

987 CE

TOLTEC INFLUENCE REACHES THE YUCATAN

In the Maya city of Chichen Itzá, the appearance of Toltec-style architecture from Tula, including chacmool offering altars, Atlantean warrior statues, and the temple-pyramid of Kukulkán, suggest the movement of people from central Mexico to the Yucatán Peninsula. It is not clear whether these people came as invaders, settlers, or as a new elite, or if the local Maya rulers simply assimilated Toltec culture.

△ Toltec warrior statue

▷ Basil II, the "Bulgar-slayer"

996 CE
BASIL II CAMPAIGNS AGAINST THE BULGARS

Basil II was a highly effective Byzantine emperor, who cemented imperial authority both at home and abroad. Most notably, he neutralized the ambitious Bulgarian kingdom, capturing key Bulgar strongholds such as Skopje. In 1014, he inflicted a devastating defeat on the Bulgar Tsar Samuel at Kleidion, killing 15,000 Bulgars and reputedly blinding 99 out of 100 survivors. The First Bulgarian empire collapsed and the Bulgars posed little threat to Byzantium for 150 years.

1001 Stephen becomes first king of Hungary, establishing it as a powerful European state

1009

△ Pueblo Bonito

c. 1000
CHACO CANYON PUEBLO CIVILIZATION FLOURISHES

The ancient Puebloans of the American southwest reached their zenith with the construction of "great houses" such as Pueblo Bonito, road networks, and irrigation systems that allowed crops to grow in the harsh climate. Within a century, the Chacoan culture had declined, probably as a result of ecological change.

1001
MAHMUD OF GHAZNI INVADES INDIA

Mahmud's actions were the first major Muslim incursions into the Indian subcontinent. In 17 campaigns his armies ranged as far south as Kannauj and Gwalior and sacked the temple of Shiva at Somnath in Gujarat. Although many Indian rulers were reduced to vassalage, his Ghaznavid state only occupied parts of the northwest.

▷ Mahmud of Ghazni

1010

1014 Irish king Brian Boru defeats a Viking coalition at the Battle of Clontarf

1018 The Chola king Rajendra I conquers Sri Lanka and the Maldive islands

1010 Foundation of the Ly dynasty in Vietnam by Ly Thai To

1017 The Danish ruler Cnut is crowned the king of England

974 CE-1028
EMPEROR LY THAI TO

Commander of the Dai Viet palace guard in Thang Long (Hanoi), Ly seized power after the death of the last Le emperor. He relocated his court to the Red River Delta and promoted Buddhism in his kingdom.

△ Boleslaw I enters Kiev

1024

BOLESLAW CROWNED KING OF POLAND

Boleslaw (later known as the Great) inherited the principality of Greater Poland on the death of his father, Mieszko I, in 992 CE and then expanded his territories through campaigns to the east, west, and south. He secured an archbishopric that was independent of German control, and was crowned Poland's first king in 1024, six months before his death.

1021
TALE OF GENJI WRITTEN

Considered to be the first Japanese novel, the *Tale of Genji* took Princess Murasaki Shikibu ten years to complete. The work is an exquisite examination of the life, customs, and etiquette of Heian Japan at the height of the Fujiwara Regency. The story is seen through the eyes of a courtier, Genji, a member of the royal family who is demoted to the rank of commoner.

◁ **Butterflies,** a chapter from *The Tale of Genji* depicted on a panelled screen

"Real things in the darkness seem no more real than dreams."

TALE OF GENJI, *MURASAKI SHIKIBU, 1021*

1041-48
INVENTION OF MOVABLE TYPE

Wooden blocks had long been used in China to print whole pages, but Bi Sheng, a Song dynasty artisan, devised a system in which blocks, each inscribed with a single character, could be arranged and rearranged to create and print many different pages of text.

◁ **Movable type,** hand-carved blocks

1031 The Umayyad caliphate of Córdoba collapses, beset by civil war

1049

1040
SELJUQS DEFEAT THE GHAZNAVIDS

The Seljuqs – originally nomadic Oghuz Turks from Central Asia – invaded Khurasan (territories in modern Iran, Turkmenistan, and Afghanistan) in 1037. Led by Tughril Beg, they defeated the Ghaznavids at Dandanaqan in 1040. After the Ghaznavid sultan Mas'ud fled to India, the Seljuqs began establishing a new Islamic empire that would ultimately stretch as far as Asia Minor.

▷ The Golden Shwedagon Pagoda, Pagan

△ **The Battle of** Dandanaqan

1044
PRINCE ANAWRAHTA BECOMES KING OF PAGAN

Anawrahta turned his small principality in Upper Burma into a united Burmese empire. He conquered the Mon kingdoms of the south, and expanded north to the borders of Nanzhao and west to Arakan. His conversion to Theravada Buddhism in 1056 led to religious reforms and the building of many pagodas on the Pagan plain, while his strengthening of the army helped secure the future of Burma.

960–1279
LIFE IN SONG CHINA

While much of Europe laboured under a feudal system, citizens of Song China lived in peace in a land of thriving cities and expanding trade. Under a succession of eight emperors, the Northern Song dynasty employed a meritocratic bureaucracy to oversee civic life. Peasants were attracted to live in the wealthy cities, some of which grew to house more than a million people. Commerce flourished along newly built canals, and entrepreneurs financed trading expeditions to Japan and southeast Asia in multi-decked junks guided by the world's first magnetic compasses. Transactions were made simpler by a money economy of copper coins and the world's first printed banknotes.

The metropolitan elite enjoyed a lifestyle featuring theatres, restaurants, and social clubs devoted to pursuits including poetry, art, cuisine, and horse-riding. Widespread literacy was encouraged by large-scale paper production and the introduction of woodblock printing. Technological innovations included gunpowder and the first firearms, while booming industry saw cast-iron production reach a record 125,000 tonnes (138,000 tons) in a year.

Even after the northern lands were lost to invaders in 1127, prosperity continued under the Southern Song centred on Lin'an (today's Hangzhou). A further century and a half passed before the dynasty finally succumbed to Mongol invaders in 1279.

KEY MOMENTS

1005 Keeping the peace
After 25 years of intermittent warfare, the Song signed a treaty with the Liao Empire on their northern border, paying them an annual tribute in silver and raw silk (*left*) in return for an end to hostilities.

1070 New economic policies
Faced with a growing budget deficit, the Song appointed the philosopher Wang Anshi (*left*) as chancellor. His reform programme targeted tax evasion by the wealthy and addressed growing social inequality. The policies were resisted by landowners and the merchant guilds but proved successful.

1127 Jurchen invaders capture Bianjing
China's northern border was breached when Jurchen raiders took the capital and captured the emperor and his heir. The emperor's younger son set up a new court south of the Yangzi River, initiating the Southern Song period (*Southern Song dragon pictured left*).

A Northern Song painting depicts a water-powered mill. This was a time of major technological innovation and commerce. Much of the trade was water-borne: it was possible to travel for thousands of kilometres (miles) on a system of inland waterways.

c. 1050

YORUBA CULTURE FLOURISHES IN IFE

The city of Ife (in today's Nigeria) was the centre of the ruling *oni*, the divine-descended ruler of all Yoruba. It developed a sophisticated urban culture and a tradition of sculpture, particularly heads in terracotta or bronze.

◁ **Ife head** sculpture in bronze

1054

THE GREAT SCHISM

The formal separation of the church into the Eastern Orthodox and Roman Catholic churches occurred in 1054 after a period of argument over the creed. A demand by Pope Leo IX's legate that Patriarch Michael Celularius recognize papal supremacy resulted in a mutual excommunication, which was only lifted in 1965. Despite many efforts, reunification of the churches has never occurred.

◁ **Patriarch Michael Cerularius** is excommunicated

1053 The Normans win the Battle of Civitate to establish their dominance in southern Italy

1055 Grufudd ap Llewelyn becomes king of all Wales

1062 The Berber Muslim Almoravid Emirate is established at Marrakech

1050

1066

THE NORMAN CONQUEST OF ENGLAND

After the death of the Anglo-Saxon king Edward the Confessor, Duke William of Normandy believed that he was the rightful heir to the English throne. The succession was, however, disputed and, in January 1066, the English earl Harold Godwinson had himself crowned. Duke William invaded England and defeated and killed Harold at the Battle of Hastings. The events surrounding the succession and battle were depicted in the famous Bayeux Tapestry.

Around 15,000 men fought at the Battle of Hastings

▷ Battle of Manzikert

1071
BATTLE OF MANZIKERT

Responding to continual Seljuq raids on the frontiers of his empire, Byzantine Emperor Romanus IV Diogenes marched his army into eastern Anatolia. Caught by surprise by a large Turkish force, Romanus was captured and his army destroyed, opening the way for the permanent Seljuq conquest of much of Asia Minor.

> "My punishment is far heavier. I forgive you, and set you free."

SULTAN ALP ARSLAN TO ROMANUS DIOGENES AFTER MANZIKERT, 1071

1075 Pope Gregory VII issues a decree forbidding lay investiture

1079

1077 The Seljuk sultanate of Rum is established in Asia Minor

△ The Bayeux Tapestry, panel depicting the death of King Harold

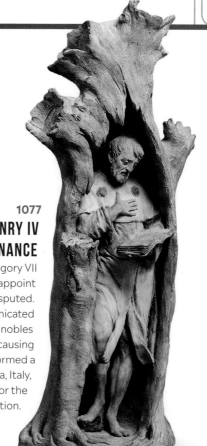

1077
HOLY ROMAN EMPEROR HENRY IV PERFORMS PENANCE

Henry IV argued with Pope Gregory VII over the right of secular rulers to appoint bishops, which the pope disputed. In response, Gregory excommunicated Henry in 1076, so freeing Henry's nobles from their oaths of loyalty and causing them to revolt. Henry performed a humiliating penance, at Canossa, Italy, waiting for three days in a storm for the pope to revoke his excommunication.

▷ Emperor Henry IV's penance

▽ Alfonso VI of Leon

1086

DEFEAT OF ALFONSO VI OF LEON AND CASTILE

Alarmed at Christian gains on the Iberian peninsula, the emir of Seville called for help from the Almoravids – a Berber Muslim dynasty from North Africa. Almoravid forces under Yusuf ibn Tashfin defeated Christian armies under Alfonso VI at the Battle of Sagrajas in 1086. Although Yusuf ibn Tashfin temporarily withdrew to Africa, the Almoravids soon returned to reunite Islamic Spain and begin a northwards advance.

▽ Song astronomical clock

1092

A CHINESE WATER CLOCK

The Chinese polymath and engineer Su Song built a water-driven clock in the Song capital of Kaifeng. Housed in a tower that was 12 m (40 ft) tall, the clock was powered by the fall of water between a series of buckets. It indicated the time of the day, the day of the month, and phase of the Moon. It was destroyed by invading Jurchens in 1126.

1080

1088 Bologna University, Europe's oldest, is founded in Italy

1092 The Seljuq Empire begins to break up after the death of Sultan Malik Shah

1085

DOMESDAY BOOK COMMISSIONED

William of Normandy commissioned a great land survey to help assess the tax he could raise from his new English kingdom. Commissioners were sent out to record the current owners of land areas and the numbers of livestock and serfs on that land, and who had held that land at the time of Edward the Confessor (r. 1042–66). The results were compiled in a central ledger.

◁ The Domesday Book

The Domesday Book records 13,418 settlements

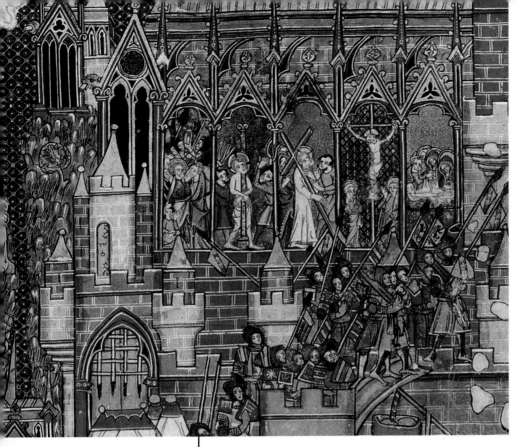

1099
THE ARMY OF THE FIRST CRUSADE TAKES JERUSALEM

A crusader army led by Raymond of Toulouse, Godfrey of Bouillon, and Bohemond of Taranto set out in 1096 in answer to a call to arms from Pope Urban. Their goal was to re-establish Christian control of the Holy Land. The army fought its way across Asia Minor and engaged in a lengthy siege at Antioch, before storming Jerusalem amid a massacre of its Muslim residents and local Christians.

◁ **The capture** of Jerusalem

1109

1098 The Cistercian Order is founded by former Benedictine monks

c. 1100 The Sican culture of north Peru flourishes in a new capital at Túcume

◁ **Thule** comb handle

1100
GREAT ZIMBABWE BUILT

The city of Great Zimbabwe in southern Africa probably served as a royal capital, growing rich on the gold trade between the interior and the East African coast. Ringed by great dry-stone walls, it housed up to 20,000 people and remained the dominant centre in the region until about 1400.

c. 1100
THE THULE INUIT BEGIN A MIGRATION

The Thule began to move eastwards from their ancestral homelands in Alaska into the Canadian Arctic. With their advanced harpoons and seal-skin boats they could hunt bowhead whales and seals far out to sea, and they displaced the Dorset Eskimo people who had previously inhabited the eastern Arctic, reaching Greenland by about 1200.

△ **Great Zimbabwe** ruins

1121
ALMOHAD CAMPAIGNS OF CONQUEST BEGIN

Founded in North Africa by Muhammad ibn Tumart, the Almohad Islamic reformist movement soon gained support among the Berbers of the Atlas Mountains. Ibn Tumart (who was killed in a failed attack on Marrakech in 1130) and his successors overthrew the ruling Almoravid dynasty in Morocco and by the 1170s controlled most of Muslim Iberia.

▷ **Almohad** council of war

1110 The Byzantine empire begins persecution of the Bogomil heresy in the Balkans

1110

1112 Accession of Alaungsithu, in whose reign the Pagan kingdom (in modern Myanmar) reaches the height of its power

1113 Prince Mstislav orders the building of Saint Nicholas Cathedral in Novgorod, the oldest in Russia

▷ Angkor Wat under construction

1113
ANGKOR WAT TEMPLE IS BUILT

The vast temple complex of Angkor Wat was built at the royal capital of Angkor during the reign of the Khmer King Suryavarman II (r. 1113–50). Dedicated to the Hindu god Vishnu, its towers represented the sacred Mount Meru, while its extensive galleries were decorated with carved scenes from Hindu epics.

With an area of 82 hectares (202 acres), Angkor Wat is the largest religious monument in the world

1122
CONCORDAT OF WORMS

The agreement, or concordat, signed by Pope Calixtus II and Holy Roman Emperor Henry V put an end to the Investiture Controversy. It stated that bishops were to be chosen by the pope and invested with their spiritual regalia by the clergy, but needed to do homage to the emperor for lands they held; in the case of disputed elections the emperor would hold sway.

▷ Concordat of Worms, commemorated in stained glass

1139
CIVIL WAR IN ENGLAND

After the death of English king Henry I, supporters of his daughter, the Empress Matilda, and those of his nephew, Stephen of Blois, fought for the throne. Central authority collapsed in a period known as "The Anarchy", which ended only in 1153 when Stephen signed the Treaty of Winchester, agreeing that Matilda's son Henry would inherit the throne after him.

◁ **Empress Matilda** (Maude)

1139

1125 The election of Lothair II as Holy Roman emperor begins a civil war between Guelphs and Ghibellines in Italy

1127
JURCHENS OVERRUN NORTHERN CHINA

The Jurchens, a confederation of tribes on China's northeastern borders, overran Kaifeng and captured the Song emperor, Huizong, in 1125. The Song re-established their dynasty as the Southern Song dynasty at Hangzhou in the south. The Jurchens, meanwhile, founded the Jin dynasty in the north. They gradually adopted Chinese practices and ruled the north until they were overthrown by the Mongols in 1234.

▷ **Song dynasty** horseman

1143
AFONSO I RECOGNIZED AS KING OF PORTUGAL

After defeating the Moors in a battle at Ourique in 1139, Afonso Henriques called himself "King of Portugal", even though Portugal was, at the time, part of the Kingdom of Leon. Four years later, Alfonso VII of Castile recognized Afonso as king of Portugal.

▷ **Afonso I** statue

"This is an island resembling the head of an Ostrich, and contains flourishing cities, lofty mountains, flowing rivers and level ground."

DESCRIPTION OF BRITAIN, FROM THE CHARTA, TEXT ACCOMPANYING THE TABULA ROGERIANA, 1154

1140

1145 Suryavarman II of Angor invades the Champa kingdom, sacking the capital, Vijjaya

1148 The Second Crusade disintegrates into chaos after a failed siege of Damascus

1147 The Almohads invade Spain after Almoravid losses to the Christian states

1145
SECOND CRUSADE CALLED

When Imad al-Din Zengi, atabeg (governor) of Mosul, captured the crusader stronghold of Edessa, a second crusade was called by Pope Eugene III. Led by King Louis VII of France and German Emperor Conrad III, it set out for the Levant in 1147. A serious defeat at Dorylaeum depleted the crusader force and a botched attack on Damascus meant it achieved none of its objectives.

△ **Louis VII** embarks on crusade

1150
CITY OF CAHOKIA REACHES ITS HEIGHT

The principal settlement of the Mississippian Mound Building culture (known for their huge earthen ceremonial platforms), 12th-century Cahokia was home to 20,000 people. They engaged in the cultivation of maize, beans, and squash, and produced fine clay tobacco pipes and pottery. Their culture declined and collapsed in the 14th century, probably due to overexploitation of resources.

△ **Nursing mother effigy**, bottle from Cahokia

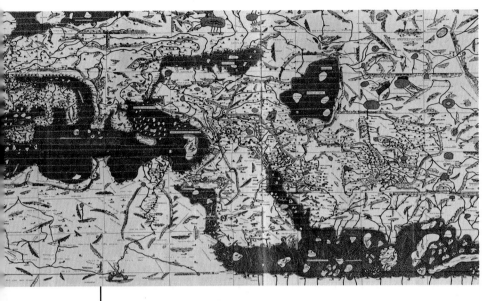

1154
TABULA ROGERIANA COMPLETED

Commissioned by King Roger I of Sicily, the Arab geographer Sharif al-Idrisi produced the *Tabula Rogeriana* ("Book of Roger"), a highly accurate world map. The map was produced after extensive research and interviews with numerous travellers. It remained the most reliable map of its kind for over two centuries.

◁ *Tabula Rogeriana* (detail)

1169

1161 Georgian King George III captures the great city of Ani from its Kurdish Shaddadid emir

1161 The Southern Song navy defeats the Jin at the Battle of Caishi, ending the Jin advance into southern China

1169
ANGLO-NORMAN INVASION OF IRELAND

Diarmaid MacMurchada, the king of Leinster who had been forced into exile by his rivals, recruited an army of Anglo-Norman knights to help him regain his throne. Led by Richard "Strongbow" de Clare, Earl of Pembroke, they recaptured his lands. Strongbow married MacMurchada's daughter, Aoife, and was declared heir to the Leinster throne. Henry II of England, fearing an independent Anglo-Norman realm in Ireland, invaded the country, securing the submission of key Irish nobles and beginning the 750-year English domination of Ireland.

▷ *The Marriage of Strongbow and Aoife,* Daniel Maclise

▽ The Martyrdom of Thomas Becket, alabaster relief

1175
MUHAMMAD OF GHUR INVADES INDIA

The Sultan of the Ghurid empire (in present-day Afghanistan) invaded northern India and later pushed into the Punjab, creating a Muslim empire. After a battle at Tarain in 1192, he captured Delhi, where his military slave and Governor of Delhi, Qutb-ud-Din Aybak, began the Qutb Minar to commemorate his victory. Struggles with the Khwarezmians in Iran slowed further conquest and after Muhammad's death in 1206, the empire fell apart.

▷ Qutb Minar, Delhi, India

1170
MURDER OF THOMAS BECKET

The Archbishop of Canterbury, Thomas Becket, was murdered inside his own cathedral by knights who believed they were carrying out the orders of the English king, Henry II. Becket had argued with the king over the monarch's attempts to extend royal control over the Church, and had his former friend and master excommunicated. The king's order to kill Beckett may have been the result of a miscommunication.

1175 The Pure Land sect of Buddhism is established in Japan

1170

1171 Henry II of England lands in Ireland to assert English overlordship

1176
DEFEAT OF FREDERICK BARBAROSSA

The Holy Roman Emperor Frederick Barbarossa was defeated at the Battle of Legnano by the Lombard League, an alliance of restive cities in northern Italy. Frederick had invaded Italy four times in the previous two decades trying to impose imperial control over the cities; this fifth expedition ended in disaster as the League's infantry stubbornly fought off imperial cavalry attacks. Frederick retreated to Germany and in 1183 was forced to recognize the autonomy of the League cities.

△ The Battle of Legnano

1187

SALADIN CONQUERS JERUSALEM

The Egyptian sultan Saladin delivered a devastating blow to the crusader states of Palestine. After destroying the main crusader army at the Battle of Hattin in 1187, he stormed a string of other fortresses, including Acre, Jaffa, Sidon, and Beirut. He then took Jerusalem after a short siege. Its fall sent shockwaves through Christian Europe, leading to the calling of the Third Crusade.

1138–93
SALADIN

Saladin became vizier to the Fatimid caliphs of Egypt, eventually overthrowing them. His acquisition of Syria and defeat of the Crusaders in Palestine made him the dominant ruler in the Middle East.

△ **Saladins' soldiers** take Jerusalem

1192 The Treaty of Ramla is made between Richard I of England and Saladin

1199

1180–85 The Minamoto and Taira clans clash in the Gempei War in Japan

1185 The revolt of Peter and Asen against Byzantine rule begins the Second Bulgarian Empire

1192

KAMAKURA SHOGUNATE ESTABLISHED IN JAPAN

Japan's Imperial government had been dominated by the Taira clan since 1160. A revolt against them led by the Minamoto clan ended in victory for the Minamoto in the Gempei War (1180–85). In 1192, the leader of the clan, Minamoto no Yoritomo , established the Kamakura shogunate (military regime) north of the imperial capital of Kyoto. By installing shogunal officials in all Japan's provinces, he ensured that hereditary Minamoto shoguns would continue to rule Japan, which they did until the 14th century.

△ **Minamoto no** Yoritomo

1206
CHINGGIS KHAN FOUNDS THE MONGOL EMPIRE

Early in the 13th century, a warrior called Temujin (c. 1162–1227) united all the nomadic Mongolian and Tatar tribes of the Asian steppe under his rule. Adopting the name Chinggis Khan ("ruler of the world"), he sent the steppe horsemen on campaigns of conquest. No army could resist them. By the time of his death, the Mongols controlled an empire stretching from the Pacific coast to the Caspian Sea.

▷ **Chinggis Khan in combat** in a miniature from *Jami' al-tawarikh*, c. 1430

1200

1206 The Delhi Sultanate, a Muslim state in north India, is founded by Qutb-ud-Din Aybak (r. 1206–10)

1209 The pope proclaims a crusade against Albigensian heretics in southern France

1204
SACK OF CONSTANTINOPLE

The Fourth Crusade, proclaimed by Pope Innocent III, degenerated into a squalid mercenary enterprise. Instead of fighting Muslims in Egypt, the crusaders looted the wealthy Christian Byzantine capital, Constantinople. The Byzantine Empire was restored but never fully recovered its territory or wealth.

△ **Mosaic floor** showing a scene from the Fourth Crusade

1209
ST FRANCIS CREATES THE FRANCISCAN ORDER

Francis of Assisi, son of an Italian merchant, adopted a life of poverty after a series of religious visions. In 1209, he was authorized by Pope Innocent III to found an order of monks who would wander the world, begging for alms and preaching. The Franciscan Order grew rapidly in reaction against the wealth and corruption of the medieval Catholic Church.

△ *Saint Francis of Assisi with Angels*, Sandro Botticelli, c. 1475

1215
MAGNA CARTA

A milestone in human rights, the Magna Carta was a triumph for powerful English barons in revolt against the ruling monarch, King John (r. 1199–1216). They forced him to sign the document agreeing not to arbitrarily imprison his subjects or impose taxes without their consent. It later became a fixed reference point in English law.

△ **Jayavarman VII,** bronze head

1218
DEATH OF KHMER RULER JAYAVARMAN VII

Considered the greatest ruler of the Cambodian Khmer Empire, which lasted from the 9th to the 15th century, Jayavarman (r. 1181–1218) successfully fought the neighbouring kingdom of Champa. He made Mahayana Buddhism the state religion, building the temple of Bayon at his capital, Angkor Thom.

△ **Magna Carta,** 1300 issue

1234 The Mongols conquer northern China, destroying the Jin dynasty

1239

1212 Spanish Christians defeat the Almohad Muslims at Las Navas de Tolosa

1235 The Mali Empire is founded by Sundiata Keita in West Africa

1221
JOKYU WAR IN JAPAN

Under the Kamakura shogunate, from 1185, the emperors of Japan were reduced to figureheads, with real power exercised by samurai warrior clans. In 1221, retired emperor Go-Toba attempted to reassert imperial authority against the dominant Hojo clan, who ruled as regents for the Kamakura shogun. With ruthless energy, the Hojo descended upon the imperial capital Kyoto in a devastating attack that swept away the emperor's supporters. Go-Toba was exiled to a remote island off western Japan.

△ **Emperor Go-Toba** forges a sword; print by Utagawa Kuniyoshi, c. 1840

"They swept through the city... like raging wolves attacking sheep."

14TH-CENTURY PERSIAN HISTORIAN WASSAF DESCRIBING THE MONGOL SACK OF BAGHDAD

1258
SACK OF BAGHDAD

Baghdad was the seat of the Abbasid caliphs, leaders of the Islamic world since 750 CE. In 1258, Hulegu, khan of the western Mongol Empire, defeated the Abbasid army in battle and encircled Baghdad, which fell after a short siege. The Mongols showed no mercy, killing the caliph and massacring the city's entire population.

1240

1241 A Mongol army defeats Christian knights in Poland at the Battle of Liegnitz

1244 Japanese Zen master Dogen founds Eihei-ji, the first temple of Soto Zen Buddhism in Japan

1242
BATTLE ON THE ICE

In April 1242, Prince Alexander Nevsky, a Russian hero, led the army of the city of Novgorod into battle against Prussian Teutonic Knights on the frozen ice of Lake Peipus. After hard fighting, the Knights were forced to retreat, many drowning as the weight of their armour caused the ice to crack. The battle ended Teutonic hopes of conquering Russia.

▷ Alexander Nevsky monument in Pskov, Russia

△ Battle of Muret in the Albigensian Crusade

1244
ALBIGENSIAN HERESY CRUSHED

Albigensianism was an unorthodox form of Christianity that had a mass following in southern France. In 1209, the Catholic Church declared a crusade against these heretics, known as Cathars. Their last stronghold at Montségur fell in March 1244. About 250 Cathars were burned to death on the spot.

△ Mongol siege of Baghdad, 14th-century Persian painting

1265
THOMAS AQUINAS WRITES SUMMA THEOLOGICA

The foremost medieval Christian thinker, Thomas Aquinas began writing his masterwork, *Summa Theologica*, in Rome in 1265. Reconciling Ancient Greek philosophy with the Christian faith, he offered rational proofs of the soul's immortality and the existence of God. His work laid the basis for modern Western philosophy.

▷ *St Thomas Aquinas,* Francesco Traini, 1363

1250 In the Seventh Crusade, French King Louis IX is captured by Muslims in Egypt

1260 The Mamluk ruler Baibars defeats the Mongols invading Palestine at Ain Jalut

1260 Kublai Khan becomes Khagan (Great Khan), the supreme ruler of the Mongol Empire

1269

1250
MAMLUKS RULE EGYPT

The Mamluks were a warrior class of slave soldiers who served the various dynasties of sultans ruling Egypt. After defeating a Crusader invasion of Egypt in 1250, Mamluk generals seized power in Cairo, overthrowing the Ayyubid dynasty. The Mamluks went on to rule Egypt for almost three centuries.

△ **Mamluk** horsemen

1215–1294
KUBLAI KHAN

Kublai was a grandson of Chinggis Khan. As Mongol Great Khan from 1260, he conquered China, founding the Yuan dynasty in 1271. Ruling from Beijing, he campaigned as far afield as Japan and Java.

△ Mongol horse archer

1270
DEATH OF SAINT LOUIS
The reign of Louis IX (1226–70) was a golden age for France, but his crusading ventures proved disastrous. Twenty years after a failed invasion of Egypt in 1250, he led an attack on the Hafsid caliphate in North Africa. Landing in Tunisia, he died of disease. He was canonized in 1297.

△ Death of Louis IX

1279
FALL OF THE SOUTHERN SONG
By 1234, the Mongols controlled northern China but the rich and populous south remained under the rule of the Song dynasty. Led by Kublai Khan from 1260, the Mongols attacked the Song, fielding a vast army and creating a navy to fight on rivers. After epic battles, the southern capital Hangzhou fell in 1276 and by 1279 all of China was under Mongol rule. Pursued as a fugitive, the last Song emperor, seven-year-old Zhao Bing, was drowned during a naval battle.

1270 Yekuno Amlak founds the Solomonic dynasty that will rule in Ethiopia until 1974

1271 Kublai Khan becomes Chinese emperor, founding the Yuan dynasty

1280
GUNPOWDER WEAPONS
Gunpowder was used in Chinese warfare from the 11th century and perhaps even earlier. Simple bombs and firecrackers evolved into flamethrowers and tubes firing projectiles. It was probably during the conflict between the Mongols and the Song in the late 13th century that guns were first widely used, in the form of metal-barrelled hand cannons. These primitive devices proved quite effective and, within half a century, imitations of the Chinese guns were being deployed in wars in Europe.

△ Yuan dynasty **Chinese** hand cannon

△ Marco Polo leaves Venice

c. 1299
MARCO POLO NARRATES HIS TRAVELS

The son of a Venetian merchant, Marco Polo travelled with his father along the Silk Road to China. He was received at Kublai Khan's court and stayed in China for 17 years, travelling widely. Returning to Venice in the 1290s, he was made a prisoner during a war with Genoa. While imprisoned he narrated the wonders he had seen to a cellmate, who later published *The Travels of Marco Polo*, a massively influential book.

"I have not told the half of what I saw."

MARCO POLO ON HIS DEATHBED, 1324

1299

1282 The Habsburg family become the rulers of Austria

1290 The Afghan Khalji dynasty seizes power in the Delhi Sultanate

1291 Acre, the last Crusader state, falls to the Mamluks

1281
JAPAN DEFIES THE MONGOLS

Already controlling China and Korea, Kublai Khan sought to add Japan to his conquests. An exploratory expedition in 1274 was followed by a full-scale invasion in 1281. Two fleets sailed from Korea and northern China carrying possibly 150,000 men. The Japanese samurai warriors fiercely resisted initial landings, restricting the Mongols to offshore islands. Then a typhoon, known in Japan as "the divine wind" ("kamikaze"), dispersed the invasion fleet, which took heavy losses. The Mongols made no further attempt to conquer Japan.

◁ **The Mongol invasion,** Japanese handscroll, c. 1300

▷ Giotto's frescoes, Arena Chapel, Padua

1306-09
GIOTTO REINVENTS ART

In the early 14th century, Italian artist Giotto di Bondone painted his masterwork, the frescoes that decorate the Arena (or Scrovegni) chapel in Padua. Illustrating the life of the Virgin Mary and of Christ, they displayed an emotional realism of gesture and expression that challenged the static Byzantine artistic tradition of the time. In retrospect, Giotto's work is seen as prefiguring the art of the Italian Renaissance.

> "Let evil swiftly befall those who have wrongly condemned us: God will avenge us."

TEMPLAR GRAND MASTER JACQUES DE MOLAY BEFORE HIS EXECUTION, 1314

1300

1302 At the Battle of Courtrai, mounted French knights are slaughtered by Flemish foot soldiers

1309 In the Avignon papacy, Pope Clement V, controlled by France, resides in Avignon instead of Rome

1314 The Knights Templar are destroyed and their Grand Master Jacques de Molay is executed by Philip IV of France

1314
DANTE'S DIVINE COMEDY

A political exile driven out of his native city of Florence, Italian poet Dante Alighieri probably began work on his poetic masterpiece *The Divine Comedy* in 1314. His decision to write in Italian rather than Latin was a crucial break with medieval tradition. Comprising 14,233 lines of verse, the epic poem follows its narrator on a journey through Hell and Purgatory to Paradise. Recognized as one of the greatest works in the Western literary tradition, it was completed a year before Dante's death in 1321.

▷ *Dante and the Three Kingdoms,* Domenico di Michelino, 1465

1274-1329
ROBERT THE BRUCE

King of the Scots from 1306, Robert was a formidable warrior. After defeating English King Edward II in 1314 he raided into England and established Scotland's right to be an independent kingdom.

1324
PILGRIMAGE OF MANSA MUSA

In 1324, Mansa Musa, ruler of the Muslim Mali empire in West Africa, embarked on a pilgrimage to Mecca. His arrival in Cairo, then the greatest city in the Muslim world, caused a sensation. No one had seen the equal of his richly clad retinue and his vast wealth in gold. When Musa returned to Mali from his pilgrimage he built fine mosques, colleges, and libraries in cities such as Timbuktu and Gao, making his empire a leading centre of Islamic faith and learning.

▽ **Mansa Musa** depicted on a Catalan chart

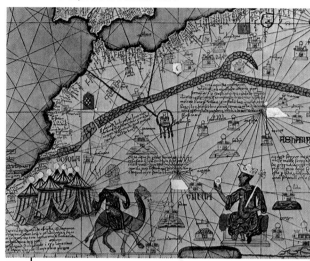

1314 Robert the Bruce leads Scotland into victory against the English at the Battle of Bannockburn

1324 Death of Osman, founder of the Turkish Ottoman dynasty

1329

▷ **Maori chevron pendant** made of whale ivory

c.1320
MAORI COLONIZE NEW ZEALAND

Although the date can never be known for certain, it was probably around 1320 that the first major wave of Polynesian settlers, now known as Maori, arrived in previously unpopulated New Zealand. They are thought to have voyaged in canoes some 4,000 km (2,500 miles) across the South Pacific from the Society Islands. Once established, the Maori developed a unique culture and social system that remained largely undisturbed by outside contact until the 19th century.

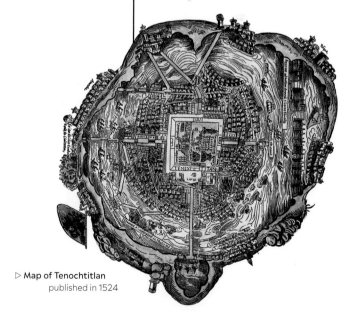

▷ **Map of Tenochtitlan** published in 1524

1325
AZTECS FOUND TENOCHTITLAN

In 1325, the wandering Aztec (or Mexica) people settled on a swampy island in Lake Texcoco, in what is now Mexico City. They chose the site as fulfilling a prophesied vision of an eagle perched on a cactus. This settlement later grew to be the largest city in Mesoamerica and hub of a powerful empire.

◁ Helmet of Ashikaga Takauji

1337

THE HUNDRED YEARS' WAR BEGINS

In 1337, Edward III, the king of England, asserted a hereditary claim to the French throne. This action started a war that lasted intermittently for 116 years. The English took the offensive, scoring victories in a naval battle at Sluys in 1340 and on land at Crécy in 1346. The French knights had no answer to England's longbowmen, but French fortunes revived under King Charles V from 1364.

△ **English coin** celebrating the victory at Sluys

△ The battle of Crécy, fought in France in 1346

1338

ASHIKAGA SHOGUNATE

Under the Kamakura shogunate established in 1185, the Japanese emperor was a powerless figurehead. In 1333, Emperor Go-Daigo called for the restoration of imperial rule. Samurai Ashikaga Takauji led the overthrow of the shogunate on Go-Daigo's behalf, but soon became disillusioned with the emperor. In 1338, Ashikaga seized power for himself, founding a shogunate that lasted for two centuries.

1330

1347 The Black Death is first reported in the West in Crimea

△ Miniature from the *Shahnameh*

1335

PERSIA'S MOST BEAUTIFUL BOOK

The illustrated version of the Persian epic poem the *Shahnameh* produced at Tabriz in the 1330s was among the highest achievements of Persian miniature painting. Produced for the country's Mongol Ilkhan rulers, it is known as the Great Mongol Shahnameh.

1354
TRAVELS OF IBN BATTUTA

Born in Tangier, Morocco, Muslim scholar Ibn Battuta was a tireless voyager. For 30 years he roamed the Islamic world, travelling from East Africa to Sumatra, from Sri Lanka to Samarkand, and from Jerusalem to Beijing. He published a famous account of his journeys after returning home to Morocco in 1354.

△ Ibn Battuta visits Tabriz, Iran

Ibn Battuta travelled 117,000 km (73,000 miles) in journeys over three decades

1351 The Red Turban revolt sees peasant guerrillas lead a Chinese rebellion against the Mongol Yuan dynasty

1356 The Battle of Poitiers sees an English victory over the French in the Hundred Years's War

1359

1355 The Bohemian king Charles IV is crowned Holy Roman Emperor

1356 The Chinese city of Nanjing falls to the Red Turban rebels

1358 The Jacquerie, a French peasant revolt, is brutally suppressed by the nobility

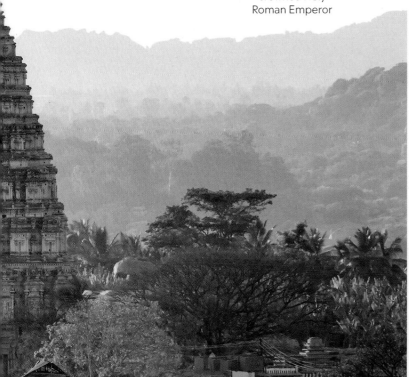

1336
VIJAYANAGARA EMPIRE

In 1336, Harihara I established an independent empire in the Deccan region of southern India. Centred on the city of Vijayanagar ("City of Victory"), this empire lasted for more than two centuries. It became prosperous through commerce, including intercontinental trade as far as the Mediterranean. By around 1500, its capital was one of the largest cities in India, embellished by palaces and Hindu temples that are considered architectural masterpieces.

◁ **Virupaksha Temple** in the ruins of the ancient Vijayanagara city

1346-51
THE BLACK DEATH

The pandemic known as the Black Death started in 1346 when an outbreak of bubonic plague struck the army of a Mongol prince laying siege to Kaffa, a Genoese trading settlement in Crimea. The Mongols lifted their siege, but after they withdrew the virus remained. Carried on the ships of Genoese traders, the plague swiftly advanced around the Mediterranean, from Syria and Egypt to Italy and southern France.

Europe's burgeoning and crowded cities were particularly vulnerable to the disease. Spread both by fleas on black rats and in the air from person to person, the plague reached England by 1348 and the Baltic by 1350. Fatality rates were terrifyingly high, with possibly 80 per cent of those infected dying. Entire villages were wiped out and the worst-hit regions may have lost three-quarters of their people. Overall some 25 million may have died in Europe by the time the plague subsided in 1351 – about one in three of the continent's total population.

The plague spread widely across Eurasia, claiming millions of victims in China in 1353. Recurrences in Europe in the 1360s and 1370s particularly struck areas spared in the first pandemic. By 1400, England's population is reckoned to have fallen to half its pre-plague level and the overall population of Europe did not fully recover until the end of the 15th century.

KEY MOMENTS

1300s Silk Road
Endemic in central Asia, bubonic plague spread along the Silk Road trade routes (*left*) that linked China to Europe. The decline of trade in the 15th century reduced virus transmission.

1349-51 Massacres of Jews
Reacting to the mass death, Christians in Germany and other parts of Europe massacred thousands of Jewish people, accusing them of causing the epidemic by poisoning wells. In cities such as Strasbourg, Cologne, Mainz, and Frankfurt whole Jewish communities were exterminated (*left*).

1358 The Jacquerie
The Black Death caused widespread social disruption, contributing to years of disorder in Europe. In France, the peasant revolt known as the Jacquerie (*left*) arose in the wake of the pandemic, causing much death and destruction before it was bloodily suppressed.

Mass burials were a familiar scene in Europe during the pandemic, as here at Tournai in 1349. The most distinctive symptoms of the plague were buboes – swellings in the neck, groin, or armpit. People neither understood the origin of the plague nor had any defence against it.

1374

RISE OF NOH THEATRE

The Japanese Noh drama, one of the world's oldest theatrical traditions, rose to prominence after the actor Kan'ami Kiyotsugu and his son Zeami Motokiyo performed before Japan's ruler, shogun Ashikaga Yoshimitsu. Zeami became a favourite at court, creating many plays that established the modern form of the genre. A subtle mix of words, music, and gesture performed by actors in masks, Noh took a central place in Japan's unique culture.

▷ **Noh mask, Mikazuki** (male deity)

▽ **Palace of the Popes,** Avignon, France

1360

1380 At the Battle of Kulikovo, Dmitri of Moscow defeats Tokhtamysh's Mongol Golden Horde

◁ **Ming dynasty** coin

1368

MING EMPIRE PROCLAIMED

Born a poor peasant, Zhu Yuanzhang made himself leader of a Chinese popular revolt against the Mongol Yuan dynasty in the 1350s. In 1368, driving the Mongols from their capital at Beijing, he assumed the imperial throne as the Hongwu Emperor. He set out to restore Chinese Confucian traditions after the period of foreign rule and strengthened the centralized state, imposing his authority with brutal ruthlessness. The Ming dynasty that he founded was destined to rule China for almost three centuries.

◁ **Emperor Hongwu,** first ruler of the Ming dynasty

1387
CHAUCER'S CANTERBURY TALES

English poet Geoffrey Chaucer was a courtier, diplomat, and official under Edward III and Richard II. His most famous work, *The Canterbury Tales*, is a set of stories told by a group of pilgrims travelling to the shrine of St Thomas Becket in Canterbury cathedral. A founding work of English literature, it presents a rich and varied portrait of its times. Begun in the 1380s, it was left unfinished at Chaucer's death in 1400.

△ The Ellesmere manuscript of Chaucer's Canterbury Tales

1378
PAPAL SCHISM

From 1309, popes resided in Avignon, dominated by the French monarchy. In 1378, Romans demanded the return of the papacy to its traditional home. Urban VI was elected pope in Rome, in opposition to Clement VII in Avignon. The two popes were joined by a third in 1409, elected in Pisa. This schism, which was finally resolved in 1417, seriously weakened papal prestige.

1383 Poland and Lithuania are unified under Wladislaw II Jagiello

1385 Portuguese victory over Castile at Aljubarrota guarantees independence under the Aviz dynasty

1389

1381 In the Peasants' revolt, English rebels led by Wat Tyler are defeated at London

1389 A Serb-Bosnian coalition meets Ottoman forces at the first battle of Kosovo

Timur's campaigns may have caused the deaths of 17 million people

1336-1405
TRIUMPHS OF TIMUR

Timur the Lame, a Mongol warrior from Samarkand, conquered land from India to Anatolia, establishing the Timurid Empire.

1387 While campaigning in Persia and Armenia, Timur sacks the city of Isfahan and reportedly kills 70,000 of its citizens.

1395 Timur defeats his rival Tokhtamysh at the battle of Terek and breaks up the Mongol Golden Horde (*helmet above*).

1398 During his invasion of India, Timur defeats the Sultan of Delhi and pillages the city, bearing off his loot to Samarkand.

1402 The Ottomans are humiliated at Ankara as Timur strikes west. He imprisons the Ottoman Emperor Bayezid I in a cage.

1392
JOSEON DYNASTY RULES KOREA

In 1388, Korean general Yi Seong-gye was ordered by Korea's ruler, King U of Goryeo, to invade Ming China. Sure that attacking the Ming would lead to military disaster, Yi instead turned his troops against the king and took control of the government. Four years later, Yi declared himself King Taejo, establishing a new dynasty, the Joseon, that would rule Korea for over 500 years.

△ **Joseon** lacquer box

▷ *The Battle of Grunwald,* Jan Matejko

1390

1396 At the Battle of Nicopolis, European knights are massacred by Ottoman forces

1402 Zhu Di becomes the Yongle Emperor in China: he is considered the second founder of the Ming dynasty

1408 The Yongle Encyclopedia, commissioned by the Ming emperor, is completed: it has 11,095 volumes

Zheng He's first treasure fleet in 1405 was crewed by 27,800 men on 317 ships

1405
VOYAGES OF ZHENG HE

In 1403, China's Yongle Emperor ordered the construction of a fleet, aiming to demonstrate China's superiority in Southeast Asia and the Indian Ocean. Commanded by the eunuch Zheng He, this "treasure fleet" made seven epic voyages between 1405 and 1432, travelling as far as Sri Lanka and East Africa and collecting treasures including live animals.

▷ **A giraffe** collected by the treasure fleet

1410
KNIGHTS DEFEATED AT GRUNWALD

The battle of Grunwald (or Tannenberg) was a decisive victory for the armies of Poland and Lithuania over the Prussian Teutonic Knights under their Grand Master Ulrich von Jungingen. A crusading military order, the Knights had been fighting to extend their power over eastern Europe for two centuries. Their decisive defeat at Grunwald began a decline from which they never recovered.

1386–1422
KING HENRY V

King of England from 1413, Henry V fought successfully for the right to rule France. Recognized as heir apparent in 1420, he was only prevented from taking the throne of France by his sudden death.

1417 Pope Martin V unites the fractured papacy and returns it to Rome

1419

1419 John the Fearless, ruler of Burgundy, is murdered by the French

1415
BATTLE OF AGINCOURT

In August 1415, English king Henry V took an army to France, asserting his claim to the French throne. After the costly siege of Harfleur, his depleted forces marched for English-held Calais. At Agincourt on 25 October he was intercepted by a far stronger French army, but the English knights and bowmen triumphed against the odds and the French nobility were decimated.

▷ Sword of King Henry V

1415
EXECUTION OF JAN HUS

As leader of a religious reform movement in Bohemia (now the Czech Republic), Hus denounced the corruption of the papacy and the Catholic clergy. Convicted of heresy by a Catholic Council at Konstanz, southern Germany, he was burned at the stake. Over the next 20 years, his Czech followers, known as Hussites, defeated papal crusades sent to suppress them.

◁ **Jan Hus** is burned at the stake

c.1400-1600
THE RENAISSANCE

During the 15th and 16th centuries, the city-states of Italy were the focus for a major flowering of the arts and new ideas. This movement is called the Renaissance as it centred around a "rebirth" of knowledge, based on the rediscovery of the thought and culture of Ancient Greece and Rome.

The material basis for the Renaissance lay in the prosperity of city-states such as Florence, Venice, and Milan, which had grown rich through trade, banking, and the manufacture of luxury goods. These cities' ruling elites, such as the Medici family in Florence, lavishly patronized scholars, painters, sculptors, and architects. They were prepared to back innovations such as linear perspective and non-religious subject-matter in painting, or statues that celebrated the beauty of the naked body. Successive popes in Rome, enriched by contributions from the Christian faithful, were another major source of patronage. Perhaps the single greatest Renaissance work, Michelangelo's ceiling of the Sistine Chapel, was painted for Pope Julius II. Although the Renaissance challenged certain Christian taboos, including the ban on dissection for the study of anatomy, it saw the ideas of pagan antiquity as an adjunct to Christian faith. The spirit of free enquiry nourished by the Renaissance spread across Europe, feeding into the Protestant revolt against Catholicism and the beginnings of modern science.

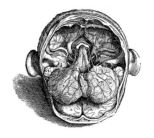

KEY MOMENTS

1485 *The Birth of Venus*
This painting (*left*) by Florentine artist Sandro Botticelli typifies the Renaissance embrace of themes from Greek and Roman mythology. Patrons of the arts revelled in the learned allegorical detail of such works, as well as the seductive beauty of the naked goddess.

c.1487-1510 Da Vinci's notebooks
Leonardo da Vinci was the total "Renaissance Man", an inspired painter, engineer, inventor, and researcher. Working chiefly in Florence and Milan, he filled notebooks (*left*) with observations and innovative ideas, including designs for flying machines and weaponry.

1543 *On the Fabric of the Human Body*
Flemish physician Andreas Vesalius published the results of his dissection of corpses, mostly conducted at the University of Padua, in a book entitled *On the Fabric of the Human Body* (*left*). His work was a giant step forward in the understanding of human anatomy.

Painted in 1509–11 by Raphael, *The School of Athens* decorates a wall in the Vatican's Papal Palace. Centred on the figures of Plato and Aristotle, it represents the greatest philosophers, mathematicians, and scientists of the Ancient World, whose works inspired the Renaissance.

◁ **The Forbidden City,**
Ming dynasty painting

1420
FORBIDDEN CITY BUILT

China's Yongle Emperor ordered Beijing to be rebuilt from scratch as a capital for the Ming empire. At the heart of the new capital lay the Forbidden City, designed as an awe-inspiring imperial palace and seat of government. The Forbidden City was the work of more than 100,000 artisans and countless labourers. Around it, Beijing soon grew to be the world's largest city, with nearly a million residents by the 1440s according to estimates.

More than 100 million tiles and bricks were used to build Beijing's Forbidden City

1420

1422 The Vijayanagara empire of South India reaches its peak under Deva Raya II

1428 A Vietnamese revolt against Ming China ends with rebel leader Le Loi taking the throne of Dai Viet

1428 The Aztec Triple Alliance brings together three city-states to rule over the Valley of Mexico

1421 At the Battle of Kutna Hora, Hussite rebels score victory over the Holy Roman Empire

1427 Portuguese sailors reach the Azores in the mid-Atlantic

1428 Ulugh Beg, sultan of Samarkand, builds an astronomical observatory

△ Joan of Arc window in Fougeres, France

"I was 13 when I had a voice from God..."

JOAN OF ARC, PUBLIC EXAMINATION, FEBRUARY 1431

1429
SIEGE OF ORLEANS

Close to winning the Hundred Years' War, the English besieged Orléans. A peasant girl, Joan of Arc, arrived in the French camp with orders from God to revive French resistance. Inspired, the French broke the siege, a turning point in the war. Joan was executed by her enemies in 1431.

1438
INCA EMPIRE FORMED

Acceding to the throne of the small kingdom of Cusco in the Peruvian Andes in 1438, Pachacuti Inca Yupanqui embarked upon a campaign of expansion that laid the foundations for the extensive Inca empire. It was Pachacuti who, in the 1450s, built the royal estate at Machu Picchu, which is now the best-known of Inca ruins. By the end of the 15th century, Inca domains stretched from modern-day Ecuador south to Chile.

◁ Inca Emperor
Pachacuti, statue
near Machu Picchu, Peru

1439

▷ Henry the Navigator

1434
EXPLORER PRINCE

In 1434, Portuguese seaman Gil Eanes passed Cape Bojador, travelling further down the West African coast than any previous European mariner. This was a triumph for Portugal's Prince Henry, known as "the Navigator", who promoted exploratory voyages, initiating Europe's Age of Discovery.

1434 Cosimo de' Medici becomes the effective ruler of Florence

1436
BRUNELLESCHI'S DOME

The residents of Florence began building a magnificent cathedral in 1296, but over a century later it still lacked a dome. In 1418, architect Filippo Brunelleschi won a competition to cap the building. Showing enormous technical ingenuity, he built an octagonal dome 42 m (138 ft) across, without any external buttresses to sustain its weight. Finished in 1436, it was an early achievement of the Italian Renaissance.

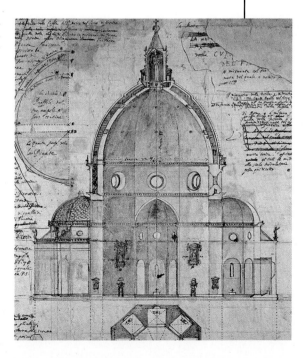

▷ Plan of Florence Cathedral
from the 16th century

1389-1464
COSIMO DE' MEDICI

Born into a rich banking family, Cosimo used his wealth to dominate the city-state of Florence for 30 years. A patron of artists and scholars, he made his city the hub of the early Renaissance.

△ Troops of Sultan Mehmed II

1453
FALL OF CONSTANTINOPLE

In 1453, the capital of the Christian Byzantine Empire, Constantinople, fell to the Ottoman Turks. Sultan Mehmed II seized the city after his heavy cannon breached walls that had resisted sieges for a thousand years. The last Byzantine emperor, Constantine XI, died in the fighting and massacre of the Christian population. The Ottoman victory was a triumph for Islam, leaving Europe open to further Turkish attacks.

1449 At the Battle of Tumu, the Chinese Yingzong Emperor is defeated and captured by Esen Khan of the Oirat Mongols

1453 The Battle of Castillon – the last in the Hundred Years' War – ends in victory for France

1440

1444 Portuguese slave traders bring the first shiploads of enslaved people from West Africa for sale at Lagos in the Algarve

▽ Bronze plaque from Benin

1432–1481
SULTAN MEHMED II
Mehmed II led campaigns that destroyed the Byzantine Empire and spread Ottoman rule over much of the Balkans. A cultured ruler, he patronized Italian Renaissance artists.

1440
RISE OF BENIN

The West African kingdom of Benin was founded by the Edo people of what is now southern Nigeria. Under the rule of Oba (king) Ewuare, who seized power in a violent coup in 1440, it expanded to control a substantial regional empire. Over the following century Benin's capital city was beautified with exquisite bronze plaques crafted by local metalworkers.

48 copies of the Gutenberg Bible survive today

△ **A Gutenberg Bible** printed on vellum

1454
GUTENBERG BIBLE

The Bibles printed by Johannes Gutenberg in the German city of Mainz in 1454 were among the first books produced in Europe using moveable metal type. The success of the Gutenberg Bible initiated a revolution in European culture. From the 1470s, presses appeared in many countries, making books widely available. By spreading knowledge and literacy beyond traditional elites, they encouraged people to challenge accepted authority.

1459

1456 The Ottomans try to subjugate Hungary, and besiege Belgrade, but are beaten back by Janos Hunyadi's forces

△ Aztec human sacrifice

1454
AZTEC FLOWER WARS

Under the rule of Moctezuma I, the Aztec Triple Alliance (of Mexico-Tenochtitlan, Tlacopan, and Tetzcoco) initiated "Flower Wars" – attacks on neighbouring peoples such as the Tlaxcala, Huexotzinco, and Cholula. The Aztecs fought to display prowess and capture prisoners for human sacrifice. These ritualized wars made the Tlaxcala bitter enemies of the Aztecs.

△ *Choosing the Red and White Roses*, Henry Payne, 1908

1455
WAR OF THE ROSES

For 30 years the English throne was contested between claimants from the House of Lancaster, represented by a red rose, and the white-rose House of York. Victory at Towton in 1461 saw Yorkist Edward IV supplant the ineffectual Lancastrian Henry VI. The Lancastrians finally triumphed when Henry VII seized power from Richard III in 1485.

1467
JAPAN'S WARRING STATES

A dispute over the succession to Japan's ruling shogun triggered fighting in the capital Kyoto between clans led by Yamana Sôzen and Hosokawa Katsumoto. The resulting Onin War was brief, but it fatally weakened the shogunate. With central authority powerless, Japan entered an era of chaotic civil strife between regional warlords, the daimyo.

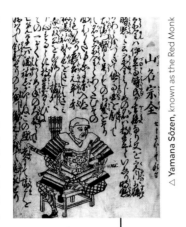

△ Yamana Sôzen, known as the Red Monk

1468
SONNI ALI TAKES TIMBUKTU

In the 15th century, the West African Mali Empire went into decline. Sonni Ali, leader of the Songhai people, seized the opportunity to capture the Malian cities of Timbuktu and Djenné. At his death in 1492, Sonni's Songhai Empire was more extensive than Mali had ever been. It lasted for a century.

△ **Mud tomb of Askia**, second ruler of the Songhai Empire

1461 French poet
François Villon writes his famous work *Le Testament*

1460

1471 The Champa kingdom
in southern Vietnam is crushed by Dai Viet in the Cham-Vietnamese War

Under the Ming, the Great Wall extended over 8,850 km (5,500 miles)

1472
MING EXTEND THE GREAT WALL

After a disastrous defeat by Mongol Oirats at the Battle of Tumu in 1449, Ming China felt increasingly menaced by incursions of nomadic warriors along its steppe border. In 1472, work began on extending the ancient Great Wall frontier defences in the north-western Ordos region. The success of the Ordos Wall in stopping raiders led the Ming to continue additions and repairs to the Wall.

△ **Section of the Great Wall of China** rebuilt under the Ming

△ *Ivan III Tearing the Deed of the Tartar Khan*, Nikolai Shustov, 1862

1476

IVAN THE GREAT DEFIES THE KHAN

From the 13th century, Russian princes accepted the overlordship of Mongol-Turkic warriors. In 1476, Ivan III, Grand Duke of Moscow, refused to pay tribute to Khan Ahmed, head of the Tatar Golden Horde. Confirmed by defeat of the Tatars at the Ugra River in 1480, Ivan's assertion of independence allowed him to claim leadership of all Russian princes. Known as "the Great", he laid the foundations of the modern Russian state.

1476 William Caxton sets up the first printing press in England at Westminster

1479

1474 Renaissance artist Mantegna paints the illusionistic bridal chamber of the Ducal Palace, Mantua

1477 At the Battle of Nancy, Swiss pikemen defeat and kill Duke Charles of Burgundy

1479

SPAIN UNITED

In 1469, Ferdinand and Isabella, heirs respectively to the Spanish kingdoms of Aragon and Castille, were married. Ten years later, having inherited their thrones, they became effectively joint rulers of a powerful united Spanish state. Known as the Catholic Monarchs, they used the Inquisition ruthlessly to root out non-believers, expelling all Jews in 1492. Defeating Muslim Granada, they extended their rule over the whole of Spain.

▷ Ferdinand V and Isabella I

△ **Spanish coin** showing Ferdinand and Isabella

1486
TEMPLE OF TENOCHTITLAN

In 1486, the Mexica (Aztec) *tlatoani* (king) Tizoc died and was succeeded by his brother Ahuizotl. In the following year, 1487, Ahuizotl reopened the great temple in Tenochtitlan, capital of the Mexican Aztec Empire, marking the event with a mass ritual sacrifice in which the victim's hearts were offered to the Aztec gods.

◁ **Aztec sacrificial stone,** c.1481–86

1492
CHRISTOPHER COLUMBUS CROSSES THE ATLANTIC

Genoese sailor Christopher Columbus won the backing of the Spanish monarchy for a plan to sail westward to Asia. On board the carrack *Santa Maria*, with two other ships, he reached the Bahamas after almost six weeks at sea. Making three other transatlantic voyages to 1504, Columbus was slow to realize he had found a continent unknown to Europeans. His voyages established a permanent link between the Americas and Eurasia.

▷ *Landing of Columbus,* John Vanderlyn, 1842–47

1480

1488 Portuguese sailor Bartolomeu Dias rounds the Cape of Good Hope and enters the Indian Ocean

1485
TUDOR DYNASTY FOUNDED

In the final stage of the York–Lancaster Wars of the Roses, Henry Tudor, a Lancastrian, invaded England to challenge the rule of Yorkist King Richard III. Exploiting discontent with Richard – who was suspected of murdering his predecessor, child-king Edward V – Henry attracted wide support. Richard was defeated and killed at Bosworth Field. Ruling as Henry VII, the new king married Elizabeth of York to consolidate his new Tudor dynasty.

◁ **Henry VII's** first act of parliament

"I have come to believe that this is a mighty continent previously unknown."

CHRISTOPHER COLUMBUS, JOURNAL OF HIS THIRD VOYAGE, 1498

1494 French King Charles VIII invades Italy and initiates a series of wars (the Italian Wars) that last for 65 years

1495 Syphilis arrives in Europe; an epidemic breaks out among French soldiers at Naples

1497 Italian mariner John Cabot, sailing from Bristol, explores the North American coast

1499

1492
FALL OF GRANADA

The Emirate of Granada was the last Muslim state on the Iberian peninsula. After ten years of campaigns by Spain's Catholic Monarchs, Granada surrendered to the Christians in January 1492. The surrender terms guaranteed the Muslims religious toleration, but they soon came under pressure to convert to Christianity. Those who refused were driven into exile.

◁ The Alhambra fortress and palace at Granada

1481–1520
PORTUGUESE EXPLORATION

Under King John II (r. 1481–1495), Portuguese sailors resumed far-reaching voyages of discovery begun by Prince Henry the Navigator.

1488 Bartolomeu Dias sails around the southern tip of Africa at the Cape of Good Hope, showing the route to India.

1497–98 Vasco da Gama commands a fleet that sails to India, via south Africa, and back, the longest oceanic voyage to that date.

1500 Pedro Cabral leads a fleet of 13 ships and makes landfall in northeast Brazil, claiming the territory for the Portuguese crown.

1519 Ferdinand Magellan sails from Spain to Asia across the Pacific. One ship completes a voyage around the globe.

△ The coronation of Sultan Selim I

1503
RENAISSANCE POPE

Julius II, pope from 1503 to 1509, was a worldly man who personally led papal troops in battle. He employed major Renaissance artists such as Raphael and Michelangelo to decorate the Vatican and plan a new St Peter's Basilica. His lavish artistic patronage was financed by the mass sale of "indulgences" – remission of sins. Such corrupt practices provoked the Protestant Reformation.

▷ **Moses,** from Michelangelo's Tomb of Pope Julius II

1517
CAIRO FALLS TO THE OTTOMANS

Reigning from 1512 to 1520, Sultan Selim I almost doubled the extent of the Ottoman Empire. His conquest of Cairo in 1517 ended Mamluk rule over Egypt and Syria, giving the Ottomans control of the heartland of the Muslim world, including the holy cities of Mecca and Medina. This allowed Selim to claim the title of caliph, leader of Islam. Selim blocked the spread of Shi'ism, massacring Shi'ites and fighting Safavid Iran.

1513 At the Battle of Flodden, King James IV of Scotland is killed fighting the English

1500

1510 The Portuguese establish a permanent base in India at Goa

1517 Portuguese merchants reach the Chinese port of Canton by sea

1501
FOUNDING OF SAFAVID IRAN

The Safavids were Sufi Muslim mystics adhering to the Shi'ite branch of Islam. In 1501, Safavid Shah Ismail I claimed rulership of politically fragmented Iran, establishing his control over a wide area in campaigns that culminated in the defeat of the Uzbeks at Merv in 1510. Ismail's Shi'ite Safavid Empire posed a direct challenge to the Sunni Ottoman Empire for leadership of Islam.

◁ **Battle at Merv,** fresco in Isfahan

1517

LUTHER TRIGGERS THE REFORMATION

In response to the sale of indulgences by the Church, the German monk and theologian Martin Luther made public his 95 Theses, which were critical of Catholic beliefs and practices. This was – in retrospect – seen as the start of the Reformation that split Christian Europe. In 1521, Luther was excommunicated by the pope, a decision confirmed by Emperor Charles V, but efforts to suppress the Reform movement failed.

△ **Martin Luther** posts his theses

> "Here I stand; I cannot do otherwise; God help me."

MARTIN LUTHER, SPEECH, 1521

1519

1519 The Spanish conqueror Hernán Cortés leads an expedition to Mexico

1485–1547
HERNAN CORTES

A minor Spanish nobleman of exceptional ambition, Cortés became a colonist in Cuba. Landing in Mexico with a small military force in 1519, he conquered the Aztec Empire on his own initiative.

1519

HABSBURG EMPEROR ELECTED

When he was elected Holy Roman Emperor in 1519, Habsburg Charles V already ruled Spain, Austria, the Netherlands, and much of Italy. With such power in his hands, he sought to become the acknowledged head of all Christian Europe. But his dominance was contested by Protestants, opposed to his Catholicism, and by the kings of France. Charles eventually gave up his unifying project after more than 30 years of warfare.

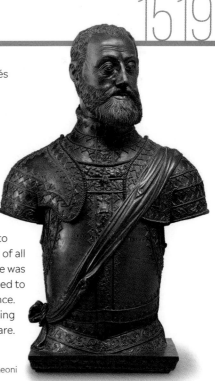

▷ **Charles V,** bust by Leone Leoni

To win election as Emperor, Charles V paid 850,000 florins in bribes

1521
CONQUEST OF THE AZTECS

Arriving in Mexico in 1519, Spanish soldier Hernán Cortés advanced to the Aztec capital Tenochtitlan. He was repulsed with heavy losses but allied with enemies of the Aztecs and returned in 1521 to besiege the city. Weakened by disease, the Aztecs were overrun in August. Emperor Cuauhtémoc was captured and later killed.

◁ **The retreat of Hernán Cortés** from Tenochtitlan in 1520

1525 The Battle of Pavia sees French King Francis I defeated and taken prisoner by Emperor Charles V

1520

1521 Martin Luther is declared a heretic, sealing the Protestant–Catholic schism

1526
MUGHAL EMPIRE FOUNDED

Babur, a Muslim warrior descended from Genghis Khan, invaded India from Afghanistan and defeated the Sultan of Delhi at the battle of Panipat in April 1526. By his death in 1530 he had extended his rule over most of northern India, founding the Mughal Empire. His descendants would preside over a golden age of stability and cultural flowering in India.

▷ **Babur** holding court

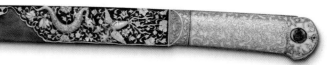

△ **Sword** from the court of Suleiman the Magnificent

1526
OTTOMAN ARMIES INVADE EUROPE

Ottoman sultan from 1520, Suleiman the Magnificent launched a series of campaigns against Christian Europe. In 1526, his invading army crushed the Hungarians at Mohacs, bringing his forces to the border of Austria. Three years later, he besieged the Austrian capital, Vienna. The city held out and Europe remained resistant to the spread of Islam.

▽ **Henry VIII,** portrait by Hans Holbein

1534
HENRY VIII BREAKS WITH ROME

Angered by the refusal of Pope Clement VII to annul his marriage to Catherine of Aragon, English King Henry VIII declared himself head of the Church of England, renouncing papal authority. Over following years monasteries were broken up and church lands confiscated by the Crown. Stubborn opponents of religious reform, such as Henry's former chancellor Thomas More, were executed.

1527 Protestant German soldiers plunder the holy city of Rome

1533 Inca ruler Atahualpa is captured and executed by Spanish Conquistadores

1534 Ignatius Loyola creates the Society of Jesus (the Jesuits) to spread the Catholic faith

1539

1534 Breton mariner Jacques Cartier begins exploring the St Lawrence River in North America

"I who am the Sultan of Sultans, the Shadow of God upon Earth…"

SULTAN SULEIMAN THE MAGNIFICENT

1522-1791
CHINA'S FOUR CLASSIC NOVELS

Printing allowed the cheap production of novels in book form, making them popular in Ming China. The best known are the "Four Classic Novels".

1522 *Romance of the Three Kingdoms* was written by Luo Guanzhong before 1400 and printed in 1522 (*painted scene above*).

1589 The roguish characters in the vivid Ming folk tales of *The Water Margin* made the book very popular when it was printed in 1589.

1592 *Journey to the West*, written by Wu Cheng'en, is most famous for the antics of the mischievous Monkey King (*pictured above*).

1791 In *Dream of the Red Chamber*, Qing era writer Cao Xueqin uses the story of an elite family to probe society.

1543

COPERNICAN REVOLUTION

In his book *On the Revolutions of the Celestial Spheres* published in 1543, Polish astronomer Nicolaus Copernicus proposed that Earth and the planets revolved around the Sun – Earth was not the centre of the universe. His theory was adopted by astronomers from the late 16th century but resisted by the Catholic Church.

1542

EUROPEANS EXPLORE NORTH AMERICA

Hernando de Soto – a Spanish soldier who had taken part in the conquest of Inca Peru – mounted an expedition to explore what is now the southern US. Advancing from Florida through lands inhabited by Indigenous peoples, he became the first European to reach the Mississippi in 1541. He died there the following year.

▽ Hernando de Soto

△ The Copernican system, 1600 illustration

1540

1541 Michelangelo completes painting the ceiling of the Vatican's Sistine Chapel

1541 Calvinism spreads as preacher Jean Calvin founds a Protestant Republic in Geneva

1545 At the Council of Trent, Catholic Church leaders plan a Counter-Reformation (to 1563)

1543

PORTUGUESE IMPACT ON JAPAN

The first European sailors to reach Japan were Portuguese traders. Their arrival in 1543 was welcomed by the Japanese because they brought goods from China. The Ming emperors had banned direct trade with Japan, so the Portuguese found a valuable niche as intermediaries. The Portuguese also introduced firearms, which were soon being manufactured in Japan, transforming samurai warfare. Jesuit missionaries, arriving from 1549, won thousands of Japanese converts, but Christianity was later suppressed.

▷ *Arrival of a Portuguese Ship,* Japanese screen, c.1620

▷ **Spanish silver** church vessel, 16th century

Spanish mines in the Americas produced 40,000 tons of silver in two centuries

1545

SOUTH AMERICAN SILVER

From 1532, Spanish Conquistadores took over the Inca Empire. In 1545 they discovered the world's richest deposits of silver at Potosí, in what is now Bolivia. Exploited with ruthless use of forced labour, the mines brought the Spanish monarchy untold wealth, financing armies that dominated Europe. Silver was also carried across the Pacific to Ming China, where it paid for goods such as silk and ceramics.

1552 Tsar Ivan the Terrible defeats the Khanate of Kazan and expands Russia into Siberia

1559

1552 China grants Portuguese traders an offshore base at Macao

▷ Gold coin of Akbar

1556

AKBAR THE GREAT RULES INDIA

Ruling from 1556 to 1605, Akbar was the greatest of India's Mughal emperors. Tripling the extent of the empire so that it covered much of the subcontinent, he followed a policy of religious tolerance, actively seeking the support of non-Muslim Indians for his Muslim regime. He gave the diverse empire a unified administration and used the wealth from taxation to patronize artists, architects, and scholars.

△ **Akbar**, Shah Jahan Album, c. 1630

◁ **Light from the galley** of the *Marqués de Santa Cruz* at Lepanto

1571
OTTOMAN DEFEAT AT SEA

The fleet of a coalition of Christian states including Spain, Venice, and Genoa inflicted a heavy defeat on the navy of the Ottoman Empire at the Battle of Lepanto. Fought off the coast of Greece, it was the last European sea battle contested by oared warships. Around 400 galleys and 150,000 men took part.

▷ *The Battle of Lepanto*, Andreas van Eertvelt, 1640

1560

1566 The Dutch Revolt against Philip II of Spain breaks out in the Low Countries

1572 The Wanli Emperor takes charge in Ming China; his reign lasts 48 years

1562 The French Wars of Religion break out between Catholics and Protestant Huguenots

1569 The Union of Lublin formally unites Poland and Lithuania in the Polish-Lithuanian Commonwealth

1572
HUGUENOT MASSACRE

France's Huguenots (Protestants) gathered in Paris, a mostly Catholic city, to celebrate the wedding of Huguenot Henry of Navarre to French King Charles IX's sister. Probably on the king's orders, leading Huguenots were murdered, and the killing of Protestants by Catholic mobs followed. This massacre on St Bartholomew's Day was the most notorious episode of France's Religious Wars (1562–98).

◁ St Bartholomew's Day massacre

Three million people are estimated to have died in the French Wars of Religion

1575
VICTORY AT NAGASHINO

A long era of civil war in Japan declined as Oda Nobunaga established dominance over all other daimyo (feudal lords). Outside Nagashino castle in 1575, he defeated the Takeda clan through his skilful use of infantry armed with primitive firearms called arquebuses. This technology transformed Japanese warfare and allowed Nobunaga to unify the country before his death in 1582.

◁ Battle of Nagashino

1576 Spanish troops, who had not been paid by the Spanish king, mutiny and sack Antwerp

1578 At the Battle of Alcacer Quibir, Moroccan ruler Ahmad al-Mansur defeats and kills Portugal's king

1579

▽ Túpac Amaru

1572
THE LAST INCA EMPEROR

After the Spanish conquered the Inca Empire in the 1530s, an Inca state survived in a remote and rugged area of Peru around Vilcabamba. In 1571, Túpac Amaru inherited the title of Sapac Inca (Inca Emperor). The following year the Spanish decided to finish off the Inca state. Their troops seized Vilcabamba and pursued the fleeing Túpac Amaru. He was captured, taken to Cuzco and publicly beheaded in September 1572.

c. 1560-1700
MUGHAL ARCHITECTURE

Rulers of much of northern India by 1550, the Mughal emperors spent lavishly on fine buildings in a blend of Central Asian, Indian, and Persian styles.

1565-73 Agra Fort, a large walled city made from brick and sandstone, took 4,000 workers eight years to complete.

1607-20 Hiran Minar, Sheikhupura, is a set of buildings commissioned by Emperor Jahangir in memory of a pet antelope.

1632-53 The Taj Mahal in Agra was built by a heartbroken Shah Jahan as a tomb for his favourite wife, Mumtaz Mahal.

1671-73 Badshahi Mosque in Lahore, commissioned by Emperor Aurangzeb, is renowned for its carved marble interior.

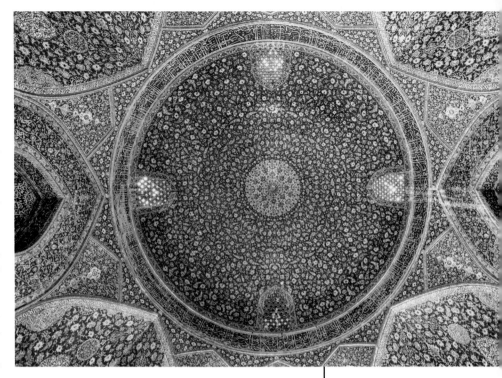

1587
SHAH ABBAS RULES IRAN

The accession of Abbas I, known as "the Great", to the throne of Iran in 1587 initiated the golden age of the Safavid dynasty. A ruthless warrior, Abbas waged successful wars against the Ottomans and the Uzbeks, expanding the borders of his empire. Persian art flourished under his patronage. He made Isfahan his capital, embellishing the city with buildings of outstanding beauty.

▷ **Ceiling,** Shah Mosque, Isfahan

1580

1582 Pope Gregory XIII replaces the Julian calendar with the more accurate Gregorian

1587 Elizabeth I of England orders the execution of her Catholic cousin Mary

1580 Philip II of Spain annexes Portugal, which loses its independence

1584 Roanoke Island becomes the first (though short-lived) English colony in North America

1588
ELIZABETH DEFIES THE ARMADA

King Philip II of Spain planned to use his army in the Netherlands to invade England. He sent a fleet of 130 ships, the Great Armada, to protect his soldiers crossing the Channel. Inspired by their stalwart queen, Elizabeth I, English mariners harassed the Armada and shepherded it into the North Sea. The invasion was abandoned. Sailing around the British Isles to return to Spain, the Armada lost many ships to bad weather.

▷ **English ships** confront the Spanish Armada

1564–1616
WILIAM SHAKESPEARE

English author Shakespeare was born and died in Stratford-upon-Avon but spent his creative years in London. Between 1589 and 1613 he wrote 38 plays and 154 sonnets, works that have made him world-famous.

1599
SHAKESPEARE AT THE GLOBE

The Globe theatre was built in London alongside the Thames to house The Lord Chamberlain's Men, a company of actors that included William Shakespeare. His *Henry V* was probably the first play performed there in 1599. Appealing both to the literate elite and the common people, London theatres were at the hub of a vigorous cultural scene that has been called the English Renaissance.

△ Shakespeare's Globe, from a UK stamp

"All the world's a stage..."

SHAKESPEARE, *AS YOU LIKE IT, 1599*

1591 At the Battle of Tondibi, the Moroccan army defeats the Songhai Empire in North Africa

1599

△ Edict of Nantes, 1598

1594
GOOD KING HENRY

A Huguenot leader in France's Religious Wars, Henry of Navarre was crowned Henry IV of France in 1594. Seeking an end to religious conflict, he declared himself a Catholic while decreeing tolerance for Huguenots through the Edict of Nantes. Known as Good King Henry for his concern for his people's welfare, he was assassinated by a Catholic fanatic in 1610.

1598
KOREA DEFEATS INVADERS

The effective ruler of all Japan, Toyotomi Hideyoshi, launched two seaborne invasions of Korea. Both failed thanks to the naval genius of Korean Admiral Yi Sun-sin. With a fleet that included "turtle ships" – cannon-armed metal-plated vessels – he repeatedly defeated the numerically superior Japanese. Yi died in November 1598 during the battle of Noryang, the final naval victory that ensured Korean independence.

△ **Admiral Yi Sun-sin,** bronze

1600
TOKUGAWA VICTORY AT SEKIGAHARA

The death of Japan's ruler Toyotomi Hideyoshi in 1598 gave the ambitious Tokugawa Ieyasu a chance to bid for power. He was resisted by regents acting in the name of Hideyoshi's five-year-old son. At the battle of Sekigahara the regents were betrayed by key allies and the Tokugawa forces triumphed. Proclaimed shogun in 1603, Ieyasu founded a regime that was to last for over 250 years.

▷ **Battle of Sekigahara,** Japanese screen

1600

c. 1600 The Dahomey kingdom is founded by the Fon people in West Africa

1600 Peruvian volcano Huaynaputina erupts, with large-scale effects on global weather

1603 Safavid Persian ruler Shah Abbas I launches a successful war against the Ottomans

1600–1602
EAST INDIA COMPANIES COMPETE

Control of the profitable trade in spices and other luxury goods from the East Indies (India and southeast Asia) was fiercely contested between European maritime nations. In 1600, the English crown authorized a group of merchants to form an East India Company with a monopoly of Asian trade. Two years later, England's commercial rivals, the Dutch, established their own East India Company. Highly competitive and aggressive, these companies acquired armed forces and became major agents of their countries' imperial expansion, governing territories in Asia.

△ **Officers of the British East India Company** in India

◁ **Arms of the Dutch East India Company** and town of Batavia

1607
FOUNDING OF JAMESTOWN, VIRGINIA

Settlers sent by the Virginia Company of London established a fort on an inlet of Chesapeake Bay, naming it Jamestown for English King James I. Starvation and disease killed four-fifths of the early colonists, but enough survived to make it England's first durable settlement in North America.

△ James Fort, 1607

1605 Emperor Jahangir succeeds his father Emperor Akbar to the Mughal imperial throne

1609

1600 Tsar Boris Godunov's death starts Russia's "Time of Troubles"

1605 The Gunpowder Plot by Catholics fails to blow up England's parliament

1606 Willem Janszoon, Dutch navigator, is the first European to reach Australia

"I discovered in the heavens many things that had not been seen before…"

GALILEO GALILEI, LETTER TO DUCHESS CHRISTINA OF TUSCANY, 1615

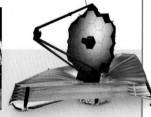

1609–2021
DEVELOPMENT OF TELESCOPES

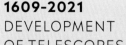

Since their invention in 17th-century Europe, telescopes have let astronomers see ever deeper into space, changing understanding of the universe.

1609 Galileo Galilei, an Italian astronomer, becomes the first to use a telescope to observe the planets.

1789 William Herschel, a German-British astronomer, builds a powerful telescope that uses mirrors rather than lenses to plot the stars.

1789 The Hooker telescope at Mount Wilson in California is used by Edwin Hubble to explore and observe many galaxies beyond our own.

2021 The James Webb Space Telescope detects radiation from the most distant objects in the universe.

1613
ROMANOVS RULE RUSSIA

The extinction of the Rurik dynasty in 1598 plunged Russia into the Time of Troubles. After the brief and brutal rule of Boris Godunov ended in 1605, various pretenders competed for the throne. In 1613, the Zemsky Sobor (parliament) elected 16-year-old Mikhail Romanov as tsar. Benefiting from a widespread desire for order, Tsar Mikhail ruled until 1645, founding a dynasty that lasted over 300 years.

◁ **Dish showing election** of Mikhail Romanov

1616
NURHACI CHALLENGES THE MING

A chieftain of the Manchu people north of China's Great Wall, Nurhaci unified the northern tribes under his rule. Creating a state organized into military sections called "banners", he laid claim to northern China. His armies scored notable victories against the Ming Chinese before his death in 1626. His successors would eventually conquer the Ming Empire.

△ Nurhaci, Manchu chieftan

1611 King Gustavus Adolphus inherits the throne of Sweden at the age of 16

1610

1610 The French king Henry IV is killed by Catholic fanatic François Ravaillac

1612 Tobacco exports begin from the Colony of Virginia in North America to England

1615 Spaniard Miguel de Cervantes completes his comic novel *Don Quixote*

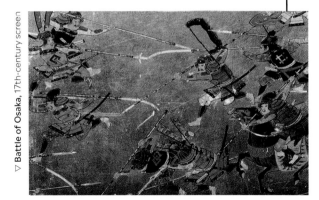

▽ Battle of Osaka, 17th-century screen

1615
BATTLE OF OSAKA

The dominance of the Tokugawa clan, shoguns (military rulers) of Japan from 1603, was contested by the Toyotomi clan. Based at Osaka Castle, Toyotomi Hideyori gathered a large army to defy the Tokugawa. Starting in winter 1614, a long siege of the castle ended with a decisive battle in May 1615 in which the Toyotomi were defeated and the castle was captured.

1547–1616
MIGUEL DE CERVANTES

Cervantes led an adventurous life, fighting the Turks at Lepanto in 1571 and later being captured by North African pirates. His books, including the novel *Don Quixote*, were written in his later years.

1618
THE DEFENESTRATION OF PRAGUE

The event that precipitated the ruinous Thirty Years' War in Europe occurred in Prague, then capital of Bohemia, in May 1618. Bohemia's largely Protestant people were at odds with their Catholic King Ferdinand, backed by Holy Roman Emperor Matthias. During a confrontation with Bohemian leaders in Hradčany Castle, two Catholic Regents sent by the emperor were thrown out of a high window. Both survived, but this act of Protestant defiance triggered a religious war.

◁ *Defenestration of Prague*, Václav Brožík, 1890

1619 German astronomer Johannes Kepler mathematically describes the movement of the planets

1619 The Dutch conquer Jakarta and impose their rule on parts of Indonesia through massacre

1619

1616
BLUE MOSQUE

When it was completed in 1616, the magnificent Sultan Ahmet Mosque – known as the Blue Mosque for the colour of its tiled interior – dominated the skyline of the Ottoman capital, Istanbul, with its six slender minarets. Commissioned by Ahmet I, sultan from 1603 to 1617, the mosque was a confident assertion of the continuing power and prestige of the Ottoman Empire.

◁ **Blue mosque** ceiling

The ceiling of the Ottoman Sultan Ahmet Mosque consists of 20,000 ceramic tiles

1615–1868
THE FLOATING WORLD

After centuries of civil strife, in the 17th century Japan entered an era of almost continuous peace under the rule of the Tokugawa shogunate. Establishing their capital at Edo (now Tokyo), the shoguns firmly controlled the regional warlords (the *daimyo*) who had once fought for power. The court of the Japanese emperors at Kyoto was relegated to decorative irrelevance. The samurai warriors, Japan's traditional fighting class, survived as paid retainers of the *daimyo*, without a function.

In conditions of peace and order, Japan's economic life flourished. Although despised in a social order that ranked them below peasants, merchants grew rich on commerce even though foreign trade was strictly controlled. Japanese craft workers and artists flourished, serving an elite that increasingly gathered in towns and cities. By the late 17th century, Japan was among the world's most urbanized countries and Edo, with a population of around a million, may have been the largest city anywhere. A vibrant urban culture, dubbed the "Floating World", absorbed the money of the merchant class and the leisure time of idle samurai devoted to pleasure instead of warfare.

Despite mounting problems with peasant revolts and plots by discontented samurai, the Tokugawa shogunate sustained a stable society for more than 250 years, before pressure from Western imperialism triggered fundamental change.

KEY MOMENTS

1629 All-male kabuki
With their melodrama, ribaldry, and flamboyant costumes, Kabuki plays (*depicted left*) became extremely popular in urban Japan. From 1629, female performers were banned, so male actors enacted both men's and women's roles.

1689 Bashō's journey
Tokugawa Japan's literary culture included the haiku verse form. In 1689, the haiku poet Matsuo Bashō (1644–94), journeyed into remote northern Honshu, recording his experiences in his masterwork *The Narrow Road to the Deep North* (*left*).

1829–32 Hokusai's Thirty-Six Views
The series of woodblock prints of Mount Fuji (*left*) by Katsushika Hokusai (1760–1849) are among the most famous Japanese artworks of the late Tokugawa period. When examples of Hokusai's prints began to filter through to Europe in the 1860s, they had a decisive influence on the evolution of Western art.

A print from Utagawa Hiroshige's series *Seven Hot Springs of Hakone*, created in 1852, illustrates the pleasures of the wealthy. Printmakers such as Hiroshige and Hokusai were labelled "artists of the Floating World" because they depicted the frivolous delights available to the privileged.

1620
PILGRIM FATHERS

In autumn 1620, a group of English Puritans fleeing religious persecution made a ten-week voyage across the Atlantic on board the *Mayflower*. Of the 102 "pilgrims" who reached Cape Cod in November, fewer than half survived to celebrate Thanksgiving with Indigenous peoples in 1621. They established the Plymouth Colony, the second permanent English settlement in North America.

▷ *Thanksgiving at Plymouth*, Jennie Brownscombe, 1925

1620 Court eunuch Wei Zhongxian begins a reign of terror over Ming China under the ineffectual Tianqi emperor

1623 The Dutch East India Company executes rival traders on Ambon Island, Indonesia

1620

1620 English philosopher Francis Bacon describes a new system of logic in his *Novum Organum*

◁ Michelangelo's plan of St Peter's, 1569

△ Battle of the White Mountain

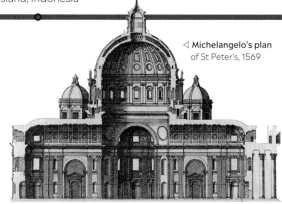

1626
ST PETER'S BASILICA COMPLETED

After 120 years under construction, St Peter's Basilica in Rome was completed in November 1626. The world's largest church, it was the work of many architects, from Donato Bramante, who made the original design, through Michelangelo, largely responsible for the vast dome, to Carlo Maderno, who added the façade. A Renaissance masterpiece, the Basilica boldly asserted the power and wealth of the Catholic Church.

1620
BATTLE OF THE WHITE MOUNTAIN

In 1619, the Bohemian (Czech) parliament chose the Protestant Elector Palatine Frederick V as their king. The Catholic Holy Roman Emperor Ferdinand II sent a large army to crush Bohemian independence. At the White Mountain outside Prague, Frederick's army was routed. The Catholic faith was brutally imposed on Bohemia but conflict between Protestants and Catholics continued as the Thirty Years' War.

The Dutch bought Manhattan Island from its native inhabitants for 60 guilders (US$2,000 today)

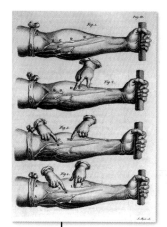

1628
HARVEY'S ANATOMICAL STUDIES

William Harvey was an English doctor who carried out thousands of dissections of human corpses and living animals. In 1628, he published a book, *De Motu Cordis* (*Of the Motion of the Heart*), demonstrating that blood circulates around the body, pumped by the heart. This was probably the greatest step forward in the understanding of human anatomy since the Ancient Greeks.

▷ **Plate illustrating** Harvey's experiments

1626 Dutch fur traders establish a settlement on Manhattan Island, calling it New Amsterdam

1626 Catholic forces under Albrecht von Wallenstein defeat the Protestants at Dessau in the Thirty Years' War

1629

1628 Cardinal Richelieu, the French chief minister, crushes a Protestant revolt at the siege of La Rochelle

△ Shah Jahan's accession, Padshahnama manuscript

1628
SHAH JAHAN TAKES THE INDIAN THRONE

The fifth Mughal emperor Shah Jahan ruled India from 1628 to 1658. His reign was a period of splendour for the Mughal court, reflected in magnificent buildings such as the Taj Mahal, commemorating the Shah's favourite wife, Mumtaz Mahal. Despite the wealth of the empire, however, millions died in a major famine in Deccan, southern India, in 1630–32.

1585-1642
CARDINAL RICHELIEU

Chief minister of France under Louis XIII, Richelieu reinforced the power of the monarchy, cracking down on the nobility and on rebellious Huguenots. He survived numerous plots on his life.

△ *Gustavus Adolphus at Breitenfeld*, Johann Walther, 1632

1631

SWEDISH VICTORY AT BREITENFELD

Under King Gustavus Adolphus, Sweden became a major European military power. In 1630, Gustavus joined in the Thirty Years' War on the Protestant side, leading his army to support Saxony against the Catholic Holy Roman Empire. At the battle of Breitenfeld, the Swedes and Saxons triumphed over the Imperial forces thanks to the Swedish king's superior generalship. Gustav Adolphus was killed in battle the following year.

1630

1631 In the Sack of Magdeburg, in the Thirty Years' War, 20,000 Protestants are massacred by Catholic troops

1630 The American colony of Massachusetts is settled by Puritans fleeing persecution in Stuart England

1633 Italian astronomer Galileo Galilei is condemned by the Inquisition for his heliocentric views

1632 Swedish king Gustavus Adolphus is killed when fighting at the Battle of Lützen

Around eight million civilians and soldiers died in the Thirty Years' War

1636

RISE OF THE MANCHU

In 1636, Hong Taiji, leader of the Manchu people, claimed the right to rule all of China as founder of a new dynasty, the Qing. In reality, the Chinese empire was still ruled by the Ming dynasty in Beijing, but the growing military might of the Manchus gave substance to their ambitions. In the winter of 1636 they invaded Korea, forcing the country to acknowledge their overlordship. A Qing invasion of China was soon to follow.

△ **Qing dynasty** imperial helmet

1637
PHILOSOPHY OF DESCARTES

Published in the Netherlands in 1637, French thinker René Descartes' *Discourse on the Method* was a founding work of the Enlightenment. Arguing that reason was the key to knowledge, Descartes saw the thinking mind as separate from the body, which was simply a physical machine. His injunction to "doubt as far as possible of all things" encouraged scientific investigation of the world.

▷ René
Descartes

1639
OTTOMANS REGAIN IRAQ

Murad IV, Ottoman emperor from 1623 to 1640, was a harsh and eccentric ruler. He was, however, successful in a war with Safavid Persia that lasted for most of his reign. Retaking Baghdad from the Safavids after a long siege in 1638, he made a peace the following year that left the Middle East divided along a line that still exists today – the current border between Iraq and Iran.

△ Sultan Murad IV receiving homage

"I think, therefore I am."

RENÉ DESCARTES, INTRODUCTION TO
DISCOURSE ON THE METHOD, 1637

1639

1639 At the Battle of the Downs, the Dutch navy destroys a Spanish fleet off the southern coast of England

1639
JAPAN REJECTS FOREIGN INFLUENCE

The influence of European traders and missionaries troubled Japanese society. In 1637-38, the Tokugawa shogunate was shaken by a major uprising in which Christian converts took part and responded by banning Christianity and limiting contact with foreigners. From then on the Dutch were the only Europeans allowed to trade with Japan, through the single port of Nagasaki.

▷ Catholics martyred
in Nagasaki

1642
ENGLISH CIVIL WAR BEGINS

Stuart king Charles I came into confrontation with many of his subjects in England and Scotland over taxation and religious issues. He tried to rule without parliament and was seen as favouring Catholicism. In 1642, the king and the English parliament raised armies and embarked on a civil war, fighting their first pitched battle at Edgehill in October. With neither side achieving a clear victory, a long conflict set in.

1640

1640 Portugal wins independence after throwing off Spanish rule

1643 Louis XIV becomes king of France at the age of four, with his mother Anne of Austria as regent

▽ Dutch drawing of the Maori, 1642

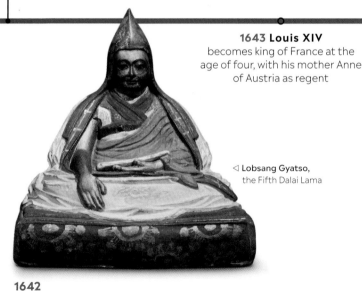

◁ Lobsang Gyatso, the Fifth Dalai Lama

1642
DUTCH REACH NEW ZEALAND

The explorer and merchant Abel Tasman was sent by the Dutch East India Company to explore the South Pacific. In December 1642, his men became the first Europeans to sight New Zealand. Anchoring off South Island they clashed with Maori warriors in canoes. The contact was fleeting. Europeans did not return to New Zealand until 1769.

1642
DALAI LAMA UNIFIES TIBET

In the early 1600s, Tibet was torn by conflict between rival Buddhist sects and warring tribal factions. In 1642, under the Fifth Dalai Lama Lobsang Gyatso, an effective government was formed in Lhasa, ending the civil strife. Lobsang Gyatso's successors ruled into the 20th century.

△ *Eve of the Battle of Edgehill*, Charles Landseer, 1845

▷ The Chongzhen Emperor with his empress

1644
FALL OF THE MING
By the 1640s, Ming China was in terminal decline. Ravaged by drought and disease, parts of the empire rose in revolt. In spring 1644, the most powerful peasant leader, Li Zicheng, marched on Beijing. The Chongzhen Emperor hanged himself from a tree in the imperial gardens and Li Zicheng was proclaimed emperor of a new dynasty. However, his triumph proved short-lived.

1644 At the Battle of Marston Moor, Parliamentarians defeat the Royalists in the English Civil War

1644

1643 At the Battle of Rocroi the French victory over Spain leaves France the leading European nation

1643 Italian physicist Evangelista Torricelli uses a mercury barometer to measure atmospheric pressure

As many as one in 25 of the English population died in the Civil Wars

△ Prince-Regent Dorgon, Manchu regent

1644
THE MANCHU INVADE CHINA
Exploiting the chaos surrounding the fall of the Ming, Manchu armies penetrated the Great Wall, asserting their claim to rule China as the Qing dynasty. With the aid of Ming generals hostile to the rebel Li Zicheng, the Manchu achieved victory at the Battle of Shanhai Pass and occupied Beijing. Led by the Regent, Dorgon, they embarked on a series of brutal military campaigns to extend their rule over the whole of the Chinese empire.

▷ Women warriors of Dahomey

1645
FIRST KING OF DAHOMEY

In the 1600s, the Fon people of West Africa formed the powerful state of Dahomey. Coming to the throne in 1645, Houegbadja is regarded as Dahomey's first king. He set up the state's characteristic institutions, including its corps of women warriors, who were called *Mino* ("Our Mothers"). Dahomey traded extensively with Europeans on the coast through the following century.

1645 At the Battle of Naseby in the English Civil War, Royalist forces are defeated by Parliament's New Model Army

1648 The Manchu Qing dynasty extends its rule into southern China, taking Guangzhou

1645

1647 Jesuits are branded subversives and expelled from the Massachusetts Bay colony

1648 Ottoman sultan Ibrahim is overthrown and replaced by his six-year-old son Mehmed IV

▷ The Manchu queue

1645
WEARING THE QUEUE

Having seized Beijing, the Manchu fought to impose their foreign rule on the Chinese. The populations of whole cities were massacred for continuing to support the deposed Ming. As a sign of submission, all Chinese men were ordered to adopt a Manchu hairstyle, with the front of the head shaved and a pigtail. The punishment for refusal of the "queue" was death.

1600–49
KING CHARLES I

King of England and Scotland from 1625, Charles believed in his divine right to rule. His marriage to Catholic Henrietta Maria and refusal to compromise on religion or politics led to his downfall.

1649
EXECUTION OF CHARLES I

Defeated in the English Civil War, Charles I was a prisoner of the Parliamentarians. After the failure of a Royalist uprising, supported by the Scots, in 1648, power lay with Oliver Cromwell and the New Model Army. On Cromwell's orders, the king was charged with treason. After a show trial, he was executed in Whitehall, London, on 30 January 1649. England became a republic for the next 11 years.

▷ **Charles I** is led to his execution

1648
THE FRONDE

During Louis XIV's childhood, his mother Anne of Austria ruled France with her chief minister, Cardinal Mazarin. In a revolt known as the Fronde, the government was challenged by the law courts and by the nobility, both claiming to defend traditional freedoms. After a five-year struggle, Mazarin restored absolute royal authority.

1648
PEACE OF WESTPHALIA

Treaties signed in the Westphalian cities of Osnabrück and Münster in 1648 ended both the Thirty Years' War between Catholics and Protestants and the Eighty Years' War between the Dutch and Spanish. A landmark in European international relations, the settlement allowed German states to determine their own policies on religion and ratified the full independence of the Netherlands and Switzerland.

◁ **Signing of** the Treaty of Münster

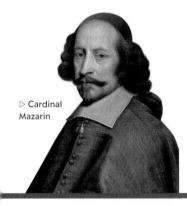

▷ **Cardinal Mazarin**

1649 Persian Shah Abbas II captures Kandahar from the Mughal Empire

1649 Cromwell's English Parliamentarian forces slaughter Irish Catholics at Drogheda during their conquest of Ireland

1649

"We will cut off his head with the crown upon it."

OLIVER CROMWELL DURING THE TRIAL OF CHARLES I, DECEMBER 1648

1653

CROMWELL BECOMES LORD PROTECTOR

A leading Parliamentarian commander in the English Civil War, Oliver Cromwell emerged as the dominant figure in Britain after the execution of Charles I. Having brutally crushed resistance in Ireland and Scotland, in 1653 he assumed almost dictatorial powers as Lord Protector of the Commonwealth. Cromwell aggressively promoted British interests abroad and maintained order at home, but he failed to create a durable republican political system. After his death in 1658 Britain soon returned to monarchy.

▷ **Oliver Cromwell** statue

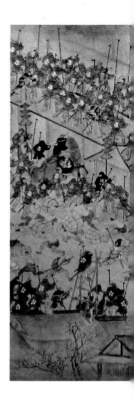

1651 Polish forces defeat Ukrainian Cossack rebels at Berestechko

1650

1654 Portuguese colonists take Brazilian sugar plantations from the Dutch

1650 Sultan bin Saif captures the port of Muscat, driving the Portuguese out of Oman

1652 French king Louis XIV enters Paris, ending the Fronde rebellion

1652

ANGLO–DUTCH TRADE WARS

By the 1650s, England and the Netherlands were commercial rivals, competing for maritime trade and colonial bases worldwide. In 1652, this rivalry turned into open warfare as Dutch and English naval squadrons battled in the North Sea and the Channel. The first Anglo-Dutch War culminated in an English victory off Scheveningen in 1653. Two more naval wars were fought before peace was made in 1674.

◁ The Battle of Scheveningen

1657
GREAT FIRE OF MEIREKI

With tightly packed houses built of wood and paper, the Japanese capital Edo (modern-day Tokyo) was notably vulnerable to fire. In March 1657, a huge conflagration – the Great Fire of Meireki – broke out, started by a burning kimono. Around 100,000 people are said to have died in three days when two-thirds of the city was destroyed by fire.

◁ **The Great Fire,** scroll painting, 1814

1655 Poland's "Deluge" begins when Swedish armies under King Charles X invade the Polish-Lithuanian Commonwealth

1656 The Ottoman Empire revives under the brutal but effective Köprülü viziers

1659

1656
ACCURATE TIME

Dutch scientist Christiaan Huygens (1629–95) was a leading figure in many fields, from astronomy to optics. In 1656, developing an idea proposed by Galileo Galilei, he devised the first pendulum clock. Built to Huygens's design by clockmaker Salomon Coster, it kept time far more accurately than any previous mechanism. Precise timekeeping eventually transformed daily life.

▷ **Christiaan Hugens'** pendulum clock

▷ **Emperor Aurangzeb** in his court

1658
AURANGZEB SEIZES POWER

As Mughal Emperor Shah Jahan grew old and ill, his four sons fought for control of India. In 1658, the third son, Aurangzeb, emerged victorious. He killed two of his brothers and placed his father under arrest. Ruling for 49 years, Aurangzeb expanded the empire, but his Muslim beliefs led to conflict with some of his subjects.

Under Aurangzeb the Mughal Empire expanded to 4 million sq km (1.5 million sq miles)

1662
PALACE OF THE SUN KING

In 1661, 22-year-old King Louis XIV took charge of France ruling as the "Sun King", an absolute monarch, accepting no limit to his God-given authority. To express his vision of royal power, he ordered the construction of a palace at Versailles, outside Paris, as a new seat for his court. The magnificent buildings and gardens were mostly completed by the late 1680s.

◁ *Palace of Versailles,*
Pierre Patel, 1668

"L'Etat, c'est moi" ("I am the State")

ATTRIBUTED TO KING LOUIS XIV

1660

1661 The Slave Code
enacted in British Barbados denies enslaved people any rights

△ 17th-century map showing Formosa

1662
KOXINGA RULES FORMOSA

Supporters of the Ming dynasty resisted the Manchu takeover of China for many years. In 1661, Ming loyalist and pirate Zheng Chenggong (Koxinga), defeated in mainland China, led his followers to Formosa (Taiwan). Capturing the Dutch fort on the island, in 1662 he set up his own kingdom as a Ming loyalist base. Koxinga's successors held Formosa until it finally fell to the Qing in 1683.

◁ **Koxinga** (Zheng Chenggong)

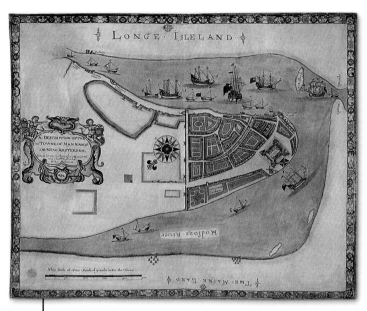

1664

BIRTH OF NEW YORK

From 1626, Manhattan Island was the site of a Dutch trading post, New Amsterdam. The settlement expanded under the energetic direction of Peter Stuyvesant. In 1664, the English sent a naval force to seize the Dutch colony. Lacking defensive resources, Stuyvesant yielded the colony without a fight. It was renamed New York after the Duke of York, heir to the British throne.

◁ Plan of New York, 1664

1665 In the Treaty of Purandar, the Marathas are forced to accept Mughal domination

1666 The death of Shah Abbas II marks the end of the golden era of Safavid Persia

1668 The Riksbank, the world's first central bank, is established in Sweden

1669

1669 Crete is conquered by the Ottoman Turks after the siege of Candia

1662

EXTINCTION OF THE DODO

The flightless dodo lived on the island of Mauritius in the Indian Ocean, which was settled by Dutch sailors in 1598. The last dodo was sighted in 1662, the species wiped out by Dutch hunters and shipborne rats. Its extinction has become a symbol of the human threat to nature.

◁ **The dodo,** *Raphus cucullatus*

1660-85
RESTORATION
ENGLAND

The son of executed King Charles I returned from exile in 1660, restoring the monarchy. His 25-year reign saw many dramatic events.

1661 The newly crowned King Charles II flouts puritanism, keeping mistresses and allowing playhouses to open.

1665 The Great Plague strikes London, killing one in six of the city's population. It is England's last major plague epidemic.

1666 The Great Fire of London destroys many buildings in September, clearing the way for major rebuilding in the city.

1675 The Royal Observatory at Greenwich is founded and contributes greatly to progress in astronomy and navigation.

▽ **Stepan Razin** heading for execution

1671
COSSACK REVOLT DEFEATED
The Cossacks were independent peoples living on the borders of the Russian Empire. From 1667, a Don Cossack, Stepan "Stenka" Razin, led an armed band on a rampage around the Volga River and the Caspian Sea. As rebellious Russian peasants flocked to join him, Razin threatened the Russian state. The well-trained imperial army defeated the Cossacks and crushed the peasant uprising. Captured, Razin was dismembered in Moscow's Red Square in June 1671.

1671 Angola is conquered as the Portuguese take over the Kingdom of Ndongo

1670

1670 England establishes the Hudson's Bay Company to trade in Canada

1672
ENGLISH SLAVE TRADE GROWS
The Royal African Company of England, established in 1672, was a venture backed by the Stuart monarchy to promote trade on the West African coast, chiefly the transport of enslaved Africans to British colonies in the New World. Wealthy figures, such as Bristol merchant Edward Colston, joined in the Company's activities. Other European countries engaged in the transatlantic slave trade, with Britain becoming the main trader.

△ **Edward Colston**, portrait by Jonathan Richardson

By 1740, some 42,000 enslaved Africans were transported in British ships every year

1672
DUTCH "DISASTER YEAR"

From 1650, the Netherlands flourished under the leadership of the brothers Johan and Cornelis de Witt but in 1672 was invaded by Louis XIV's France with naval support from England. The de Witts, blamed for military failure, were lynched by a mob. William of Orange took over as ruler and blocked the French advance by opening the dikes to flood low-lying areas. The Netherlands survived the "Rampjaar" ("Disaster Year"), but the Dutch Golden Age had ended.

◁ The de Witt brothers

1673
REVOLT OF THE THREE FEUDATORIES

The Manchu Qing dynasty faced a major revolt in southern China. Han Chinese generals who had supported the Manchu takeover had been given provinces to rule as personal fiefdoms. Three of these "feudatories" – Wu Sangui in Yunnan province, Shang Zhixin in Guangdong, and Geng Jingzhong in Fujian – rebelled and threatened to overthrow the Manchu Kangxi Emperor. It took eight years of military campaigns to suppress the revolt and finally render Qing dynasty rule in China secure.

△ Coin issued by Wu Sangui

1675 Mughal Emperor Aurangzeb has the Sikh leader Tegh Bahadur executed

1679

1678 The treaties signed at the Peace of Nijmegen end the war between France and the Dutch Republic

1674
RISE OF THE MARATHA EMPIRE

The Marathas were Hindu warrior clans living in southern India. From the 1640s, Shivaji, a member of the Bhonsle clan, proved a formidable military leader. Forced to accept the overlordship of Mughal emperor Aurangzeb in 1665, he soon resumed his campaigns and in 1674 was crowned Maratha emperor. By Shivaji's death in 1680 he controlled a swathe of southern India. Surviving Aurangzeb's counter-attacks, the Maratha empire flourished in the following century.

◁ Statue of Shivaji Bhonsle

1681
PENNSYLVANIA FOUNDED

In 1681, English king Charles II granted a large area of land in North America to the Quaker William Penn, in payment of a debt owed to his late father. Penn founded a colony based on the principle of freedom of worship for all Christian sects. He signed a treaty with Indigenous Americans, the Lenape, in 1683 and established Philadelphia as a thriving capital for his colony.

▷ *Penn's Treaty with the Indians,*
Benjamin West, 1772

1681 The Canal du Midi is completed, linking the French Atlantic to the Mediterranean

1682 Ten-year-old Peter I (the Great) takes the throne as tsar in Russia

1680

1680
PUEBLO REVOLT

Under Spanish rule since 1598, the Pueblo people of New Mexico rose in revolt in 1680, provoked by the oppression of their religious practices. The resistance, organized by Popé, a religious leader, was so effective that the Spanish were completely driven out of the region. They returned 12 years later, after Popé's death, but no longer interfered with Pueblo beliefs.

◁ **Popé,** sculpted by Cliff Fragua

1644–1718
WILLIAM PENN

As a Quaker, Penn suffered persecution in England before becoming proprietor of Pennsylvania. The principles of his *Frame of the Government of Pennsylvania* later influenced the US Constitution.

"Let men be good, and the government cannot be bad."

WILLIAM PENN, FRAME OF THE GOVERNMENT OF PENNSYLVANIA, *1682*

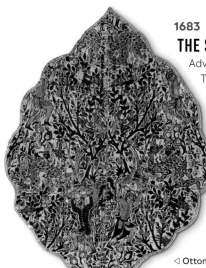

1683
THE SIEGE OF VIENNA

Advancing from Hungary, a vast Ottoman Turkish army led by Grand Vizier Kara Mustafa laid siege to Vienna, capital of the Holy Roman Empire. Polish, Austrian, and German forces led by Poland's king Jan Sobieski marched to lift the siege. Attacking the Ottoman camp, Sobieski drove the Turks into headlong flight. This defeat contributed to the decline of the Ottoman Empire.

◁ **Ottoman tent panel** from the siege of Vienna

1683 Taiwan falls to the Manchu Qing dynasty
after Taiwan-based Ming loyalists are defeated at the battle of Penghu

1684

1684 Shona warriors
of the Rozvi Empire drive the Portuguese out of Zimbabwe

▷ Cavalier de La Salle stained glass

1682
LA SALLE CLAIMS LOUISIANA

René-Robert Cavelier de La Salle was a French adventurer intent upon extending his country's territory in North America. He explored the Illinois River and in 1682 descended the Mississippi by canoe to the Gulf of Mexico. He claimed the whole region for France, naming it Louisiana. On a follow-up expedition in 1687, La Salle was murdered by mutinous followers.

▽ **Frost fair** on the River Thames, London

1683
LITTLE ICE AGE

From around 1650, the climatic period known as the Little Ice Age reached its most extreme point in Europe. Frost fairs were held on the iced-over River Thames in London, advancing glaciers destroyed villages in the Alps, and widespread crop failures led to frequent famines. The winter of 1683 was especially notable for freezing temperatures and heavy snowfall. The causes of this phenomenon remain uncertain.

More than 800,000 French Huguenots fled from persecution in Louis XIV's France

1685
EDICT OF NANTES REVOKED

In the 1680s, Louis XIV launched a campaign to eradicate Protestantism in France. The 1598 Edict of Nantes, guaranteeing the rights of the Huguenots (French Protestants), was revoked. Facing brutal mistreatment, Huguenots had to choose between forced conversion to Catholicism or emigration. Most left France, over 50,000 settling in England. The loss of their skills was a severe blow to the French economy.

◁ **Tympanum of the French Protestant Church,** London

1686 The Mughal emperor Aurangzeb conquers the sultanate of Bijapur in south India, expanding his empire

1687 Emperor Higashiyama's accession starts the Genroku era in Japan in which cities grow and the economy thrives

1685

1685 A rebellion led by the Duke of Monmouth fails to overthrow English king James II

▽ **The Parthenon** explodes

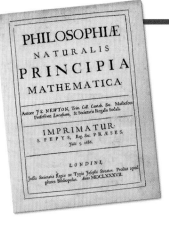

▷ **First edition** of Newton's work

1643–1727
ISAAC NEWTON

Professor of mathematics at Cambridge University and president of the Royal Society, Newton did major work in mathematics, physics, and optics. In his later years he ran the Royal Mint.

1687
NEWTON'S PRINCIPIA MATHEMATICA

Published in 1687, Sir Isaac Newton's *Principia Mathematica* was a giant step forward in the understanding of the physical universe. It stated the Laws of Motion and recognized gravity as the force that both kept the planets in their orbits and made objects fall to the ground on Earth.

1687
PARTHENON RUINED

In 1687, Venice was fighting the Ottoman Empire for control of Greece. When Venetian forces attacked Athens, the city's Turkish garrison withdrew to the heights where the ancient temple of the Parthenon stood. Using artillery to bombard the Turkish position, the Venetians ignited an ammunition store, setting off an explosion that left the famous building in ruins.

◁ **Carpet showing** the arms of William III

1688
"GLORIOUS REVOLUTION" IN BRITAIN

The succession of James II in 1685 caused a crisis in Britain because he was a Catholic and keen to rule without parliament. The political elite decided to replace him. Dutch leader William of Orange, a Protestant married to James's daughter Mary, was invited to take the throne as William III. He landed in England unopposed and James fled into exile. This "Glorious Revolution" confirmed Britain as a Protestant parliamentary state.

1689 The Grand Alliance
of England, the Netherlands, and Austria is formed against Louis XIV of France

1689

1689 The Treaty of Nerchinsk
settles the border between China and Russia along the Amur River and Lake Baikal, opening trade across Siberia

1688
SIAMESE COUP

In the 1680s, the Ayutthaya kingdom in Siam (modern-day Thailand) had extensive contact with Europeans. Its king, Naria, sent diplomats to the court of Louis XIV and welcomed French traders, soldiers, and missionaries. In 1688, Siamese nationalists opposed to foreign influence overthrew Naria in a palace coup. The French were expelled and all contacts with Europeans curtailed.

▷ **View of Ayutthaya city**, c.1665

1690
BATTLE OF THE BOYNE

After the "Glorious Revolution" of 1688, Catholics in Ireland rebelled against England's new Protestant monarch, William III. Backed by the French, deposed king James II assumed leadership of the Irish Catholic forces, which soon controlled most of the country. In 1690, William led an army to Ireland and defeated James at the Boyne River, near Drogheda. James fled to France and William reasserted Protestant ascendancy in Ireland.

▷ **William III** at the Battle of the Boyne

1690

1690 At the Battle of Beachy Head, the British and Dutch navies inflict a crushing defeat on the French fleet

1692 Spanish colonists reoccupy New Mexico, ending the Pueblo revolt

1690 East India Company agent Job Charnock establishes a fortified base at Calcutta (Kolkata)

1692
SALEM WITCH TRIALS

In the late 17th century, belief in witchcraft remained strong in the colonies of North America, encouraged by Puritans such as Cotton Mather. In 1692, teenage girls in Salem, Massachusetts claimed to have been bewitched, exhibiting fits and convulsions. Alleged cases of demonic possession rapidly spread. Some 200 people were accused of witchcraft; 14 women and six men were executed before the hysteria subsided.

△ *Examination of A Witch*, Tompkins Matteson, 1853

"Go tell Mankind, that there are Devils and Witches…"

COTTON MATHER, MEMORABLE PROVIDENCES, 1689

1693
BRAZILIAN GOLD

The discovery of gold deposits in southeast Brazil in 1693 triggered the world's first "gold rush". Tens of thousands of Portuguese migrated to their country's colony in hope of riches. By 1730, Brazil was producing 10,000 kg (22,000 lb) of gold a year.

△ **Enslaved Africans** panning for gold in Brazil

1694 The Bank of England is founded: the institution will finance the growth of the British Empire

1694 The Quilombo dos Palmares, a community of thousands of self-emancipated people, is crushed in Brazil

1694

△ **The Sicilian earthquake,** engraving

1693
SICILIAN EARTHQUAKE

A huge earthquake struck southeast Sicily on 11 January 1693. In the cities of Catania and Ragusa, worst hit by the disaster, more than half the population were killed and most buildings destroyed. Damage spread as far afield as Malta, with a tsunami following the tremor. The total death toll is reckoned to have reached 60,000.

1690-1775
EARLY STEAM ENGINES

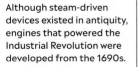

Although steam-driven devices existed in antiquity, engines that powered the Industrial Revolution were developed from the 1690s.

1690 Physicist Denis Papin, a French Huguenot living in Germany, builds the first model of a piston steam engine.

1698 Thomas Savery, an English engineer, invents a steam-powered water pump that becomes a commercial success.

1712 Thomas Newcomen, an English inventor, makes his ground-breaking "atmospheric engine" to pump water out of mines.

1763 Scottish inventor James Watt improves Newcomen's design, creating a more versatile engine to power factories.

Under the Qing, China's empire covered ten per cent of the world's land area

1696
THE QING INVADE MONGOLIA

Now firmly in control of the territory of the former empire, China's Qing dynasty launched a series of expansionist campaigns against Mongol tribes beyond the Great Wall. In 1696, the Kangxi Emperor led an 80,000-strong army across the Gobi Desert to attack the Dzungars, the most powerful Mongol confederacy. Victorious at the battle of Jao Modo, the emperor was able to extend Chinese rule over the whole of Outer Mongolia.

▷ **Qing warrior**
on horseback

1695

1697 A peace agreement,
the Treaty of Ryswick,
ends the Nine Years' War
in Europe

1696
SIEGE OF AZOV

Aspiring to make Russia a great power, Tsar Peter the Great sought access to the Black Sea, which was then controlled by the Ottoman Empire. In 1695, he laid siege to the Ottoman fortress of Azov on the Black Sea coast, but the siege failed for lack of naval power. In 1696, he returned with a fleet of galleys and took the fortress. A major southward expansion of Russian influence had begun.

◁ *Capture of Azov*, Robert Ker Porter

1654–1722
THE KANGXI EMPEROR
Ruling China for 61 years from 1661, the Kangxi Emperor unified the country. He reconciled the Han Chinese to Manchu rule by embracing Confucian traditions and promoting prosperity.

1697
OTTOMANS DEFEATED
The Ottoman Empire struggled to reverse the losses suffered after the failed 1683 Siege of Vienna. In 1697, Sultan Mustafa II led a large army northward to attack the Habsburg Austrian Empire. Crossing the River Tisza at Zenta, in what is now Serbia, the Ottoman forces were surprised by an army under Prince Eugene of Savoy and routed. The defeat confirmed Habsburg control of Hungary, expelling the Ottomans from central Europe.

◁ **The Battle of Zenta**, 1697

1699

1698 A Russian revolt led by the *streltsy* (a military caste) is crushed by Tsar Peter

▷ **Fort Jesus,** Mombasa

1698
ARABS DOMINATE EAST AFRICA
During the second half of the 17th century, the Sultanate of Oman, a state on the Arabian Peninsula, replaced Portugal as the dominant power on the Swahili coast of east Africa. By the 1690s, Fort Jesus, at Mombasa in modern-day Kenya, was the sole remaining Portuguese stronghold in the region. Omani forces seized the fort in 1698 after a lengthy siege. Much of east Africa was to remain under Arab control for almost 200 years.

△ Creation of the Khalsa

1699
SIKHS FOUND THE KHALSA
The Sikhs of northern India felt threatened by the religious intolerance of the Muslim Mughal emperor Aurangzeb. Sikh Guru Gobind Singh, whose father had been executed by Aurangzeb, decided to create a warrior community, the Khalsa, to defend religious freedom. In 1699, the first Khalsa were "baptized" in a ceremony staged at Anandpur in the Punjab. Following a strict code of dress and behaviour, the Khalsa became the core of Sikhism.

1701-1901
THE ASHANTI EMPIRE

The Ashanti Empire emerged in the 17th century in what is now Ghana. An ethnic sub-group of the Akan-speaking people, the Ashanti, or Asante, were composed of small chiefdoms established around Kumasi in the late 1600s. From 1701, Osei Tutu unified the chiefdoms and ruled as Asantehene (absolute monarch) of the most powerful political and military state on the Gulf of Guinea in West Africa. Gold was the Ashanti Empire's major product, with gold dust used as the circulating currency; even the poorest possessed gold ornaments. However, the Ashanti also became exporters of slaves, trading people captured during war raids on neighbouring enemies with the British, Dutch, and French for luxury goods and, most importantly, firearms. This technological advantage allowed the Ashanti to build their empire, which reached its greatest extent under Opoku Ware (r. 1720-50) and stretched across central east and west Ghana and some parts of Ivory Coast and Togo.

Territorial expansion brought the Ashanti into conflict with the British, who had colonized Cape Coast, in the early 19th century. From 1824 to 1899, there were five wars between the Ashanti Empire and Britain and its allies. The British slowly gained the upper hand, capturing and burning Kumasi in 1874, and deposing and exiling the Asantehene, formally annexing the empire in 1900.

KEY MOMENTS

1701 Osei Tutu unites the Ashanti people
As king of the new Ashanti state, Osei Tutu's authority was symbolized by a Golden Stool. The stool was ritually cleansed every year as part of the Ashanti Yam festival (*left*), which marked the first yam harvest.

1720-50 Trade and expansion
Under Osei Tutu's successor, Opoku Ware, the Ashanti Empire expanded, contributing to a commercial network that spread north across the Sahara, trading ivory, kola nuts, and – most notably – gold, which was weighed using ornate weights (*left*).

1824-1901 Wars with the British
The Ashanti came into conflict with the British (*left*) after they claimed land belonging to the Fante – a prosperous British client state. Four more wars followed until the last – prompted by British disrespect of the Ashanti Golden Stool – resulted in a British victory and their dominion over the entire Gold Coast.

This photograph from 1896 shows King Kobina and members of his tribe wearing traditional Kente cloth. This fabric became hugely popular with 18th-century Akan royalty, who wore it like a toga. Kumasi – the Ashanti capital – became a centre for Kente production in the 19th century.

1701
WAR OF THE SPANISH SUCCESSION BEGINS

In 1701–13, France and Spain fought a Grand Alliance that included England, the Netherlands, and Austria over the Spanish crown. This had been left to Philip of Anjou, grandson of King Louis XIV of France after the death of Charles II of Spain.

△ Louis XIV proclaiming his grandson king

1709
FIRST USE OF COKE TO SMELT PIG IRON

Abraham Darby (1678–1717) transformed iron production by smelting iron ore with coke – a substance made from coal rather than charcoal. This fuelled the Industrial Revolution by allowing larger blast furnaces to be made and reducing Britain's reliance on rapidly disappearing woods for charcoal.

△ **Iron production** at blast furnaces in Coalbrookdale, Shropshire

1704 Christian leader Dona Beatriz Kimpa Vita leads resistance to the Portuguese slave trade in the Kongo Empire

1708 Gobind Singh, the last human Sikh guru, is assassinated

1701 The Ashanti empire rises in modern-day Ghana

1700

1700
NORTHERN WAR BEGINS

The Northern War (1700–21) began when Russia and its allies challenged the supremacy of the Swedish Empire in northern and eastern Europe. The Swedish emperor, Charles XII, defeated his opponents by 1706 and invaded Russia in 1707. He was beaten at the Battle of Poltava (1709) by the forces of Peter the Great, who drove the Swedes out of the Baltic region. The war ended with the Treaty of Nystad (1721), which gave Sweden's Baltic provinces to Russia.

▷ **Peter the Great,** painted by Paul Delaroche

△ **Aurangzeb,** Mughal Emperor

1707
DEATH OF AURANGZEB

The last of the Mughal Empire's great emperors, Aurangzeb (b. 1618), seized the throne from his father, Shah Jahan, in 1658, declaring himself "Conqueror of the World". He was a devout Muslim, and expanded the empire to its greatest extent, warring frequently with the Marathas. After his death, the Mughal Empire fragmented, but lasted in name until 1858.

△ Mausoleum of Mirwais Hotak, Kandahar

1709
AFGHAN UPRISING

In 1709, Mirwais Hotak (1673–1715) freed Loy Kandahar (Greater Kandahar) in southern Afghanistan from its Persian Safavid rulers. Hotak's dynasty went on to rule an area that included Afghanistan, Iran, and western Pakistan until 1738, when Persia's new ruler, Nadir Shah Afshar, reconquered Kandahar.

"Let the path of the pure prevail all over the world."

GOBIND SINGH, c. 1699

1714

1709 The Great Frost affects Western Europe; icebergs are seen in the North Sea

1710 The first European porcelain is produced at Meissen in Germany

1713
BRITAIN'S SLAVE TRADE EXPLODES

In 1713, Spain awarded Britain a contract to send 4,800 enslaved Africans to Spanish America every year for 30 years. This, along with the opening up of Africa to all English merchants in 1698 and increasing demand for labour for the New World's sugar plantations, helped Britain become the dominant slave-trading nation in the 18th century. Between 1640 and 1807, Britain transported an estimated 3.1 million enslaved Africans, creating wealth for the port cities of London, Bristol, and Liverpool.

△ A Liverpool-based slave ship

▷ Shackles from the slave ship *Amistad*

1774 The Spinning Mule, invented by Samuel Crompton, revolutionized the cotton industry. It was able to produce hundreds of spindles of yarn at once and make different qualities and types of yarn. By 1812, over 4 million mule spindles were in use, producing textiles on a vast scale.

1700-1799
INDUSTRIALIZATION

In the 18th century, technological innovation and widespread societal changes collided to transform Britain's economy. Better agricultural methods made farms more productive, creating a ready supply of labour, while new banking practices freed up capital for investment. Steam engines replaced horses and water as the source of power for factories and transport, and allowed mines to efficiently produce the raw materials for Britain's expanding iron industry. The iron industry was transformed by the shift from charcoal to coal furnaces in 1709, and new puddling and rolling techniques for removing impurities from iron were developed in 1783, unlocking large-scale iron production.

Inventions such as the spinning jenny and Arkwright's water frame took the textile industry out of artisans' cottages and into giant factories. As iron foundries and textile mills moved near to Britain's coalfields in the Midlands and north of England and South Wales, a network of canals and roads sprang up to carry goods across the country.

Industrialization gave Britain an economic advantage that translated into political power, and also brought social change as workers came together, often striking or destroying machinery, in the fight for better pay and working conditions. By the 19th century, Germany, France, the US, and Japan had joined the Industrial Revolution, transforming the modern world.

KEY MOMENTS

1712 Newcomen's engine transforms mining
Coal was the fuel of the Industrial Revolution, key to the production of iron and steel. Its mining was transformed in 1712 when Thomas Newcomen developed his atmospheric steam engine, which cheaply and efficiently pumped water from Britain's mines, allowing them to be exploited to ever greater depths. By 1729, over 100 engines were at work in Britain and across Europe. The vast amounts of coal so produced transformed the industrial landscape (*right*).

1779 World's first iron bridge constructed
Built over the River Severn in Shropshire, England, the Iron Bridge (*right*) was a turning point in engineering, demonstrating what could be achieved with cast iron – the material that defined the new industrial age. Demand for iron for steam engines and military hardware in the Napoleonic Wars meant that Britain's iron production quadrupled between 1793 and 1815.

1715
YAMASEE WAR

The war between British settlers and the Yamasee Indigenous Americans of South Carolina nearly destroyed the colony and contributed to the emergence of the powerful Muscogee Creek and Catawba confederations.

▽ **Yamasee War,** wood engraving, 1844

1720
BAJI RAO BECOMES PESHWA

At the age of 20, Baji Rao became the seventh Peshwa (prime minister) of the Maratha Confederacy of Hindu warriors. An extraordinary cavalry general, he was undefeated in battle. His tactics, including encircling the enemy quickly and attacking from unexpected directions, kept his enemy off-balance and the Marathas in control of the battlefield. By moving swiftly and living off the land, the Maratha army under his leadership secured a series of conquests that threatened the Mughal Empire.

◁ **Baji Rao I,** who lived from 1700 to 1740

1716 The Spanish establish the fort of San Antonio to protect east Texas from the French in Louisiana

1715

1721 Japanese dramatist Chikamatsu Monzaemon publishes his classic play *The Love Suicides at Amijima*

▷ **Sultan Ahmed III Fountain,** Topkapi Palace, Istanbul

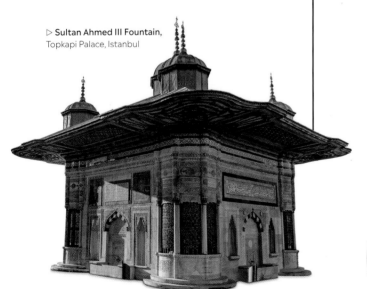

1653–1725
CHIKAMATSU MONZAEMON
Author of over 100 *kabukui* and *joruri* puppet theatre plays, Chikamatsu is considered one of Japan's most influential dramatists for his portrayal of complex, realistic characters and interest in human nature.

1718–1730
OTTOMAN TULIP PERIOD

This period saw a flowering of Ottoman arts and culture, with architecture and decoration becoming more elaborate and open to the influence of Western styles, such as Baroque. The period was named after the popularity of the tulip flower at the time, and the frequent use of the tulip motif in design.

1722
YONGZHENG EMPEROR IN CHINA

Yongzheng (1678–1735) became the emperor of China's Qing dynasty in 1722, succeeding his father, Kangxi. He centralized power under the Grand Council and sought to reduce European influence in China, expelling Christian missionaries, banning the sale of opium, and restricting foreign traders to the port of Canton (Guangzhou).

△ The Yongzheng Emperor

1721
VARIOLATION INTRODUCED IN THE WEST

Variolation – in which a small amount of pus from smallpox pustules is placed in cuts in the skin to inoculate against the disease – was a well-known practice in Asia and Africa. It was introduced to Europe by the British writer Lady Mary Wortley Montagu after she successfully inoculated her own children. Self isolation after inoculation was essential, but many European doctors disregarded this, sending infectious people back into society.

△ Lady Mary Wortley Montagu

1722 Persia's Safavid dynasty is overthrown by Afghan forces under Mahmud Hotak

1724

1724 The Mughal Empire in India further fragments, losing Awadh and Hyderabad to rival dynasties

> "A ruler that has but an army has one hand, but he who has a navy has both."
>
> *PETER THE GREAT, c. 1700*

1721
PETER THE GREAT BECOMES EMPEROR OF ALL RUSSIA

The founder of modern Russia, Peter (1672–1725) oversaw Russia's transition from tsardom to empire following victory in the Great Northern War. He looked to Western Europe for ideas on modernizing Russia, building St Petersburg, creating the Russian navy, and basing promotion on merit rather than inheritance. Under Peter, Russia became a major power and a threat to the Turkish and Persian empires.

◁ **Peter the Great** on the shore of the Baltic Sea, contemplating the idea of building Petersburg

1725

PEAK OF STRADIVARIUS VIOLIN PRODUCTION

From 1700, Italian instrument-maker Antonio Stradivari (1644–1737) produced violins, cellos, and violas of unsurpassed tone, craftsmanship and beauty. Around 650 instruments have survived.

▷ Stradivarius violin

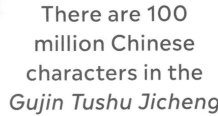

There are 100 million Chinese characters in the *Gujin Tushu Jicheng*

1725

1725 Austria and Spain sign the Treaty of Vienna, shifting the balance of power in Europe

1726 *Gujin Tushu Jicheng*, China's largest pre-modern encyclopaedia is published; it fills 10,000 volumes

1728

GREAT NORTHERN EXPEDITION

The Russian Emperor Peter the Great was determined to discover the extent of his lands to the east. He commissioned Danish seaman Vitus Bering (1681–1741) to follow the Siberian coast northwards from the Kamchatka Peninsula. In 1728, Bering sailed into the strait that separates Siberia and Alaska – now named after him – and established that it was the eastern limit of Siberia. A second expedition in 1733–43 involving 3,000 people mapped Russia's vast northern coastline.

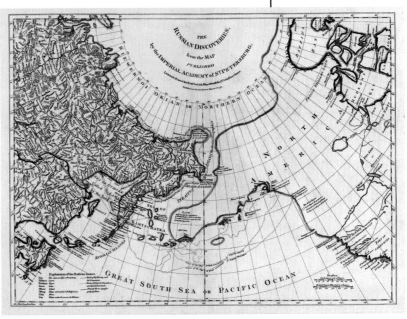

△ A map made at St Petersburg's Imperial Academy shows the limits of Russian exploration

1730
RESURGENCE OF SHINTO IN JAPAN

By the 18th century, Shinto had moved away from its roots as a cult of nature worship to become intertwined with Buddhism and Confucianism. In the 1730s, a reform movement led by Kada Azumamaro (1669–1736) and Kamo Mabuchi (1697–1769) sought to free Shinto of these elements, stressing instead its morality of pure simplicity and reviving the ancient rites. Shinto shrines proliferated and, by the early 19th century, the Japanese government required every family to belong to one.

◁ **Itsukushima** Shinto shrine

1731 The Kingdom of Dahomey accepts the suzerainty of the Yoruba Oyo Empire of West Africa

1734

1733 Invention of the flying shuttle improves the speed of weaving

1729
PERSIANS UNITE UNDER NADIR SHAH

In the chaos that followed the overthrow of the last Safavid shah of Iran, Sultan Husayn, in 1722, Nadir Shah (1688–1747) took control of northern Iran before defeating the Afghan Hotak ruler at the Battle of Damghan (1729) and uniting all Persia under his authority. Declaring himself Shah in 1736, Nadir drove the Russians and Ottomans from Persia and built a vast empire that his dynasty ruled until 1796.

△ **Nadir Shah** in battle

△ The 13 colonies, woodcut

1732
GEORGIA BECOMES THE LAST OF BRITAIN'S COLONIES IN NORTH AMERICA

Named after Britain's King George II, the province of Georgia was founded in 1733. The last of the 13 colonies established by Britain on America's Atlantic coast, Georgia was intended to strengthen the British presence in the south.

▷ Augustus III of Poland

1735
END OF THE WAR OF THE POLISH SUCCESSION

A major conflict followed the death in 1733 of Poland's king, Augustus II, as Bourbon France and Spain on one side, and Habsburg Austria, Prussia, and Russia on the other sought to install their own candidate on the throne. Fighting continued until a peace was agreed in 1735. In 1738, Habsburg Austria's choice was confirmed as King Augustus III.

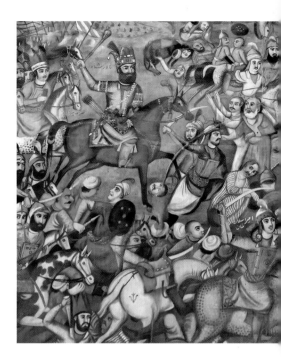

1735 Fulani Muslims create the Futa Jallon, a West African confederation of Islamic provinces

1735 Charles Marie de la Condamine undertakes the first scientific exploration of the Amazon River's entire navigable length

1735

1707–78
CARL LINNAEUS

A Swedish natural scientist known as the "father of taxonomy", Linnaeus organized all known organisms into a single hierarchical system that reflected the differences between species.

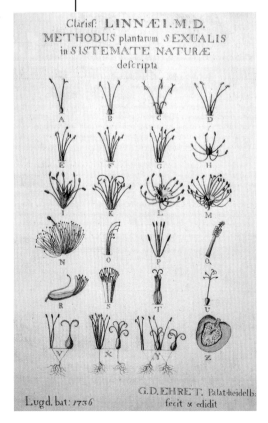

1735
CARL LINNAEUS PUBLISHES SYSTEMA NATURAE

In *Systema Naturae*, Linnaeus introduced his taxonomy, classifying living organisms into groups according to their structure and characteristics. He standardized the binomial system, which gave two Latin names to every organism. Linnaeus' system was refined in further publications, including *Genera Plantarum* (1742) and *Species Plantarum* (1753). His division of the natural world into kingdoms and his classification of organisms according to class, order, genus, and species still guides how we organize our understanding of the natural world.

◁ Plate from *Systema Naturae*

1738

NADIR SHAH INVADES MUGHAL INDIA

After conquering Kandahar in Afghanistan, the Persian ruler Nadir Shah invaded Mughal India, then already under pressure from the Sikhs and Hindu Marathas. At the Battle of Karnal (1739), he defeated a larger Mughal force and captured their ruler, Muhammad Shah. He plundered Delhi, carrying away treasure – including the Peacock Throne and Koh-i-Noor diamond – worth 700 million rupees. The plunder meant Nadir could continue his campaigns against the Ottoman Empire and in the North Caucasus.

◁ **Battle of Karnal** fresco

> "If the names are unknown, knowledge of the things also perishes."

CARL LINNAEUS, PHILOSOPHIA BOTANICA, *1751*

1739 The Russo-Turkish war ends; Russia abandons its claims to Crimea but gains a Black Sea port at Azov

1739

1735 The French begin establishing sugar plantations in Indian Ocean islands

△ *The Capture of Puerto Bello*

1739

WAR OF JENKINS' EAR BEGINS

War broke out when Britain was goaded into action over the case of Robert Jenkins – a captain whose ear was cut off by Spanish coastguards attempting to curb illicit trade in their New World colonies. Britain attacked Spanish possessions, capturing Puerto Bello naval base in Panama, and fighting continued until 1748, when it was subsumed by the War of the Austrian Succession.

1735-96
QIANLONG
CHINA

In his 60-year reign, the Qianlong Emperor (1711–99) developed China into a vast, multi-ethnic empire, whose diversity he celebrated.

1735 Qianlong becomes emperor, succeeding the Yongzheng Emperor, and announces a reign of liberal magnanimity.

1750 The emperor gains renown as a poet, calligrapher, and patron of literature, commissioning works to glorify Manchu culture and history.

1755 Qianlong begins the Ten Great Campaigns that expand the Qing Empire to its greatest extent, albeit at huge financial cost.

1770 Qianlong assembles a great collection of art at his summer palace, including his own writings as shown on this vase (above).

1740
FREDERICK THE GREAT BECOMES KING OF PRUSSIA

Frederick the Great (1712–86) transformed Prussia into a significant European power, expanding its territories, notably through the first partition of Poland (1772). An Enlightenment monarch, Frederick published his own writings and was a keen patron of the sciences and arts, supporting musicians including Johann Sebastian Bach and building the Berlin State Opera.

> "... there shone Frederick, the pole star around whom Germany... even the world seemed to turn."

JOHANN WOLFGANG VON GOETHE, GERMAN WRITER, ON FREDERICK THE GREAT, c. 1833

△ **Frederick the Great** playing the flute at Sanssouci

1740

1740 Baal Shem Tov develops Hasidism, an influential Jewish revivalist movement, in Poland

1741 Johann Sebastian Bach publishes the *Goldberg Variations*, a key work of Baroque music

△ **Austrian camp** on the River Danube

1740
WAR OF THE AUSTRIAN SUCCESSION BEGINS

The death of the Holy Roman Emperor Charles VI in 1740 sparked a series of conflicts (to 1748) over his daughter Maria Theresa's right to succeed to his Austrian lands and her husband to his title. The war drew in Prussia, Bavaria, France, Spain, Sweden, Russia, Britain, and Hanover. Maria Theresa secured her inheritance, ruling with her husband and then her son as emperor until 1780, but Austria was weakened and many issues remained unresolved.

1742
THE CELSIUS TEMPERATURE SCALE

Swedish physicist Anders Celsius (1701–44) proposed a temperature scale with 100 degrees between the freezing and boiling points of water on a mercury thermometer. Celsius set the boiling point at 0 and freezing point at 100, but this was reversed by his colleague Martin Strömer in 1750.

△ **Mercury in a glass** Celsius thermometer from c. 1790

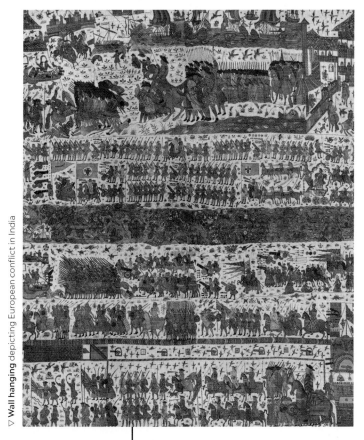

▷ **Wall hanging** depicting European conflict in India

1744
FIRST CARNATIC WAR

Rivalry between Britain and France in the War of the Austrian Succession played out in a struggle between the British and French East India Companies for control of the region's trading posts. After a British attack on the French fleet, the French attacked British-held Madras and Fort St David, and the British besieged the French at Pondicherry. Hostilities ended in 1748, but peace was short-lived.

1749

1744 The emir of Diriyah, Muhammad ibn Saud, and Muhammad ibn Abd al-Wahhab create the first Saudi state

1746 An earthquake and tsunami destroy Lima and Callao in Peru

1746 Ahmad Shah Durrani unites the Afghan peoples, founding modern Afghanistan

▷ **The Female Spectator** title page

1745
ELIZA HAYWOOD FOUNDS THE FEMALE SPECTATOR

The first periodical for women written by women was published. Each issue tackled one topic, with comments from the "spectator'" and her "assistants", who represented the various stages in a woman's life.

1746
BATTLE OF CULLODEN

Since the exile of King James II in 1688, his supporters – the Jacobites – had sought to reinstall a member of the Stuart royal family on the British throne. In 1745, Bonnie Prince Charlie (Charles Edward Stuart) and a Jacobite force took Scotland, advancing to Derby before retreating. The rebels were slaughtered by the British at Culloden, near Inverness, in the last pitched battle fought on the British mainland.

◁ **Charles Edward Stuart** (1720-1788)

1700–1789
THE ENLIGHTENMENT

A broad philosophical and cultural movement, the Enlightenment dominated intellectual and artistic endeavour in Europe and North America in the 18th century. It was rooted in the Scientific Revolution and the works of political theorists such as John Locke – who believed that men are free and equal by nature – and touched on many areas of life including politics, religion, and economics. Enlightenment thinkers championed rationality and freedom of thought over the "darkness" of dogma, faith, and superstition. For theorists such as Voltaire, Jean-Jacques Rousseau, Immanuel Kant, and Thomas Paine, reason was the primary source of authority and legitimacy. They explored ideas of liberty, equality, progress, tolerance, and constitutional government, challenging the power of Europe's monarchies and the Church and driving the revolutions of the 18th century. Paine and Rousseau argued against absolutist monarchy and the divine right to rule and so influenced the French Revolution and American Declaration of Independence. Yet for all the emphasis on equality and freedom, such concepts were often only selectively applied. Equality came slowly to include women and people of colour; indeed, the Enlightenment's scientific approach helped establish a pseudo-scientific basis for racism that was used to justify slavery and colonial oppression.

KEY MOMENTS

1763 Diderot publishes his *Encyclopédie*
French philosopher Denis Diderot's *Encyclopédie, ou dictionnaire raisonné des sciences, des arts et des métiers* (*sample page shown left*) attempted to catalogue all human knowledge in science, philosophy, politics, and religion. Its assertion that the government's main concern should be the common people provided the rationale for the French Revolution.

1784 Kant's "What is Enlightenment?" defines the movement
In this 1784 essay, German philosopher Immanuel Kant (*left*) defined enlightenment as "man's emergence from self-incurred immaturity". He suggested that people found it difficult to throw off this immaturity, and easier to accept the status quo, because they lacked the courage to think for themselves. The cultivation of the mind, which Kant summarized with the motto "Dare to be wise", was key to Enlightenment thinking.

An Experiment on a Bird in the Air Pump, painted by the English artist Joseph Wright in 1768, offered a vivid metaphor of the Enlightenment, depicting a scene in which a rational investigation of the world literally illuminates, "enlightening" the observers in the room.

▽ **Illustration of Guarani Indian life** by Jesuit missionary Florian Baucke

1750
TREATY OF MADRID
Signed on 14 January 1750, the Treaty of Madrid attempted to settle the colonial boundary between Spain and Portugal in the New World, superseding the earlier Treaty of Tordesillas (1524). In the hope of containing Portuguese expansion, Spain ceded much of what is now Brazil to Portugal. The treaty faced intense resistance from both Jesuit missionaries in South America and the native Guarani peoples; the boundary was finally agreed in the First Treaty of San Ildefonso (1777).

1750

1750 Hannah Snell is honourably discharged from the British armed forces after serving for several years disguised as a man

1751 British East India Company forces take Arcot in the Second Carnatic War against the French

1752 Burma unites under Alaungpaya; his Konbaung dynasty rules until 1885

1751
BRITISH GIN CRAZE
The consumption of gin increased rapidly in Great Britain in the early 18th century. Cheap and easily available, gin fuelled a social crisis, satirized by artist William Hogarth in his prints comparing the evils of gin consumption with the merits of beer drinking. After several unsuccessful attempts to curb consumption, the 1751 Gin Act limited gin sales, and the gin craze petered out.

> ## "Gin, cursed fiend, with fury fraught, makes human race a prey."
>
> *VERSE WRITTEN FOR HOGARTH'S* GIN LANE *BY JAMES TOWNLEY, 1751*

△ *Gin Lane*, **William Hogarth's** satire of the gin crisis

1754
FRENCH AND INDIAN WAR

The War of 1754–63 was one of several fought by France and Britain over supremacy in North America. The British lost several forts before going on the offensive in 1758 and securing a victory at Quebec in September 1759. The war ended with the Seven Years War, in 1763. It gave Britain control of North America but also fuelled resentment of British exploitation among American colonists.

▽ Battle scene from the French and Indian War

1706-90
BENJAMIN FRANKLIN
A successful writer and scientist from Philadelphia who demonstrated the electrical nature of lightning and invented bifocal spectacles, Franklin was also among the creators of the US Constitution.

1754

1753 Scottish doctor James Lind outlines his theory that citrus fruit can cure scurvy among sailors

1754
BENJAMIN FRANKLIN PROPOSES UNITY OF THE AMERICAN COLONIES

At the Albany Congress of June–July 1754, Benjamin Franklin presented his Plan of Union, suggesting that the colonies unite in a loose confederation, presided over by a president general and with authority to levy taxes. The plan was not implemented, but it contained the seeds of American independence.

△ Benjamin Franklin cartoon

1750-85
ART FOR THE PUBLIC

Many of Europe's great museums were founded in the 18th century as Europe's royalty put their collections on public display.

1750 The Musée du Luxembourg displays pieces, including work by Leonardo (*above*) from the collection of Louis XV.

1753 Sir John Soane donates 71,000 objects to Britain; they form the basis of the British Museum, the first public national museum in the world.

1764 The Hermitage Museum is created by Catherine the Great in St Petersburg to house Russia's vast royal collections.

1785 The Prado Museum is built to house the Natural History Cabinet of King Charles III (*above*): it opens to the public in 1819.

△ Depiction of Lisbon earthquake and tsunami

1755
LISBON EARTHQUAKE AND TSUNAMI

On 1 November, a powerful earthquake shook Lisbon, destroying thousands of homes and large buildings, including churches, where worshippers had gathered to celebrate the Feast of All Saints. The resulting tsunami swept across the Atlantic, hitting Martinique 10 hours later. Around 60,000 died in the earthquake, or drowned or perished in the fires that ravaged Lisbon for six days.

1755

1756 Wolfgang Amadeus Mozart, the influential composer, is born in Salzburg, Austria

1756 Prussia defeats Austria at Lobositz, Bohemia, in a prelude to the Seven Years' War

"I assure you that this extensive and opulent city is now nothing but a vast heap of ruins."

REVEREND CHARLES DAVY, ON THE LISBON EARTHQUAKE AND TSUNAMI, 1755

△ Samuel Johnson's *Dictionary*

1755
SAMUEL JOHNSON PUBLISHES HIS DICTIONARY OF THE ENGLISH LANGUAGE

It took Samuel Johnson and six assistants just nine years to put together his two-volume work; the equivalent French dictionary took 40 years. The *Dictionary* included over 40,000 definitions and around 114,000 literary quotations. Johnson's definitions were often subjective, reflecting his humour and prejudices. The work was only surpassed by the Oxford English Dictionary in 1884.

1756
SEVEN YEARS' WAR BEGINS

Colonial rivalries between France and Britain, and unresolved issues from the War of the Austrian Succession, erupted in 1756 in a conflict fought on land and at sea around the world – in India, North and South America, the Caribbean, Europe, and West Africa. The end of the war in 1763 left Prussia as a major European power and Britain with the upper hand in North America and India.

△ The British army at Quebec

1759
BRITAIN'S ANNUS MIRABILIS

In 1759, the British won several important victories in the Seven Years' War. At Pondicherry on 10 September, the British chased the French fleet from India. On 12–13 September, General James Wolfe captured Quebec with just 3,000 men, securing Canada for the British. And on 20 November, the Royal Navy prevented a planned invasion of Britain by destroying the French navy at Quiberon Bay.

△ *An Allegory of the Victory at Quiberon Bay*

1758 Halley's Comet returns, proving Edmond Halley correct in theorizing that comets orbit the Sun

1757 Muhammed III stabilizes Morocco after 30 years of unrest and curbs the Berber pirates

1758 The Al Sabah dynasty takes control of Kuwait after the chieftains of the Utub confederation make Sabah bin Jaber emir

1759 Suppression of the Jesuits begins in European colonies amid suspicion of their power and loyalty to the Pope

▷ The nawab's forces at Plassey

1757
NAWAB OF BENGAL DEFEATED AT PLASSEY

On 23 June, a force of the British East India Company under Robert Clive defeated the Nawab of Bengal's much larger army at the Battle of Plassey. The victory allowed the British to take control of Bengal and then expand the Empire over much of the subcontinent.

1725–74
ROBERT CLIVE

A British general and administrator, Clive was a controversial figure. He established British control over Bengal but was accused of corruption and exacerbating the devastating famine of 1770.

1762
CATHERINE THE GREAT SEIZES POWER IN RUSSIA

A German princess, Catherine (1729–96) married Emperor Peter III of Russia in 1745. She developed a deep love for the country and, on 28 June 1762, led a coup to rid Russia of its erratic, reactionary emperor and was proclaimed empress. She proved to be an enlightened monarch, reforming Russia's administration, raising its prestige in Europe, and extending its territories.

▷ Empress Catherine II of Russia

1760 Tacky's War sees a major uprising of enslaved West Africans brutally crushed in Jamaica

1760

1763 John Harrison's chronometer transforms navigation at sea by allowing longitude to be determined

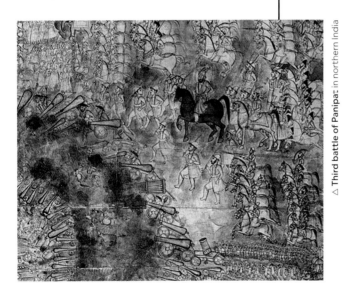

△ Third battle of Panipat in northern India

1761
BATTLE OF PANIPAT

Ahmad Shah Durrani led the Afghans to victory in a bloody battle against the Marathas, who dominated much of India. The battle of Panipat ended the Afghan-Maratha War (from 1757) and destroyed Maratha hopes of succeeding the Mughals as rulers of India, but left a dangerous power vacuum in northern India that Britain would exploit.

▷ First edition, title page

1762
JEAN JACQUES ROUSSEAU PUBLISHES HIS SOCIAL CONTRACT

Declaring that "man is born free but is everywhere in chains", Rousseau argued that people could only experience true freedom by living in a civil society that ensured the rights and well-being of all its citizens – a revolutionary idea at the time.

> "Ambition leads me...
> as far as I think it possible
> for man to go."

JAMES COOK, 1774

1769
JAMES COOK REACHES NEW ZEALAND

On 25 August 1768, James Cook and 96 men set sail aboard the *Endeavour* to search for the fabled southern continent of Terra Australis. Cook reached New Zealand on 6 October 1769, where his first encounter with the Maoris, at Poverty Bay on North Island ended in the death of four or five of them. After charting both islands, Cook continued westward.

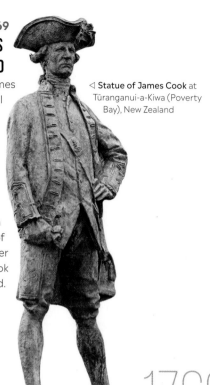

◁ **Statue of James Cook** at Tūranganui-a-Kiwa (Poverty Bay), New Zealand

1769

1765 China attempts the first of four unsuccessful invasions of Burma

1766-69 The First Anglo-Mysore war pits the British against Hyder Ali, Sultan of Mysore, in southern India

1766 Botanist Jeanne Baret is the first woman to circumnavigate the globe; she travels disguised as a man

1765
STAMP ACT SPARKS PROTESTS IN NORTH AMERICA

In 1764–65, the British government passed a series of taxes aimed at raising money from America's colonists. These included the Stamp Act, which taxed every piece of paper colonists used. Angry at having no say over taxation, the American colonists raised petitions and protested. They secured the act's repeal, but anti-British feeling festered.

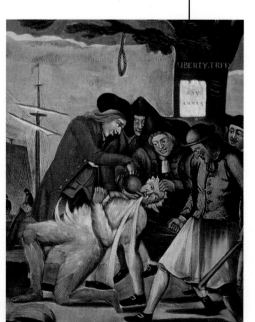

△ **American protesters** tar and feather a tax agent

1728-79
JAMES COOK

A skilled navigator and cartographer, James Cook captained three expeditions to the Pacific between 1768 and 1779. He died during a quarrel in Hawai'i, leaving a contested legacy.

1770

COOK EXPEDITION REACHES MAINLAND AUSTRALIA

On 29 April, Cook and the *Endeavour* made landfall at the Kurnell Peninsula. He named the area Botany Bay after Joseph Banks and Daniel Soleander, the expedition's naturalists, recorded 30,000 specimens of plant life, 1,600 of which were unknown to science. While there, they met Aboriginal Australians for the first time.

▷ **Joseph Banks**, botanist on Cook's expedition

1772

THE FIRST PARTITION OF POLAND

By the 18th century, the once powerful Polish-Lithuanian Commonwealth was near anarchy. In 1772, its neighbours Austria, Prussia, and Russia agreed to annex portions of the Commonwealth to avoid a war over expansion. Poland lost half its population and almost a third of its land in the partition. Two more partitions, in 1793 and 1795, dismantled Poland altogether.

△ **The division of Poland,** engraving

1770

1771 The Great Yaeyama tsunami hits Japan, killing 12,000 people in Okinawa

1771 Plague in Moscow kills 200,000; riots break out when the authorities enforce quarantines

"Just trust yourself and you'll learn the art of living."

JOHANN WOLFGANG VON GOETHE, FAUST, PART ONE, *1808*

1770-1850
ROMANTIC MOVEMENT

Romanticism was a European artistic and intellectual movement. A response to the Enlightenment, it explored emotion and nature.

1774 Johann Wolfgang von Goethe publishes *The Sorrows of Werther*, a highly influential, sentimental novella.

1781 Henry Fuseli paints *The Nightmare*, a disturbing evocation of obsession that hints at the supernatural and at dark sexuality.

1790 William Blake publishes *The Marriage of Heaven and Hell*: written like a prophecy, it outlines his Romantic and revolutionary beliefs.

1801 Ludwig van Beethoven completes his *Moonlight Sonata*, abandoning traditional constraints to create music that embodies the emotions.

1774

LOUIS XVI BECOMES KING OF FRANCE

At the age of just 19, Louis succeeded his grandfather, Louis XV, to become the last king of France before the French Revolution (1789). He inherited a kingdom deeply in debt, in which resentment of the monarchy was growing. A weak, indecisive man, Louis proved unable to combat the forces working to thwart much-needed economic and social reforms. His decision to convoke the States-General (a gathering of the Church, nobility, and commons) set the Revolution in motion.

◁ Bust of Louis XVI

1774 The Ottoman Empire cedes Crimea to Russia at the end of the Russo-Turkish War

1774

1772 The Qianlong Emperor orders the creation of the *Siku Quanshu*, the largest series of books in Chinese history

1773 James Cook circumnavigates Antarctica on his second voyage to the Southern Hemisphere

△ Depiction of the Boston Tea Party, engraving

1773

BOSTON TEA PARTY

A key grievance of American colonists against the British was that they had to pay taxes, yet had no representation in the British parliament. In protest, a group of Massachusetts colonists tipped a cargo of tea from British ships into Boston harbour on 16 December. British retaliation prompted the colonists to call the First Continental Congress (1774) to discuss America's future.

1738-1820
GEORGE III

King of Great Britain and Ireland (1760–1820), George III's hard line against dissent in the colonies after the Boston Tea Party precipitated their loss in the Revolutionary War.

▽ **Battle of Lexington,** the first engagement of the American Revolutionary War

1775
AMERICAN REVOLUTIONARY WAR BEGINS

As discontent in America grew, the British began to fear an armed rebellion. On 19 April, General Thomas Gage led a group of British soldiers to seize guns and ammunition being held by American "patriots". Rebel militia clashed with the British at Lexington and Concord, and fighting soon spread throughout New England. George Washington was appointed commander-in-chief of the revolutionary Continental Army, leading it until the war for independence ended in 1783.

1775 The First Anglo-Maratha War breaks out in India

1775

1775
DEATH OF FUKUDA CHIYO-NI (KAGA NO CHIYO)

One of Japan's greatest haiku poets, Fukuda Chiyo-ni was a scroll-mounter's daughter from Kaga Province. She began writing at the age of seven and developed her own style after studying the poems of Matsuo Bashō. She became a Buddhist nun in 1754, taking the name Soen.

◁ **Lady Chiyo,** woodblock print

△ Liberty Bell, Philadelphia, Pennsylvania

1776
AMERICA DECLARES INDEPENDENCE

On 4 July 1776, Congress adopted the Declaration of Independence, celebrating the "self-evident truths" of the rights to life, liberty, and the pursuit of happiness, denouncing King George III as a "tyrant", and dissolving "all political connection" between Britain and its American colonies. Bells, including the Liberty Bell (*above*), rang to announce the news.

▷ Flintlock pistol

1779
XHOSA WARS BEGIN
From 1779 to 1879, European settlers in South Africa's Eastern Cape were embroiled in a series of nine wars involving the Xhosa Kingdom that arose from tensions between Xhosa chiefs, or between settlers and the Xhosa. The first war (1779–1810) arose from Boer allegations that the Xhosa were stealing cattle.

◁ **A colonial depiction** of the Xhosa Wars

1781 William Herschel discovers Uranus, the first planet found since ancient times

1782 Rama I of Siam founds the Chakri Dynasty, which still rules Thailand

1784

1776 Adam Smith publishes *The Wealth of Nations*, which lays the foundations of modern Western capitalism

1783
LAKI VOLCANO IN ICELAND ERUPTS
The Laki eruption was the greatest seen in historical times. For nearly one year (June 1783 to February 1784), the volcano spewed out lava, which spread over about 565 sq km (220 sq miles). The gases released caused a haze that reached Syria, western Siberia, and North Africa, and killed most of Iceland's domestic animals. In the ensuing famine, one-fifth of Iceland's population died.

△ **The Laki crater**, part of the Lakagígar fissure in Iceland

"It began with the Earth... splitting asunder, ripping and tearing as if a crazed animal were tearing something apart."

ACCOUNT OF THE LAKI ERUPTION BY PASTOR JÓN STEINGRÍMSSON, 1783

1787
RUSSO-TURKISH WAR RESTARTS

After previous wars between Russia and the Ottomans, the Russian empress Catherine annexed the Crimean peninsula. Fearing that her plan was to partition their empire with the Austrian Habsburg empire, the Ottomans went to war. The conflict ended in 1791 with the Ottomans ceding the entire western Ukrainian Black Sea coast to Russia.

△ **The Imperial Russian Army** besieging the Turkish port of Ochakov

1787
CALLS INCREASE FOR THE ABOLITION OF SLAVERY

As questions were raised – particularly by the Religious Society of Friends (Quakers) – about the moral justifications for slavery, several societies emerged in Europe calling for its abolition. These included the French Société des Amis des Noir and the British Society for the Abolition of the Slave Trade.

▷ A popular abolitionist image

1785

1785 The invention of the power loom revolutionizes the textile industry

1785 English social reformer Jeremy Bentham argues for the decriminalization of homosexuality

1786 The collapse of a dam on the Dadu River in China causes a flood that kills around 100,000 people

1787 Formerly enslaved people colonize Sierra Leone, arriving from England, Nova Scotia, and Jamaica

1732-99
GEORGE WASHINGTON

A signatory of the US Constitution, George Washington was the United States' first president (1789–97), serving two terms before retiring to his family estate at Mount Vernon, Virginia.

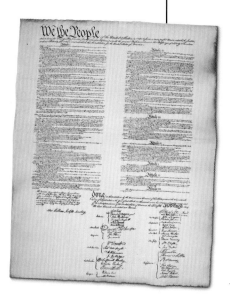

1787
US CONSTITUTION SIGNED

On 17 September 1787, 39 delegates of the Constitutional Convention met in the Assembly Room of the Pennsylvania State House to sign the US Constitution. Beginning "We the people", it laid out the rights of American citizens and defined the tripartite structure of the federal government: the legislative (Congress); the executive (the president and government officers); and the judicial (Supreme Court and other federal courts).

◁ **The US Constitution** parchment

▷ **Phyrgian cap,** a symbol of the revolution

1789
FRENCH REVOLUTION

In June 1789, representatives of the Third Estate (the French people) declared themselves a National Assembly, vowing in a tennis court at Versailles to establish a written constitution. When a mob stormed the Bastille prison (a symbol of the king's tyranny) on 14 July, the government was forced to agree to the abolition of the aristocracy. The day marked the end of the Ancien Régime, France's centuries-old political and social system.

△ *The Tennis Court Oath*, Auguste Couder

1789

1788 Hungary revolts against the Holy Roman Empire

1788 The first colonists arrive in Australia: they include 732 convicts and 22 children

1789 Revolutionaries in France issue the *Declaration of the Rights of Man and of the Citizen*

△ **John Fitch's vessel** sails the Delaware River

1787
FIRST STEAMBOAT ON AMERICA'S RIVERS

On 22 August 1787, American inventor and engineer John Fitch made the first successful trial run of his steamboat *Perseverance* on the Delaware River. He went on to establish the first regular steamboat service in US history, laying the foundations for the great age of steamboat travel on America's rivers.

1788-1807
THE END OF THE SLAVE TRADE

From the 16th to the 19th centuries, an estimated 12 million Africans were forcibly transported across the Atlantic to the Americas, where they were sold as slaves. As this trade grew in the 18th century, reaching a peak in 1750–1800, so did arguments for its abolition based on moral and economic grounds. Black people took up leading roles in the fight to end the institution that systematically dehumanized them for profit. In the 17th century, Angolan prince Lourenço da Silva Mendonça travelled to Rome to convince the Pope to end the slave trade, and in 1792, *The York Herald* reported that Africans had blown up the slave ship *Le Couleur* on the coast of Guinea.

Guerrilla actions, such as arson and poisoning, were a threat to plantation owners, while open revolts such as that in Saint-Domingue (*see below*) made the establishment question the viability of slavery. Formerly enslaved people added their voices to the growing movement for abolition. The slave trade was outlawed in Britain 1807, but more than a million Africans were illicitly shipped across the Atlantic after this date.

KEY MOMENTS

1788 Slave Trade Act
After lobbying by the Sons of Africa, a group of 12 Black men including Olaudah Equiano (*left*), and the Society for the Abolition of the Slave Trade, Britain passed a law regulating the Atlantic slave trade, limiting the number of people British ships could transport.

1791-1804 Haitian Revolution
Formerly enslaved Toussaint Louverture led thousands of enslaved people in the colony of Saint-Domingue (*left*) to victory over European colonial armies to establish Haiti as the first independent Black republic in the Americas.

1807 Abolition of the Slave Trade Act
In March 1807, Britain became the first major European nation to abolish the slave trade. However, British slave merchants found ways to circumvent the ban using intermediaries (*left*), and slavery itself remained legal in Britain's colonies until 1833.

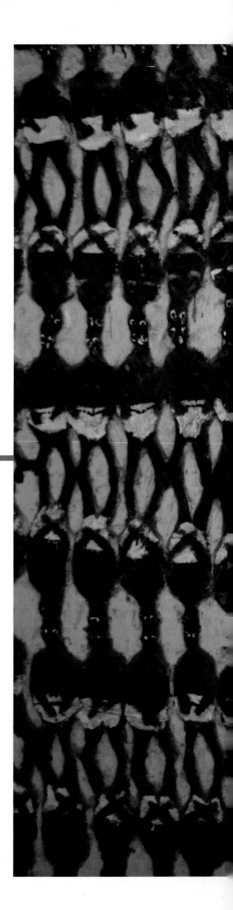

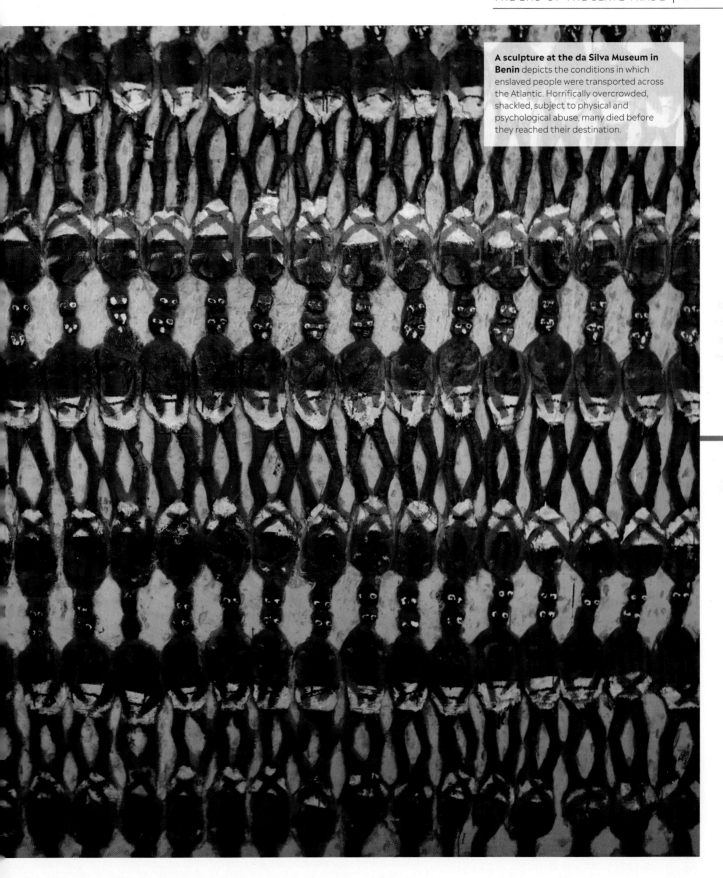

A sculpture at the da Silva Museum in Benin depicts the conditions in which enslaved people were transported across the Atlantic. Horrifically overcrowded, shackled, subject to physical and psychological abuse, many died before they reached their destination.

1791
DREAM OF THE RED CHAMBER
One of China's four great classical novels, *Dream of the Red Chamber* was written by Cao Xuequin and published in 1791. A semi-autobiographical novel featuring hundreds of characters, it provides rich insight into Qing dynasty society in its story about the wealthy Jia family.

◁ Scene from *Dream of the Red Chamber*, a Chinese classic

1790

1792 Denmark abolishes the slave trade, becoming the first country in the world to do so

1791 The Haitian Revolution sees enslaved people overthrow the system of slavery and form the first Black Republic in the Americas

1792 Mary Wollstonecraft publishes *A Vindication of the Rights of Woman*, an early feminist text

> "I do not wish them [women] to have power over men; but over themselves."

MARY WOLLSTONECRAFT, A VINDICATION OF THE RIGHTS OF WOMAN, 1792

1792
WAR OF THE FIRST COALITION
From 1792 to 1802, France was embroiled in a series of wars with Britain, the Holy Roman Empire, Prussia, and Russia, all keen to stop the revolution from spreading. The War of the First Coalition (1792–97) began with a short-lived Austro-Prussian invasion of France that was turned back at the Battle of Valmy in September 1792. After a series of defeats, the French secured major victories from 1794, including against the Austrians at Fleurus (1794). The Austrians sued for peace after the French general Napoleon Bonaparte decimated their forces in Italy (1796–97).

△ Battle of Valmy, 20 September 1792

▽ Storming of the Tuileries Palace

1792
FRANCE DECLARES A REPUBLIC

The French Revolution reached its climax in September 1792. After Louis XVI vetoed radical measures agreed by the revolutionary Legislative Assembly, armed revolutionaries stormed the Tuileries Palace on 10 August, imprisoning the king and his family. On 21 September, the monarchy was formally abolished and a Republic established on the next day.

1793 China rejects British demands to open more trading ports to Britain's merchants

1794 The Battle of Fallen Timbers ends the Northwest Indian War, opening up Ohio to white settlement

1794

1794 The Warsaw Uprising aims to throw off Russia's control of the Polish capital

▷ Admiral Arthur Phillip depicted on a Wedgewood urn

1794
HAWKESBURY AND NEPEAN WARS BEGIN

The Hawkesbury and Nepean Wars (to 1816) arose from British attempts to colonize the area around Sydney, Australia. While the first British Governor of New South Wales, Arthur Philip, attempted to maintain good relations with the indigenous Australians, continued raids on British settlements prompted the third Governor, Philip Gidley King, to authorize settlers to shoot indigenous people on sight.

△ Mosaic from the Qajar era

1794
QAJAR DYNASTY SEIZES POWER IN IRAN

In 1794, Mohammad Khan Qajar (r.1789–1797) deposed Lotf 'Ali Khan (r.1751–94), the last Shah of the Zand dynasty, which ruled much of Iran as well as areas of Armenia and Iraq. He subdued the Christian Kingdom of Georgia, and then conquered the Khorasan region, long the stronghold of Nader Shah's Afsharid dynasty, uniting Iran under the Quajar, who ruled until 1925.

1796
GEORGES CUVIER ESTABLISHES EXTINCTION AS FACT

Naturalists of the 18th century could not countenance that creatures – then believed to have been created by a perfect God – could become extinct. By comparing the anatomy of fossilized animals with living ones, the French zoologist Cuvier established that many species had indeed vanished. Extinction was a fact.

▷ Statue of Georges Cuvier

1795

1795 The British seize territory from the Dutch in the Cape of Good Hope, South Africa

1796 The Qianlong Emperor abdicates, sending China's Qing empire into decline

1797 French soldiers land in Fishguard, Wales, in the War of the First Coalition

▽ Members of the White Lotus Society

1796
WHITE LOTUS REBELLION

The millenarian White Lotus Society was a cult dedicated to overthrowing the Manchu Qing dynasty. In response to famine and persecution, the Society led a rebellion against the Qing that took eight years and enormous expense to quell. Around 100,000 rebels died during the revolt, as did the myth of Manchu military invincibility.

△ Hanaoka Seishū, *Surgical Casebook*

1796
GENERAL ANAESTHESIA DEVELOPED IN JAPAN

Hanaoka Seishū, a Japanese surgeon of the Edo period, began developing a plant-derived compound named *tsūsensan* that could render patients unconscious for 6–24 hours. By 1804, he had perfected his formula and was able to successfully perform the world's first surgery using general anaesthesia.

1798
NAPOLEON BONAPARTE INVADES EGYPT

In May 1798, Napoleon sailed for Africa, planning to annex Ottoman Egypt and disrupt British influence in the area. His victory at the Battle of the Pyramids was balanced by defeat at the naval Battle of the Nile (1–2 August). After an unsuccessful expedition in Syria (1799), Napoleon evaded the British at Aboukir Bay and escaped to France (July 1799).

◁ **Battle of the Pyramids,** 21 July 1798

1799 Napoleon Bonaparte overthrows the French First Republic and makes himself First Consul

1799

1798 The Society of United Irishmen rebel against British rule, aiming to form a republic

1799 Tipu Sulta, the "Tiger of Mysore", dies defending his stronghold at Srirangapatna against a British, Maratha, and Hyderabadi force

1799
ROSETTA STONE UNEARTHED

The Rosetta Stone was uncovered by French soldiers in the town of Rashid (Rosetta), Egypt, in 1799, and then captured by the British in 1801. Inscribed with a decree issued in 196 BCE written in three ways – ancient Greek, Egyptian demotic, and hieroglyphics – the stone helped scholars decode ancient Egyptian hieroglyphics.

Deciphering the Rosetta Stone took 20 years

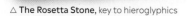

△ **The Rosetta Stone,** key to hieroglyphics

1801
FIRST BARBARY WAR BEGINS

States trading across the Mediterranean were forced to pay tribute to North Africa's Barbary states to gain protection from pirates. American refusal to pay triggered conflict between the US and Tripoli, which ended only after US forces captured Derna in Tripoli in 1805.

▽ US Marines board a Tripolitan gunboat

1802
NGUYEN ANH UNITES VIETNAM AND BECOMES EMPEROR

After capturing Saigon in 1788, Nguyen Anh struck at the Tay So'n rulers of Vietnam from his base in the south. He slowly united the country after centuries of internal conflict and ruled as Emperor Gia Long until his death in 1820. His dynasty was Vietnam's last; by 1883 Vietnam was part of French Indo-China.

◁ **Emperor Gia Long** (1762–1820)

1800

1800 Napoleon crosses the Alps to beat the Austrians at the Battle of Marengo

1801 The Act of Union unites Great Britain and Ireland as the United Kingdom

"The word impossible is not French."

NAPOLEON BONAPARTE, 1813

1800–1991
BATTERY TECHNOLOGY

The invention of batteries, which convert chemical energy into electric energy, unlocked the possibilities of portable power.

1800 Alessandro Volta, an Italian physicist, develops a pile that produces a steady electrical current.

1859 The lead-acid battery is invented by French physicist Gaston Planté. It is a reversible, rechargeable, electrochemical cell that soon finds many uses.

1886 Georges Leclanché develops longer-lasting dry-cell batteries using zinc-carbon electrodes and ammonium chloride paste.

1991 Lithium-ion batteries are produced commercially. Rechargeable, light, and powerful, they are used in used portable electronic devices.

▷ The Battle of Trafalgar, 21 October 1805

1769–1861
NAPOLEON BONAPARTE

One of the world's most famous military leaders, Napoleon Bonaparte saved revolutionary France from destruction by its enemies in 1792–1802 and proclaimed himself Emperor of France in 1804.

1803
THE NAPOLEONIC WARS BEGIN

In 1803, Britain declared war on France in an attempt to curb Napoleon Bonaparte's expansionism. Austria, Russia, and Sweden were drawn into the conflict, and various coalitions of Europe's major powers were involved in a series of wars with France that ranged across the world from India to America over the next 12 years. After an early, spectacular British victory at the Battle of Trafalgar in 1805, the tide only turned against Napoleon in 1812.

1804 Haiti becomes a Republic after the last battle of the Haitian Revolution at Vertières

1804

1803 Mecca falls to the Wahhabi First Saudi State

1803
LOUISIANA PURCHASE

By 1803, France had lost interest in its New World possessions and needed to raise funds for its war with Britain. Accordingly, Napoleon sold the whole of Louisiana – 2,144,500 sq. km (828,000 sq. miles) of land between the Mississippi River and the Rocky Mountains – to the United States for the sum of 60 million francs (US$15 million). The purchase doubled the area of the United States.

▷ Map of the Louisiana Purchase in 1803

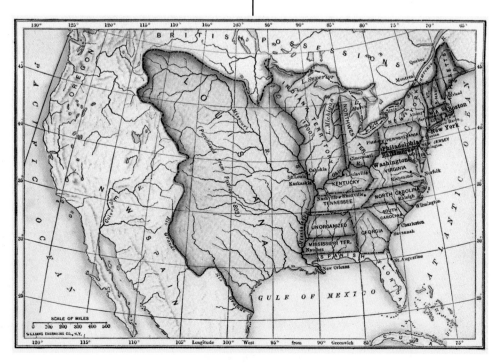

△ Napoleon at the Battle of Austerlitz

LATIN AMERICAN WARS OF INDEPENDENCE

After 300 years of Spanish rule, all of Spain's American colonies except Cuba and Puerto Rico gained independence between 1810 and 1826, largely through the leadership of Simón Bolívar in the north of South America and José San Martín in the south. They converged in Peru and Bolivia, forcing the last Spanish troops to leave South America in 1826.

1805
FRENCH VICTORIOUS AT AUSTERLITZ

After a dismal defeat by the British at Trafalgar on 21 October, Napoleon secured one of his most brilliant victories against the Russians and Austrians at Austerlitz on 2 December. With tactical genius and hard fighting, Napoleon outwitted a much larger enemy force. Austria was forced to make peace and the anti-French Third Coalition was broken.

1808–14 The Peninsular War pits France against Spain, Portugal, and Britain

▷ **José San Martín**, Battle of Chacabuco, Chile, 1817

1805

1807 Britain abolishes the slave trade (although slavery itself remains legal); the US enacts a similar ban in 1808

1810
MEXICAN WAR OF INDEPENDENCE

On 16 September 1810, the priest Miguel Hidalgo y Costilla issued a revolutionary tract known as the *Grito de Dolores* (*Cry of Dolores*), calling for the end of Spanish rule in Mexico. A peasant army gathered around Hidalgo, nearly capturing Mexico City before being defeated at the Battle of Calderón Bridge in January 1811. More uprisings followed, leading to the establishment of a short-lived empire and, in 1823, the Republic of Mexico.

▷ **Miguel Hidalgo's** *Cry of Dolores*, mural

1783-1830
SIMON BOLIVAR

Known as *El Libertador*, Bolívar was a Venezuelan military and political leader who led Venezuela, Bolivia, (named after him), Colombia, Ecuador, Peru, and Panama to independence from Spain.

1810
RED FLAG FLEET SURRENDERS

The South China Sea was terrorized by a great Pirate Confederation led, from 1808, by Zheng Yi Sao. She personally commanded the Red Flag Fleet of hundreds of war junks and was strong enough to threaten the East India Company, Portuguese Empire, and Qing China. In November 1809, a combined Portuguese and Qing fleet blockaded Zheng's fleet at Tung Chung Bay; in April 1810, she finally surrendered and the confederation crumbled.

△ **Pirate fleet** in the South China Sea

1812 Ali of Egypt
begins a campaign to retake Mecca and Medina from the Wahhabis and curb their power in Arabia

1814

1812-14 War between the US and Britain is triggered by the British seizure of American ships

1812
NAPOLEON INVADES RUSSIA

In a turning point in the Napoleonic Wars, Napoleon invaded Russia with a vast army, hoping for a quick victory against the empire. Instead, the Russians drew the French army deeper into Russia, where it was decimated by hunger, thirst, extreme heat, and freak blizzards. Following an indecisive battle at Borodino in September, Napoleon was forced to retreat through the Russian winter and arrived in Paris with just 50,000 men.

△ **French Napoleonic uniform**

Around 85,000 Napoleonic soldiers died on their march back to Paris from Moscow in 1812

1815
BATTLE OF WATERLOO

In a gruelling battle near Waterloo (in Belgium) on 18 June 1815, Anglo-Allied and Prussian armies under the Duke of Wellington and General Blücher finally ended the Napoleonic Wars. Wellington's forces endured a fierce French assault before Blücher's Prussians arrived, freeing Wellington for a final offensive that drove the French from the field. Napoleon was caught and exiled to Saint Helena.

▷ Battle of Waterloo

1815

1816–58 The Seminole Wars between the US and the Seminole Tribe in Florida are the bloodiest of the US–American Indian Wars

> "Believe me, nothing except a battle lost can be half so melancholy as a battle won."

ARTHUR WELLESLEY, THE DUKE OF WELLINGTON, ON THE BATTLE OF WATERLOO; LETTER FROM THE FIELD OF WATERLOO, JUNE 1815

1769–1852
DUKE OF WELLINGTON

Arthur Wellesley, the Duke of Wellington, was a veteran of the Peninsular War and Napoleon's greatest rival. He was deeply affected by the horrors of Waterloo; it was his last battle.

1816
SHAKA BEGINS BUILDING THE ZULU EMPIRE

The son of Senzangakhona, King of the Zulus, Shaka transformed the kingdom through a series of military, social, and political reforms. He quadrupled the size of the Zulu army and introduced a system of promotion by merit rather than birth, creating a highly trained and disciplined force that would go on to conquer large areas of southern Africa and challenge the British army.

▷ **Shaka,** King of the Zulus

1817
FIRST CHOLERA PANDEMIC

An outbreak of cholera in Bengal in 1817 spread across India, and gained attention in the West when hundreds of thousands of Indians and around 10,000 British troops died. The pandemic reached China, Indonesia, and the Caspian Sea before receding. It was the first of several cholera pandemics to ravage the world in the 19th century.

◁ **"Monster Soup"**, a contemporary cartoon commenting on the poor quality of London's water

1819 The first bicycles are invented; Karl Drais's velocipede sparks the first of many cycling crazes

1819

1817
RUSSIA ANNEXES NORTH CAUCASUS

The invasion of the Caucasus by the Russian Empire began a series of conflicts against the native Circassian peoples of the Caucasus that lasted until 1864. Many Muslims from the Caucasus were massacred or forcibly deported, most of them to Anatolia.

◁ **Circassian dagger,** or khanjali

1819 Singapore is established as a British trading post by Sir Stamford Raffles

1819 Spain cedes the Pacific Northwest and Florida to the US; New Spain's (Mexico's) boundaries are set

1818
END OF THE MARATHA CONFEDERACY

After dominating a large portion of the Indian subcontinent during much of the 18th century, the Hindu Maratha Confederacy came under pressure from the British in the 19th century. It lost control of Delhi in 1803 and was broken by the surrender of Peshwa Baijirao II to the British East India Company in the Third Anglo-Maratha War, opening the way for British domination in India.

◁ **Maratha ceremonial** mace head

1820
SINKING OF THE
WHALER ESSEX

A sperm whale rammed the US whaler *Essex* in the Pacific Ocean, crushing the ship's bow. The crew abandoned ship and attempted to reach land in three small boats. After three months at sea, having endured storms and been forced into cannibalism, only five men survived. The story inspired the American novel *Moby Dick*.

△ **A whale** rams the *Essex*

1820
COLONY OF LIBERIA FOUNDED

In 1820, the white American Colonization Society began sending volunteers from among America's formerly enslaved people to establish a colony on West Africa's Pepper Coast. Nearly half the first settlers died; more arrived and the colony declared independence in 1847.

△ **Colonization Society** membership certificate

1820

1821 Mexico becomes a sovereign country, but Spain does not recognize its independence until 1836

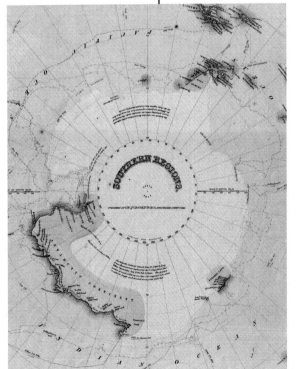

△ **Colton's map** of the South Pole, 1872

1820
FIRST RECORDED SIGHTING
OF ANTARCTICA

The ancient Greeks postulated the idea of a southern land mass and, in 1773, Captain James Cook unknowingly crossed the Antarctic Circle. The first sighting of Antarctica, however, was by the Russian explorer Thaddeus von Bellingshausen, who saw the ice-fields of the Antarctic coast on 28 January 1820. Two days later, Irishman Edward Bransfield sighted the northernmost point of the Antarctic mainland.

1822-1943
EARLY
COMPUTING

Developments in computer theory in the 19th century laid the foundations for modern computing, paving the way for the earliest digital machines in the 20th century.

1822 Charles Babbage, an English inventor, designs a "Difference Engine" – a steam-driven calculating machine, arguably the first computer.

1821
GREEK WAR OF INDEPENDENCE BEGINS

Greece had been under Ottoman rule since the 15th century when the Greek War of Independence broke out on 21 February 1821. The war turned in Greece's favour when Britain, France, and Russia joined the conflict on its side and destroyed the Ottoman-Egyptian fleet at Navarino in October 1827. A Russian invasion forced the Ottoman Empire to accept Greek independence, which was formally recognized in the London Protocol of February 1830.

◁ **Lazaros Kountouriotis,** patriot of the Greek War of Independence

1822 Brazil declares independence as the Empire of Brazil, ruled by Pedro I

1823 Beginning of the Anglo-Ashanti Wars between Britain and the Ashanti Empire of West Africa

1824 New Holland is renamed Australia by the British colonial authorities

1824

"The Analytical Engine weaves algebraic patterns just as the Jacquard loom weaves flowers and leaves."

ITALIAN MATHEMATICIAN LUIGI MENABREA, ON BABBAGE'S ANALYTICAL ENGINE, 1843

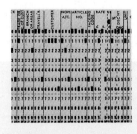

1843 Ada Lovelace, an English mathematician, writes the first programme for Babbage's more advanced Analytical Engine.

1854 English mathematician and philosopher George Boole develops the Boolean algebra that underpins computer programming.

1890 Herman Hollerith's tabulating punch card system processes the US census results, spawning the data processing industry.

1936 Alan Turing describes his "universal machine" – a system of rules and states that tests the limits of what can be computed.

1943 Colossus, the first programmable, electronic digital computer, helps British code-breakers in World War II.

1825–1900
THE TRANSPORT REVOLUTION

Advances in steam power, iron and steel production, and engineering fuelled a revolution in transport in the 19th century. Large-scale works such as the Erie Canal, linking New York City and the midwest, and the Suez Canal, joining the Mediterranean and Red seas, boosted development in the US and intercontinental trade respectively. While steamboats plied their trade along the US's great lakes and rivers, steam ships carried passengers around the world, furthering the aims of imperialism. However, the biggest impact on 19th-century mobility was made by the railways.

The pioneer of rail was British engineer George Stephenson, whose locomotive was the first to carry passengers on a public rail line, the Stockton and Darlington Railway, opened in 1825. Within decades, lines were crossing continents, revolutionizing the speed at which goods and people could be moved. These developments fuelled waves of immigration: thousands of indentured workers from Japan and China came to build America's railways; the Irish poor escaped famine on the transatlantic steamships; and many others sought their fortunes in India and South Africa.

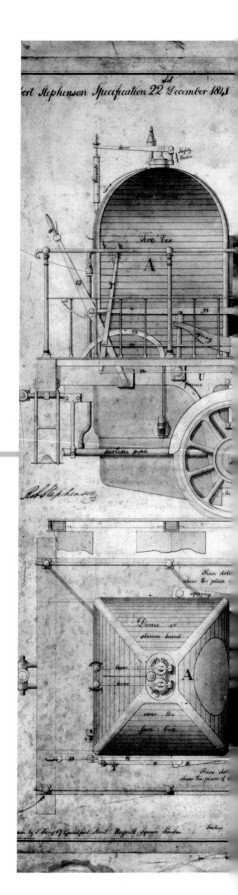

KEY MOMENTS

1838 SS *Great Western* crosses the Atlantic
The first steamship purpose-built for crossing the Atlantic, Isambard Kingdom Brunel's SS *Great Western* (*left*) reached New York from England in 15½ days, beginning the first regular transatlantic steamship service.

1859 Construction of the Suez Canal begins
Overseen by French engineer Ferdinand de Lesseps, thousands of forced labourers began digging out the 193 km (120 mile) long channel (*left*) that would link Port Said on the Mediterranean Sea with Suez, on the Red Sea. The canal was completed in 1869, cutting the need to round the Cape of Good Hope.

1869 US Atlantic and Pacific coasts linked
Combining two railways – the Central Pacific (starting from San Francisco) and the Union Pacific (starting from Omaha, Nebraska) – the Transcontinental Railway (*left*) linked the US east and west coasts. It was an invaluable trade conduit that helped fuel exports across both the Pacific and Atlantic oceans.

the arrangement and combination of the parts of Locomotive Engines

Lateral Elevation

Figure 1

Cylindrical part of the boiler
C

Smoke box

frame

Main Wheel
K

Chimney

Cylinder   Cylinder   Chimney

These dotted lines show the place of the Main wheel

These dotted lines show the place of the fore wheel

Figure 4

These dotted lines show the place of the Main wheel

These dotted lines show the place of the fore wheel

Figure 2   Horizontal Plan
Scale of Feet and Inches

Figure 3

Engineering plans from 1841 show the "Long-boiler" locomotive designed by Robert Stephenson, son of the "Father of railways", George Stephenson. Powerful and efficient, such engines were rather slow, but many remained in service for several decades.

1829
LOUIS BRAILLE PUBLISHES HIS RAISED DOT WRITING SYSTEM

Blinded in an accident at the age of three, French inventor Louis Braille was just 15 years old when he began developing his six-dot "cell" system that enabled the blind to read by touch. He went on to invent Decapoint, a 100-dot system by which the blind could write to sighted people.

▷ **Foucault apparatus** for printing Decapoint

1830
BOOK OF MORMON PUBLISHED

At the age of 24, the American religious leader Joseph Smith published what he claimed to be a history of an ancient American civilization revealed to him by an angel – the *Book of Mormon*. Smith's new religion, Mormonism, attracted thousands of followers, many of whom moved to Utah to found a society based on their beliefs in 1847.

▷ **Joseph Smith,** Mormon prophet

1825 The Java War, a guerrilla war against the colonial Dutch empire, claims 200,000 lives over five years

1830 The French invade the Ottoman Regency of Algiers; fighting continues until 1847

1825

1828 Queen Ranavalona I of Madagascar (r. 1828–1861) begins a brutal reign in which half the population perishes

1826
THE FIRST PHOTOGRAPHS

French inventor Joseph Nicéphore Niépce captured the earliest surviving photograph using his heliography ("sun writing") technique, in which a plate coated with light-sensitive bitumen was left in a camera obscura for several days to produce an image. Louis Daguerre refined the process and was credited with the invention of photography until Niépce's photograph *View from the Window at Le Gras* was rediscovered in 1952.

◁ *View from the Window at Le Gras,* the earliest surviving photograph of a real-world scene

◁ **Niépce's camera**

1830
REVOLUTIONS OF 1830

A wave of revolution swept through Europe in 1830. It affected Poland, the Italian states, Portugal, Switzerland, and, most dramatically, Belgium and France. Belgium freed itself from the United Kingdom of the Netherlands, becoming an independent nation ruled by King Leopold I, while France overthrew the Bourbon king, Charles X, for his cousin the Duke of Orléans in the July Revolution.

◁ *Liberty Leading the People,* by Eugene Delacroix, commemorates the July revolution

1831 Pedro I abdicates as emperor of Brazil in favour of his five-year-old son Pedro II, who reigns for nearly 59 years

1833 The Carlist Wars in Spain begin between supporters of Queen Isabella II and those loyal to the pretender, Infante Carlos of Spain

1834

1830 The Indian Removal Act forces Indigenous American tribes to move to reservation lands

1831 Muhammad Ali establishes a dynasty in Egypt after going to war with the Ottoman Empire; his dynasty rules Egypt to 1952

"I leave my brush in the East And set forth on my journey."

UTAGAWA HIROSHIGE, POEM BEFORE HIS DEATH IN 1858

1833–34
UTAGAWA HIROSHIGE PUBLISHES THE FIFTY-THREE STATIONS OF THE TŌKAIDŌ

The last great master of the *ukiyo-e* ("pictures of the floating world") genre of Japanese art, Hiroshige created a series of woodcut prints documenting his journey along the Tōkaidō road between Edo (now Tokyo) and Kyoto. His work fuelled Japonisme, a craze for Japanese art that influenced Western artists including Van Gogh, Degas, and Whistler in the mid-19th century.

▷ *Sudden Shower at Shōno,* woodblock print by Hiroshige

1836
CHARLES DICKENS PUBLISHES HIS FIRST NOVEL

Already a successful writer, Dickens published his first novel *Pickwick Papers* as a serial over 20 months. The book was a huge success that established Dickens' reputation as one of Britain's greatest writers and made him internationally famous.

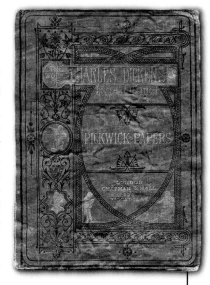

▷ The *Pickwick Papers*, early cover

1839-42
FIRST ANGLO-AFGHAN WAR

In the first major conflict of the Great Game – Britain and Russia's struggle for influence in Central Asia – Britain intervened in Afghanistan, installing Shah Shujah Durrani as ruler. The British army was annihilated during its retreat from Kabul in 1842. A second British expedition destroyed parts of Kabul but quickly withdrew, leaving Afghanistan to Durrani's rival, Dost Mohammed.

▷ Shah Shujah Durrani

1835

1835 The Black War between British colonists and Aboriginal Australians in Tasmania ends

1835 Dutch settlers leave the British Cape Colony, moving further north into Southern Africa on the Great Trek

1837 Queen Victoria begins her 63-year reign of the UK

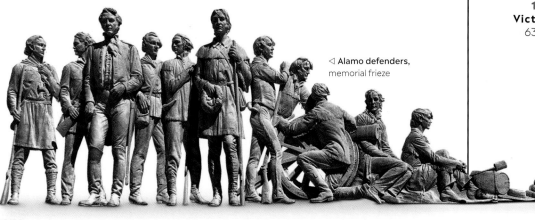

◁ Alamo defenders, memorial frieze

1836
TEXAS REVOLUTION ENDS

Fighting between the Republic of Mexico and American and Hispanic colonists in Texas broke out in October 1835. After the Mexicans killed the Texan defenders of the Alamo Mission in March, the Texan army defeated Mexican forces at the Battle of San Jacinto, securing independence for the Republic of Texas.

1838-1953
ADVANCES IN BIOLOGY

In the 19th century, several key discoveries in cell biology and heredity helped unlock the secrets of life, paving the way for the decoding of DNA in the 20th century.

1838 Cell theory is developed as German biologists Matthias Schleiden and Theodor Schwann postulate that the cell is the basic unit of life and all living organisms are composed of cells.

△ British ships attack Chinese junks, 1841

1839-42
THE FIRST OPIUM WAR

For years, Britain had been flooding China with opium, causing an addiction crisis. Tasked with stamping out the illegal trade, Chinese official Lin Zexu confiscated 20,000 chests of opium in Canton in 1839. The British invaded, capturing Canton and, by July 1842, threatened the city of Nanjing.

1839-1901
QUEEN VICTORIA

Victoria was Britain's queen from 1837 to 1901 and Empress of India from 1877. Her nine children with Prince Albert married into Europe's royalty, earning her the name "Grandmother of Europe".

1839 Charles Goodyear vulcanizes rubber, creating the pliable, waterproof material used in tyres

1839 A cyclone devastates the port of Coringa, India for the second time, killing 300,000; the city is not rebuilt

1839

"How can you bear to go further, selling products injurious to others... to fulfill your insatiable desire?"

LIN ZEXU, LETTER TO QUEEN VICTORIA ON THE OPIUM TRADE, 1839

1859 The variety of beak form in finches observed in the Galapagos Islands helps lead Charles Darwin to propose his theory of evolution through natural selection.

1866 Gregor Mendel, an Augustinian friar, studies inheritance in pea plants and discovers that they pass on their characteristics through invisible "factors".

1869 Swiss biologist Friedrich Miescher, identifies "nuclein", now known to be deoxyribonucleic acid (DNA), in blood cells; he suggests it has a role in inheritance.

1953 Scientists Rosalind Franklin, Francis Crick, and James Watson describe the double helix structure of a DNA molecule that suggests how biological information is transmitted.

1842
TREATY OF NANJING

The First Opium War ended in defeat for China in 1842. Under the punitive terms of the Treaty of Nanjing – the first of several "unequal treaties" – China was forced to open more ports to British trade, pay 21 million silver dollars compensation, and cede the island of Hong Kong to the British. The British-controlled territory later expanded to include part of the Kowloon Peninsula.

▷ **Treaty of Nanjing**, August 1842

1841 War erupts between Siam and Vietnam in Cambodia when Vietnam absorbs Cambodia and demotes the Khmer rulers

1845–52 The Great Famine in Ireland claims the lives of one million as potato blight devastates crops and the British government exacerbates the crisis

1840

1844 Samuel Morse sends the world's first telegraph message, from Washington, D.C. to Baltimore, Maryland

1840
TREATY OF WAITANGI

New Zealand's founding document, The Treaty of Waitangi, was an agreement between the British Crown and 540 Maori *rangatira* (chiefs) in which control over New Zealand was ceded to Britain. The New Zealand Wars broke out when the colonial government took increasing control over Maori affairs in 1845. They lasted until 1872.

▷ **Waitangi Sheet**, one of nine copies of the Treaty

1848
A YEAR OF REVOLUTIONS

A wave of revolutions spread through Europe affecting France, Italy, Hungary, Austria, and Prussia, among others. Driven by multiple factors, including nationalism and demands for the removal of old monarchical structures, the revolutions largely ended in repression but did bring about the abolition of serfdom in Austria and Hungary, the end of absolute monarchy in Denmark, and the establishment of the Second Republic in France.

1848
KARL MARX AND FRIEDRICH ENGELS PUBLISH THE COMMUNIST MANIFESTO

In the Communist Manifesto, Marx and Engels laid out their theory of history, which they interpreted as a series of class struggles that would inevitably see the workers (proletariat) overthrow the ruling class (bourgeoisie). Arguments soon raged across Europe about what shape this revolution would take and what the state's role should be, contributing to the development of socialism, Communism, and anarchism.

▷ **Marx and Engels** monument

1818–83
KARL MARX
A German philosopher, social theorist, and economist, Marx is among the world's most influential thinkers; his theories have shaped intellectual, economic, and political history.

1848 The first US women's rights convention is held at Seneca Falls, kickstarting the women's suffrage movement

1849

1847 Liberia declares independence from the US, becoming Africa's first modern republic

1848 California's gold rush begins when gold is found at Sutter's Mill, Coloma

△ Hungarian revolution, battle scene

1849
END OF THE SIKH EMPIRE
Formed in 1799 by Ranjit Singh, the Sikh Empire fell to the British after Singh's death in 1839. Having disposed of the Empire's formidable regent, Jind Kaur, in the first Anglo-Sikh War (1845–46), the British secured the Empire's dissolution in the second (1848–49), breaking it into several princely states and the British province of Punjab.

▷ **Maharani Jind Kaur**

1850-64
TAIPING REBELLION
Under the leadership of Hong Xiuquan, the Taiping rebels raged across 16 provinces in their quest to bring down China's Qing rulers. In 1853, Nanjing became capital of their Heavenly Kingdom, a utopian social experiment that promoted the equality of men and women. From 1856, the Qing army under Zeng Guofan began retaking Taiping-held areas, finally capturing Nanjing in 1864 and ending a conflict in which over 20 million died.

◁ Taiping Rebellion

1850

1851 US Congress passes
the Indian Appropriations Act that confines Indigenous Americans to reservations

▽ **Crystal Palace** in London's Hyde Park

1851
GREAT EXHIBITION IN LONDON
Great Britain held the Great Exhibition of the Works of Industry of All Nations in the Crystal Palace – a vast hall made of glass and iron sited in London's Hyde Park. There were 100,000 objects from 15,000 exhibitors, half of them British. Around six million people came to see items including the Koh-i-Noor diamond, Samuel Colt's pistols, Axminster carpets, and precision machinery.

London's Crystal Palace had 293,655 panes of glass

1851
GOLD STRUCK IN AUSTRALIA

Edward Hargraves, a veteran of the California gold rush, discovered flecks of gold in a waterhole near Bathurst, New South Wales, in February 1851. Larger nuggets were soon discovered in Victoria, and a huge influx of gold diggers from Britain, America, Germany, Poland, and China arrived in Australia, quadrupling the population in just 20 years.

△ Panning for gold

1814-64
HONG XIUQUAN

A religious leader and revolutionary, Hong challenged China's Qing dynasty, establishing the Taiping Heavenly Kingdom, and declaring himself both "Heavenly King" and Jesus Christ's younger brother.

1854 London-based physician John Snow discovers that cholera is a waterborne disease; this finding transforms public sanitation

1854

1854
CRIMEAN WAR BEGINS

After Russia occupied Turkish territory in 1853, France and Britain, determined to preserve the Ottoman Empire as a bulwark against Russian expansion, invaded the Crimea and besieged the Russian naval base at Sevastopol in 1854. Both sides were hampered by incompetent leadership and fought in terrible conditions. Sevastopol was captured in 1855 and Russia surrendered its claims to Ottoman lands in 1856.

▷ **British veteran** of the Crimean War

▷ A Ferry expedition ship, Japanese painting

1854
JAPAN ENDS POLICY OF SECLUSION

In 1853–54, Commodore Matthew Perry led a fleet of US warships into Tokyo Bay to force Japan to open itself to foreign trade after 200 years of seclusion under the Tokugawa Shogunate. This act of gunboat diplomacy revealed to Japan that it was ill-equipped to defend itself against the modern weapons and ships of the industrialized West.

1857–1900
IMPERIALISM

In the late 19th century, the world was reshaped as Western nations embarked on an unprecedented scramble for overseas territories. Competition between nations played a part in this drive for control: Britain hoped to recover its stature after losing its American colonies; France wanted to rebuild its power after the Napoleonic wars; Russia continued to push east into the weakening Qing Empire in China; and from the 1860s, the young nations of Germany, Italy, and the United States sought to become world powers. Rapidly modernizing after centuries of isolation, Japan was also keen to gain access to resources and territory it lacked. A misguided moral mission was also used to justify the conquest of, and increasing control over, lands across Asia, Africa, the Caribbean, and Australasia.

Industrialization was a key force behind imperialism because it demanded access to raw materials, labour, and new markets. Industrialization also made imperialism possible. Modern weapons and rapid transport meant that local resistance could be quashed in what sometimes became genocide, while telegraphic communication meant that large areas could be easily controlled. Modern medicine, particularly the discovery of quinine as a treatment for malaria, aided the spread of imperialism because the colonizers were less susceptible to the disease.

KEY MOMENTS

1857–58 The British take control of India
After suppressing a major revolt in 1857–58 (*left*), the British government placed British India and its princely states under direct rule by the Crown – the Raj. In 1876, Queen Victoria became Empress of India.

1876 Scramble for Africa
In 1876, King Leopold II of Belgium began colonizing the Congo, prompting Europe's powers to gather at the Berlin Conference (1884–85) to decide how they could carve up Africa between them. By 1900, Europeans ruled over 90 per cent of Africa (*left*) and its valuable natural resources.

1870s Social goals
Underpinning Western imperialism was a pseudo-scientific belief in the superiority of the white man and a perceived moral duty to rule, civilize, educate (*left*), and Christianize "native" peoples. The resulting policies typically wrought havoc on Indigenous cultures around the world.

This nationalistic map created in 1886 shows the extent of the British Empire (in pink) at the time. At the bottom of the map, Britannia sits symbolically on top of the globe, ruling over her colonies, while colonized people are illustrated as reductive stereotypes.

MAP OF THE WORLD.
SHOWING THE EXTENT OF THE BRITISH TERRITORIES IN 1786.

1855
TEWODROS II CROWNED EMPEROR OF ETHIOPIA

The architect of modern Ethiopia, Tewodros II, unified the Ethiopian kingdoms under his control, ending the Zemene Mesfint (Era of the Princes), during which the emperor was little more than a figurehead. He was determined to modernize the country but frequently faced opposition. He took his own life after the British attacked his forces at Maqdala in April 1868.

▷ Emperor Tewodros II

1855

1855 David Livingstone is the first European to see the Mosi-oa-Tunya waterfalls on the Zambezi River; he renames them "Victoria Falls"

> "… scenes so lovely must have been gazed upon by angels in their flight."

DAVID LIVINGSTONE DESCRIBING THE MOSI-OA-TUNYA FALLS, 1855

▷ Plan of areas destroyed by the earthquake

1855
EDO EARTHQUAKE

The last of three powerful earthquakes to hit Japan in 1854–55, the Edo earthquake struck on 11 November. Its epicentre was near the mouth of the Arakawa River, close to Edo. Much of the city was destroyed by fire; more than 6,600 people died and a further 2,700 were injured. Woodcut prints depicting the earthquake quickly appeared, some showing Namazu, the giant catfish said to be the cause of earthquakes.

1856–60
SECOND OPIUM WAR

Between 1856 and 1860, China was at war with the British and French empires over issues relating to the opium trade. Despite significantly outnumbering the foreign forces, the Qing army proved unable to prevent them capturing the imperial capital Beijing and destroying the Summer Palace. Defeated, the Qing had to legalize the opium trade, open more ports to foreign traders, and cede the Kowloon Peninsula to the British.

◁ **Anglo-French forces** land at Beitang, China

1856 Bones found in the Neander Valley, Germany, are recognized as a distinct hominid species, later named *Homo neanderthalensis*

1859 Spain declares war on Morocco over attacks on the Spanish enclave there

1859

1858 Mexico's War of the Reform pits liberals against conservatives; it ends in 1860

1859 The French conquer Saigon in Vietnam during the Cochinchina Campaign

◁ **A Bessemer converter**

1855
BESSEMER TRANSFORMS STEEL PRODUCTION

English inventor Henry Bessemer patented his converter for making steel. Molten pig iron was poured into the vessel and blasted with air to burn off impurities. Highly efficient, it marked the beginning of mass steel production.

△ The Sepoy Rebellion, illustration

1857–58
INDIAN REBELLION

A mutiny among the Indian sepoys (soldiers) over cartridges for the new Enfield rifles at the British garrison at Meerut on 10 May 1857 ignited a revolt against the British in India's Gangetic heartland. In the revolt's wake, British Crown rule – the Raj – was established across India.

1861
DOWAGER EMPRESS CIXI TAKES CONTROL OF CHINA

When her young son succeeded Chinese Emperor Xianfeng as the Tongzhi Emperor, the Empress Dowager seized control in a bloodless coup. She adopted the name Cixi ("motherly and auspicious") and dedicated her life to the survival of the fragile Qing Empire. She ruthlessly manipulated events to control the succession of two more emperors before she died in 1908.

◁ Dowager Empress Cixi

1861 Victor Emmanuel II of Piedmont-Sardinia becomes king of Italy, beginning the country's reunification

1860

1862 Umar Tall conquers Massina in Mali and founds the Toucouleur Empire

1860
FLORENCE NIGHTINGALE FOUNDS THE FIRST SCHOOL FOR NURSES

Famous for organizing the nursing of wounded soldiers during the Crimean War, Florence Nightingale transformed nursing into a profession and increased women's participation in the workforce by founding the Nightingale Training School in London.

◁ Florence Nightingale, relief

1861-65
CIVIL WAR RAGES IN AMERICA

Angry at US President Abraham Lincoln's anti-slavery stance, several states withdrew from the Union, forming the Confederate States of America in 1860. Civil war broke out as the Union sought to reunite the US.

12-13 April 1861 The first shots of the war are fired when the South Carolina militia bombard the US garrison at Fort Sumter, near Charleston.

17 December 1862 At the Battle of Antietam, a Union army stalls the Confederate invasion of Maryland; it is the bloodiest single day of battle in American history.

1863 In the Emancipation Proclamation, Lincoln changes the legal status of enslaved people in the Confederacy; 3.5 million African Americans are made free.

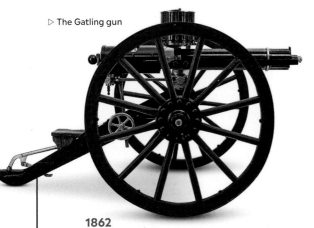

▷ The Gatling gun

1862
GATLING GUN PATENTED

Invented by Richard Gatling, this hand-cranked gun had ten rotating barrels capable of firing 400 rounds per minute. Gatling hoped the weapon's power would discourage war; instead, it was used to devastating effect against the indigenous peoples of the US, Africa, and Asia in the process of colonization.

1864–70
WAR OF THE TRIPLE ALLIANCE

The War of the Triple Alliance (or Paraguayan War) was the bloodiest interstate war in Latin American history. It was fought between Paraguay, which was then intent upon proving its strength in the region, and the alliance of Argentina, Brazil, and Uruguay. An estimated 60 per cent of Paraguay's population (around 270,000 people) died, along with some 56,000 from the Alliance, before the war ended in 1870.

▷ The Paraguayan war

1864

1863 The Football Association (FA) is founded in London; the first such body in the world, it introduces standardized rules for the game

1863 The Second Mexican Empire is created after Emperor Maximilian is executed

The US Civil War cost the Union $6.2 billion and the Confederate states $4 billion

1864 Union general Sherman captures Atlanta, an important Confederate centre, and marches south to the sea, destroying Confederate property as he goes.

1865 The Civil War ends when Union forces surround the Confederate army in Virginia; General Lee surrenders at Appomattox on 9 April.

1839–1915
ROBERT SMALLS

A formerly enslaved African American, Smalls stole the Confederate ship *Planter* from Charleston and piloted it through the Confederate checkpoints to the Union blockade and freedom.

1866
FYODOR DOSTOYEVSKY PUBLISHES CRIME AND PUNISHMENT

One of the greatest works of Russian literature, *Crime and Punishment* explored the psychology of crime, guilt, and redemption through the story of impoverished murderer Raskolnikov. It drew on Dostoyevsky's own experiences in a Siberian prison camp.

◁ ***Crime and Punishment,*** first edition cover

△ **Franz Joseph** takes his oath of office in Budapest

1867
AUSTRO-HUNGARIAN EMPIRE FORMED

After a series of foreign policy failures and military defeat by Prussia, Austria's Franz Joseph sought to strengthen the Austrian Empire. To pacify a rebellious Hungary, he made Austria and Hungary autonomous states under a common sovereign in a "Dual Empire" – the Austro-Hungarian Empire. The system ignored the claims of other nationalist minorities in the Empire, including the Croatians, Serbs, and Slovaks, fuelling tensions in Europe.

1865

15 April 1865
US President
Abraham Lincoln
dies after being shot

1867 The US purchases Alaska from Russia

1866–71
UNIFICATION OF GERMANY

In 1866, Prussian Chancellor Otto von Bismarck began removing the last obstacles to the unification of the various German states under Prussian rule. First, he engineered the Seven Week War (June–July 1866) with Austria. It left Austria isolated and weakened and Bismarck in control of a North German Confederation. Then, Prussian victory in the Franco-Prussian War (1870–71) neutralized the last opponent (France) to unification. On 18 January 1871, King Wilhelm IV of Prussia became Wilhelm I, Emperor of Germany.

◁ Proclamation of the German Empire

△ Mutsuhito, Meiji emperor, 1867–1912

1868
MEIJI RESTORATION

In 1868, a group of ambitious young samurai gathered at the imperial court in Kyoto planning to wrest power from the Tokugawa Shogunate and restore the Emperor's authority. Following victory in the Boshin War between the imperial army and reactionary forces, the young Meiji ("enlightened rule") Emperor oversaw reforms that transformed Japan from an isolationist, feudal country into a modern industrial nation.

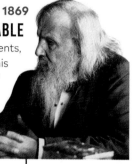

△ Dmitri Mendeleev

1869
MENDELEEV CREATES THE PERIODIC TABLE

Seeking a way to organize the known chemical elements, Russian chemist Dmitri Mendeleev published his periodic table. He arranged the elements in order of increasing relative atomic mass and grouped those with similar properties. Noting trends in the properties of elements, he left gaps for undiscovered elements, predicting what characteristics they would have.

1869

1867 The British Dominion of Canada is created from the provinces of Canada, Nova Scotia, and New Brunswick

1868 Cuba begins the "Ten Years' War" (1868–78) for independence from Spain

1815–98
OTTO VON BISMARCK

Architect of the German Empire, Bismarck (nicknamed the "Iron Chancellor") led Germany in a period of industrialization, social reform, and colonization before being forced to resign in 1890.

△ Suez Canal opening ceremony

1869
SUEZ CANAL OPENS

The Suez Canal linking the Mediterranean and Red seas was opened – four years behind schedule – on 17 November 1869. After Christian and Muslim blessings at Port Said the French imperial yacht, *L'Aigle* led a procession of ships through the canal. On the first night, the French ship *Péluse* grounded at the entrance to Lake Timsah, where the ships were to anchor for more celebrations.

1870

CONSTRUCTION BEGINS ON THE BROOKLYN BRIDGE, NEW YORK

Linking New York and Brooklyn across the East River, the Brooklyn Bridge was the world's longest suspension bridge at the time of construction. The work on was overseen by Emily Roebling, wife of the bridge's designer, John A. Roebling, who died following a freak accident in 1869. Carrying a rooster in her arms, Emily was the first to cross the bridge when it opened on 24 May 1883.

◁ **Construction workers** on the unfinished bridge

The Brooklyn Bridge is 1,834 m (6,016 ft) long and 83 m (272 ft) high

1871 Gold is discovered in South Africa following the discovery of diamonds there in 1867

1872 American suffragette Susan B. Anthony votes in the US election and is arrested

1872 Louis Ducos du Hauron, a French physicist, pioneers modern colour photography

1870

1871 Rome becomes part of the kingdom of Italy, finishing the process of reunification

1872

YELLOWSTONE, THE WORLD'S FIRST NATIONAL PARK, OPENS

After photographs and paintings of Yellowstone helped raise interest in the area's unique natural wonders, President Ulysses S. Grant signed the Yellowstone National Park Protection Act into law on 1 March 1872. It withdrew the "headwaters of the Yellowstone River" from "settlement, occupancy, or sale" and made the area a "public park or pleasuring-ground for the benefit and enjoyment of the people".

▷ **Grand Canyon** of the Yellowstone River

1841–95
BERTHE MORISOT

French painter Berthe Morisot was one of few women among the early Impressionists. The Académie des Beaux-Arts accepted her work, but she also exhibited with the Impressionists in their shows.

1874
FIRST IMPRESSIONIST EXHIBITION

After years of rejection by the French Académie des Beaux-Arts, a group of Impressionist painters organized their own exhibition in Paris. It showed 165 works by 30 artists, including Claude Monet's *Impression, Sunrise*. Critics mocked the broad, unblended brushstrokes and bright colours that characterized Impressionism; some called the paintings the work of "lunatics" or comedians.

▷ *Impression, Sunrise*, Claude Monet

1873 Spain becomes a republic after King Amadeo I abdicates during the Third Carlist War (1872–76)

1874

1873–96
WORLDWIDE DEPRESSION

For more than two decades, the world was gripped by a financial crisis caused by panics on the Vienna, New York, and Paris stock markets, a tariff war between France and Italy, and an increase in protectionism. The crisis realigned the world's economies, with the US emerging first from the slump and replacing Great Britain as the world's leading industrial power.

◁ **New York Stock Exchange** panic

1874
THE ASHANTI CAPITAL, KUMASI, IS DESTROYED

Between 1824 and 1900, there were five wars between the Ashanti Empire of West Africa and Great Britain. In 1874, a British force destroyed the earth and stone palace of the *Asantehene* (king) at Kumasi and imposed an indemnity of 50,000 ounces of gold, which the Ashanti paid in part by handing over gold masks, jewellery, and other treasures.

▷ **Solid gold head** from Kumasi

1876
THE FIRST TELEPHONE CALL IS MADE

On 10 March, Scottish inventor Alexander Graham Bell made the first call using his "speaking telegraph" device, which converted sound waves into a fluctuating electric current that could be reconverted into sound at the other end of the circuit. He called his assistant in another room to say: "Mr Watson – come here – I want to see you."

▷ Bell's telephone

1879–84
WAR OF THE PACIFIC

Chile went to war against Bolivia and Peru in a struggle for control of the mineral-rich area of the Atacama Desert on the Pacific coast. In February 1879, Chile occupied the Bolivian port of Antofagasta and the subsequent conflict ranged across the Pacific Ocean, Peruvian deserts, and the Andes. The war finally ended in 1883–84; Chile annexed Peruvian and Bolivian land along the Pacific coast.

1876–78 The Great Famine in central and southern India affects 58 million people; 8.2 million die

1875

1875 Ethiopia repels an Egyptian invasion force, guaranteeing its independence from foreign interference

1876 Porfirio Díaz seizes the Mexican presidency and serves for 31 years, overseeing Mexico's modernization

1876
BATTLE OF LITTLE BIGHORN

On 25–26 June, US General Custer and 600 cavalry rashly attacked the camp of the Northern Plains Indians' leader, Sitting Bull, on the Little Bighorn River. Custer's men were soon caught in a running battle with 2,000 warriors led by Sioux war leader Crazy Horse. Custer made his "last stand" on high ground above the Sioux village and died along with 210 of his men in the fighting.

▷ **George Custer** and scouts

1831–90
SITTING BULL

A Lakota Sioux warrior, Sitting Bull united America's Great Plains Indians against the white settlers. His victory at Little Bighorn made the government determined to quell the Indigenous Americans.

△ Battle of Angamos Madera, War of the Pacific

1877 The Qing Empire suppresses the Dungan Revolt begun by Hui Muslims and other ethnic groups

1879

ZULUS DEFEAT THE BRITISH AT ISANDLWANA

In January 1879, the British invaded Zululand after the king, Cetshwayo ka Mpande, refused to disband his army and join a federation of British colonies in South Africa. On 22 January, 20,000 Zulus attacked the British camp near Isandlwana, killing over 1300. Shocked by the Zulus' discipline and fighting skill, the British began a more aggressive campaign against them.

◁ Cetshwayo ka Mpande, Zulu king

1879

1878 The Treaty of San Stefano ends the Russo-Turkish War; the Ottoman Empire grants Serbia, Romania, and Montenegro freedom

"One does not sell the earth upon which the people walk."

CRAZY HORSE, QUOTED BY DEE BROWN IN BURY MY HEART AT WOUNDED KNEE, *1970*

1879-98
REALISM

Realism was an artistic movement that sought to represent truthfully the everyday experience of people's lives.

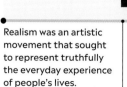

1879 The "father of realism" Henrik Ibsen publishes *A Doll's House*, his controversial portrayal of women's lives in a male-dominated society.

1880 Emile Zola outlines the elements of a "naturalist" novel, embracing determinism, scientific objectivism, and social commentary.

1896 Giacomo Puccini premiers *La Bohème*, a "Verismo" (Italian: "realism") opera, marked by plots with everyday characters.

1898 Konstantin Stanislavski creates method acting, encouraging actors to identify with a character's inner motivation and emotions.

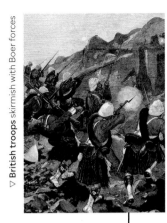

▷ **British troops** skirmish with Boer forces

1880
FIRST BOER WAR

After Britain annexed the Boer republic of the Transvaal in southern Africa in 1877, tensions grew. The Boers, descendants of mainly Dutch settlers, declared independence and, using guerrilla tactics, defeated British troops in a series of engagements. The Pretoria Convention of 1881 recognized Transvaal independence.

1882
GERMANY, AUSTRIA-HUNGARY, AND ITALY FORM A SECRET ALLIANCE

The three countries came together in what became known as the Triple Alliance. Under its terms, Germany and Austria-Hungary (close allies since 1879), agreed to support Italy should France make an unprovoked attack. Italy in turn would support Germany if France attacked. And in the event of war between Austria-Hungary and Russia, Italy was to remain neutral.

▷ **Peace shield** showing the heads of state of the Triple Alliance

1880

1881 The Tennessee State Legislature votes for segregated rail passenger cars. It is one of the earliest "Jim Crow" laws

1881 Pioneering nurse Clara Barton founds the American Red Cross

1881 France invades and seizes control of Tunisia, North Africa

▷ Booker T. Washington

1881
COLLEGE FOR AFRICAN AMERICANS OPENS AT TUSKEGEE, ALABAMA

Formerly enslaved, Booker T. Washington battled to obtain an education, entering the Hampton Institute, Virginia, in 1872. He believed education was essential for African American liberation and, starting with a small shack as premises, opened the Tuskegee Normal School, later the Tuskegee Institute, to provide teacher training for Black Americans.

▷ **Krakatoa** before its eruption, woodcut

The Krakatoa eruption shot gas and debris 24 km (15 miles) up into the atmosphere

▷ **Jibbeh (tunic)** worn by Madhists, c. 1880

△ **Mahdists clash** with British forces

1883
MAHDISTS FIGHT AN ANGLO-EGYPTIAN ARMY IN SUDAN

In 1881, Islamic cleric Muhammad Ahmad declared himself Mahdi (spiritual leader) and led an uprising against Egypt, which had controlled Sudan since 1819. In 1883, Egyptian and British forces were defeated by the Mahdists at El Obeid. Khartoum fell to the Mahdists in 1885.

1884

1882 Anti-Jewish pogroms occur in Russia, following the assassination of Tsar Alexander, which was blamed on the Jews

△ **Delegates** at the Berlin conference

1883
KRAKATOA ERUPTS IN INDONESIA

From 20 May 1883, the volcanic island of Krakatoa, between Java and Sumatra, began erupting for the first time in 200 years. In August, a series of four explosions almost completely destroyed the island. Eruptions sent vast quantities of earth into the air, created vast tsunamis, and killed 36,000 people.

1884
EUROPEAN POWERS DIVIDE UP AFRICA

Marking a new stage in their imperialist ambitions, European powers met in Berlin in November 1884 to effectively partition Africa into European colonies. Organized by German chancellor Otto von Bismarck, the conference continued until February 1885. Some 14 nations attended, including France, Belgium, Portugal, and Britain. No African leaders were consulted or invited to attend, nor was any consideration given to existing cultural, social, ethnic, and language borders. Within a few years, European powers controlled more than 80 per cent of Africa.

1885
INDIAN NATIONAL CONGRESS FOUNDED

Also known as the Congress Party, this was the first modern nationalist party to emerge within the British colonized countries in Africa and Asia. Meeting for the first time in Bombay (Mumbai) in December, its aim was to achieve greater political representation for educated Indians and political control within the British Raj. After 1920, under Mahatma Gandhi, it campaigned first for major political reform and then spearheaded the movement for Indian independence.

◁ **The first** Indian National Congress meets

1885

1887 Buffalo Bill's Wild West show comes to Britain to celebrate Queen Victoria's Jubilee

1885 The Canadian Pacific Railway reaches British Columbia and is completed

1888 Slavery is abolished in Brazil after more than 300 years of slave labour

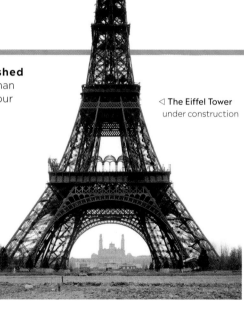

◁ **The Eiffel Tower** under construction

1885
LEOPOLD II CLAIMS THE CONGO

Following the Berlin Conference, King Leopold II of Belgium seized the rubber-rich Congo, which was renamed the Congo Free State. Unlike other European colonizers, Leopold ran the region as a privately owned state for personal gain. His administration became infamous for its excessive brutality, forced labour, and the torture and murder of the Congolese.

▷ Leopold II

1889
EIFFEL TOWER OPENS

Towering 312 m (1,024ft) over Paris, the Eiffel Tower was unveiled at the World Fair to commemorate the centenary of the French Revolution. Designed by engineer Gustav Eiffel and built by his company, it was the world's tallest man-made structure of the time and took 22 months to complete. The huge wrought-iron structure was criticized by public and artists, but when opened it was an instant success, attracting nearly 12,000 visitors every day.

1889
IMPERIAL EXPANSION IN AFRICA

European control over Africa grew rapidly as Italy colonized Eritrea and Britain tightened its grip on southern Africa. Expansion was led by speculators such as the controversial imperialist Cecil Rhodes. Granted a charter for his British South Africa Company, he increased British-controlled territory, later named Rhodesia after himself, and extracted mineral rights from leaders, such as King Lobengula of the Ndebele.

◁ **Cecil Rhodes** as a symbol of imperial greed, *Punch* magazine

1889 Socialists from 20 countries meet in Paris for the Second International

1889

1889 Japan adopts the Meiji constitution, which introduces some political reforms

1889 American journalist Nellie Bly travels around the world in 72 days

Between 1913 and 1927, Ford factories produced more than 15 million Model Ts

1886–1908
EARLY MOTORING

Early motor cars were expensive, but the arrival of mass production in 1908 lowered prices, triggering the age of the automobile.

1886 German engineer Karl Benz patents the first true petrol-powered automobile. With its four-stroke engine and three wire-spoked wheels, it is the first practical car.

1890 Frenchmen René Panhard and Émile Levassor produce the first car with a front-mounted engine. It has rear wheel drive and a sliding gear transmission.

1908 The first Model T-Ford rolls off the production line. Designed and produced by American Henry Ford, it is nicknamed "Tin Lizzie" and is the first mass-produced and affordable car.

1891
TRANS-SIBERIAN RAILWAY BEGUN

Brainchild of Tsar Alexander III, the railway was designed to run 9,198 km (5,715 miles) from Moscow to the eastern port of Vladivostok. Construction started eastward from Moscow and westward from Vladivostok. Tens of thousands worked on the railroad, including skilled workers, peasants, and prisoners. Trains had to be ferried over Lake Baikal but by 1904 all sections were completed, opening up Siberia.

▽ Engineers on the Trans-Siberian railway

1892
ELLIS ISLAND OPENS

With an ever-increasing number of immigrants from Central, Eastern, and Southern Europe making their way to the US, a federal immigration station was opened on Ellis Island in New York Harbour, close to the Statue of Liberty. Seven hundred immigrants passed through on the first day, followed by nearly 450,000 over the course of the year. They included Jews fleeing pogroms in Russia and Italians escaping poverty. In 1900-1914, some 1,900 immigrants arrived daily.

▷ **Immigrants arriving** in New York

1890

1891 Eugene Dubois, a Dutch paleoanthropologist, finds bone fragments in Java; he names them *Pithecanthropus erectus*, later known as "Java Man"

1890
MASSACRE AT WOUNDED KNEE

Devastated by the loss of their lands and livelihoods, Sioux people adopted a ritual Ghost Dance, believing their lands and culture would be restored. The US government saw this as a provocation and sent forces to Wounded Knee Creek, Dakota, to disarm the Lakota Sioux. Between 150 and 300 Sioux were killed.

◁ **Chief They-Fear-His-Horse,** negotiator after Wounded Knee

"Soldiers cut down my timber... kill my buffalo... my heart feels like bursting."

SANTANA, KIOWA CHIEF, 1867, FROM BURY MY HEART AT WOUNDED KNEE, *DEE BROWN*

1893
ART NOUVEAU ARRIVES

Reacting against the fussiness of Victorian decoration, European architects and designers developed a style known as Art Nouveau – literally New Art. It was characterized by flowing organic lines, natural forms, and modern materials. Architects such as Belgian Victor Horta, who designed the Hotel Tassel, popularized the style. Art Nouveau featured at the 1900 International Exhibition in Paris.

▷ **Hotel Tassel,** Brussels, Belgium

1893 France expands colonial rule over much of West Africa

1894

1892 Homer Plessy, a Louisiana Creole, challenges discriminatory US "Jim Crow" laws by sitting in a whites-only carriage

1894 Christian Armenians are massacred when they demand reforms within the Ottoman Empire

◁ **Memorial** shows Kate Sheppard, Meri Te Tai Manqakahia, and other campaigners

1893
NEW ZEALAND WOMEN WIN THE VOTE

In September 1893, women in New Zealand became the first to win the right to vote in parliamentary elections. Their success followed a long campaign headed by women such as Kate Sheppard who presented petitions to parliament, until finally the law was passed giving white and Maori women voting rights. New Zealand women could not, however, stand for parliament until 1919.

1848–1943
KATE SHEPPARD

Born in Liverpool, Sheppard moved to New Zealand in her early twenties. Committed to women's rights, she campaigned strenuously for the vote, crisscrossing the country, lobbying, and organizing petitions.

1840s-2021
VOTES FOR WOMEN

Women fought a long campaign to win the right to vote, especially in Britain and the US where the struggle was particularly intense. By the 1860s, women's suffrage movements – linked to women's growing demands for equality – were developing in the UK and US. These suffragists campaigned using respectable law-abiding methods, such as petitioning and lobbying parliamentarians, holding meetings, organizing marches, and writing to the press. However, as time went on, some – the suffragettes – turned more to direct action and civil disobedience to achieve their goals.

Campaigning faltered towards the end of the 19th century but was galvanized when New Zealand women won a right to vote in 1893. Australia followed in 1902 and four years later Finnish women won the vote – the first to do so in Europe. Most women gained the vote during the inter-war years, with some enfranchised following constitutional or revolutionary changes. Russia, for instance, extended the vote to women as part of the 1917 revolution.

Between 1893 and 2021, most of the world's women gained the vote but not always equally. Age, property ownership, literacy, or ethnicity could restrict rights. In Britain, only propertied women over 30 had the vote in 1918; equal rights had to wait until 1928. In South Africa and Australia, white women gained the vote before indigenous women and women of colour.

KEY MOMENTS

1893 Casting a vote
New Zealand women were the first to gain the vote in 1893; others, especially in the Middle East, had to wait longer. Kuwaiti women were able to vote in 2005 and Saudi women (*left*) in 2015 (in municipal elections only).

1903 Growing militancy
In the UK from 1903, suffragettes – members of the Women's Social and Political Union (WSPU) led by Emmeline Pankhurst (*left*) – turned to militancy. They rushed the Houses of Parliament, chained themselves to railings, and broke windows. About 1,000 suffragettes were imprisoned.

1917 Political participation
Women's access to political office came later than a right to vote. The first woman to be elected to the parliament of an independent nation was Jeannette Rankin (*left*), who entered the US House of Representatives in 1917. Today, many women are visible in the political arena but in fewer numbers than men.

In the US, women's fight for the vote began in 1848. By 1890, the National American Woman Suffrage Association was the main campaigning group, holding parades and lobbying the Supreme Court. The vote was won in 1920 but most African Americans and Indigenous Americans were excluded.

1895
JAPANESE VICTORY AT WEIHAIWEI

The Chinese Qing dynasty fought Japan for supremacy over Korean waters. Japanese forces quickly achieved a series of victories and, in February 1895, defeated and destroyed the Chinese fleet at Weihaiwei. War ended in April and the Treaty of Shimonoseki was signed. Japan gained influence over Korea, annexed Taiwan, and became the dominant force in East Asia.

▷ Battle of Weihaiwei

1895

1895 Cuban revolutionaries rise up against Spanish colonial rule

1895 British forces under Starr Jameson enter Transvaal in an unsuccessful attempt to overthrow the Boer government

1895 Italian engineer Guglielmo Marconi invents the wireless telegraph

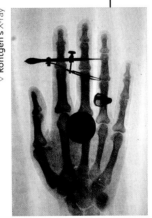

▷ Röntgen's X-ray

1895
X-RAYS DISCOVERED

While experimenting with cathode rays, German physicist Wilhelm Röntgen discovered a type of radiation that was blocked only by dense materials. Projecting these rays through an object onto a photographic plate produced a shadow image of the dense parts. Experimenting with parts of the body, Röntgen found that the rays, which he called X-rays ("X" for unknown), passed through flesh but left shadows of the bones, which were clearly visible.

1896
ETHIOPIA BATTLES ITALY

Since 1885, Italian interests in Africa had grown. Italy had colonized Eritrea and wished to take over a famine-stricken Ethiopia. Under the Treaty of Wichale, Italy proposed to make Ethiopia a protectorate. Emperor Menelik II rejected the treaty, mobilized forces, and defeated the Italians at Adwa. Ethiopia remained the only major African nation to avoid European colonization.

△ Emperor Menelik II observes the Battle at Adwa

▷ Olympic stadium, 1896

1896
FIRST MODERN OLYMPIC GAMES

Under the International Olympic Committee (IOC), the Ancient Olympic Games were revived in a modern form and staged in Athens. Male athletes from around the world (but mainly Europe, Chile, Australia, and the US) took part, competing in events such as track and field, shooting, gymnastics, cycling, and fencing.

241 athletes took part in the first modern Olympic Games

1896 The US Supreme Court upholds racial segregation in public places in the Plessy v Ferguson case

1897 Greece and the Ottoman Empire go to war over the status of Crete

1899 Sigmund Freud, an Austrian psychoanalyst, publishes *The Interpretation of Dreams*

1899

1898 The physicist Marie Curie isolates the radioactive elements polonium and radium

1867–1934
MARIE CURIE

Born in Poland, physicist Marie Curie was famous for pioneering work on radioactivity. She discovered radium and polonium and, in 1903, won the Nobel Prize for Physics jointly with her husband.

1898
US DECLARES WAR ON SPAIN

Tensions between the US and Spain over Cuba grow when the USS *Maine* exploded in Havana harbour. Blaming the Spanish, the US sent troops to support Cuba's struggle for independence. Spain capitulated ten weeks later. Cuba gained independence, although US forces remained in Cuba, finally taking over the country in 1902.

▷ **US cavalry** in action in Cuba

"The interpretation of dreams is a royal road to a knowledge of the unconscious activities of the mind."

SIGMUND FREUD, THE INTERPRETATION OF DREAMS, *1900*

1900

THE BOXER REBELLION

By 1900, major European powers had extended their influence throughout China. Fuelled by resentment, a Chinese organization — the Society of the Righteous and Harmonious Fists (known to Westerners as Boxers) – led an uprising in northern China, killing diplomats, civilians, and Christian missionaries, and destroying foreign property. They besieged China's capital Beijing until an alliance of international forces broke the siege and put down the uprising.

▷ **Allied armies storm Beijing,** by Torajirō Kasai

1900

1900 The Ashanti in West Africa rise up against British occupation, but are suppressed

1901 Italian inventor Guglielmo Marconi sends the first radio transmission across the Atlantic

1900

FIRST ZEPPELIN TAKES OFF

After years of planning, German inventor Ferdinand von Zeppelin's first successful airship, LZ-1, took to the air from a floating hangar on Lake Constance. Consisting of a cylindrical rigid frame containing 17 gas cells and powered by two internal combustion engines, the Zeppelin was 128 m (420 ft) long. It was steered by fore and aft rudders. Its maiden flight lasted 17 minutes. In 1909, von Zeppelin developed the LZ-6 that carried 20 passengers on pleasure trips.

◁ The first Zeppelin

1904
JAPAN AND RUSSIA AT WAR

Japanese-Russian tensions had mounted because of rivalry over Korea and Manchuria. Having made a surprise attack on the Russian fleet at Port Arthur, Manchuria, Japan declared war on Russia. Japanese forces defeated the Russians in a series of battles on land and at sea, finally destroying the Russian fleet at Tsushima Strait, ending the war in 1905. Japan gained Port Arthur and, in 1910, took over Korea.

▷ **Naval battle** in the Tsushima Strait, from an Italian newspaper

1904 Herero and Nama people rebel against German imperial rule in South West Africa (Namibia); they are put down brutally

1904

1904 The US begins construction of the Panama Canal; it will open in 1914

△ **Boer War** army discharge certificate

1902
SECOND BOER WAR ENDS

After more than two years of fighting between the British and Boers for control of the Transvaal and Orange Free State, the war ended with victory for the British. The Boers were initially successful, besieging Ladysmith, Kimberley, and Mafeking in 1900. However, British forces broke the siege and implemented a "scorched earth" policy, destroying Boer farms and incarcerating dispossessed Boer families in concentration camps.

1903-58
POWERED FLIGHT

Inventors of flying machines had little success until the early years of the 20th century. By the 1920s, passenger flights had begun.

1903 American inventors Orville and Wilbur Wright achieve the first sustained heavier-than-air flight; it lasts 12 seconds.

1915 The first all-metal aeroplane is designed by German engineer Hugo Junkers. It achieves a speed of 170 kph (105 mph).

1939 German engineer Hans von Ohain installs a jet engine in the experimental Heinkel He 178 plane, creating the world's first jet plane.

1958 The Boeing 707 sets the design for passenger jet airliners. With four engines, it can carry 190 passengers between continents.

1905
REBELLION IN EAST AFRICA

Following years of oppression and forced labour, Africans in German East Africa (Tanzania) rose up. Warriors armed with arrows and spears attacked garrisons and destroyed crops. The rebellion spread, bringing together 20 different ethnic groups. It peaked at Mahenge when several thousand Maji Maji warriors unsuccessfully attacked a German stronghold. By 1907, the rebellion had been crushed and some 75,000 Africans had been killed.

◁ Fighting at Mahenge

1879–1955
ALBERT EINSTEIN

One of the greatest theoretical physicists of all time, Einstein developed two theories of relativity: special and general. They revolutionized understanding of space, time, motion, and the universe.

1906 The city of San Francisco is hit by a devastating earthquake that kills over 2,000 people

1905

1905 German-born physicist Albert Einstein publishes the Special Theory of Relativity

1906 Upton Sinclair's novel *The Jungle* exposes appalling working conditions in the US meat packing industry

1905
REVOLUTION IN RUSSIA

Protests and strikes broke out in Russia, fuelled by discontent with the Tsar's autocratic rule, economic hardship, and Russia's humiliation in the Russo-Japanese War. After troops fired on unarmed protesters, parts of the Russian military joined the unrest, sailors mutinying on the battleship *Potemkin*. Revolutionaries established Soviets (councils) before Tsar Nicholas II agreed to reform and the establishment of a *duma* (elected legislature).

△ The First Revolution depicted on a poster

The 1906 San Francisco earthquake made more than 225,000 people homeless

1907
CUBISM ARRIVES

Spanish artist Pablo Picasso and French painter Georges Braque pioneered a new artistic approach known as Cubism. Influenced by the work of Paul Cézanne, they abandoned the traditional idea of a single viewpoint and instead combined multiple views of their subject in one image, as in *Les Demoiselles d'Avignon,* resulting in an abstracted form. Cubism had a huge impact on the development of art in the 20th century.

▷ Picasso's seminal Cubist work,
Les Demoiselles d'Avignon

1906 US anarchist Emma Goldman launches the journal *Mother Earth*

1909

1909 Imprisoned suffragettes in the UK begin a hunger strike and are force fed

1906
NAVAL ARMS RACE ESCALATES

From 1898, Kaiser Wilhelm II set out to make Germany a great military power. He instructed Admiral Tirpitz to develop a fleet to rival Britain's, which was the world's strongest navy at the time. Tirpitz focused on developing warships to compete with Britain's dreadnoughts – huge big-gun battleships. Seeing Germany as a threat, Britain too built more warships. Tensions mounted in Europe as the naval arms race escalated.

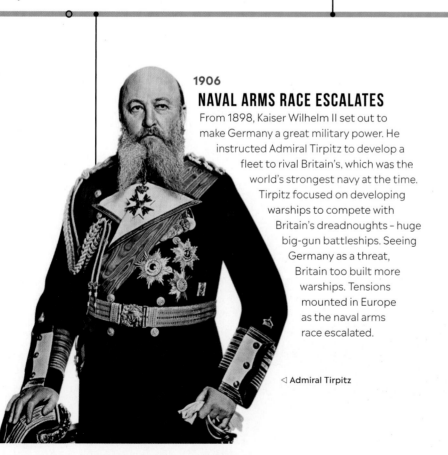

◁ Admiral Tirpitz

△ Flag of the Young Turks

1908
YOUNG TURKS DEMAND REFORM

A group of liberals, students, and revolutionaries, the Young Turks demanded an end to absolutism in the Ottoman Empire. They rebelled against Sultan Abdulhamid II, who had dissolved parliament and suppressed dissent. The Young Turk movement expanded, drawing in civil servants and army officers. They marched on Istanbul, forcing Abdulhamid to reinstate parliament.

△ **Pancho Villa** and his fighters

1910
MEXICAN REVOLUTION

Under Mexican dictator Porfirio Díaz, poverty became widespread and opposition was crushed. Reformer Franciso I. Madero stood for election against Díaz but was jailed. Managing to escape, he called for an armed revolution. Guerrilla peasant armies led by Emiliano Zapata and Pancho Villa attacked wealthy landowners, seized towns, and battled presidential forces. Díaz was ousted and by 1911 Madero was president.

1912
THE TITANIC SINKS

Completed in 1911, the RMS *Titanic* was the world's largest, most luxurious ocean liner. With 16 watertight compartments in the hull, it was believed to be unsinkable. However, four days into its maiden voyage from Southampton to New York, it collided with a large iceberg, which tore gashes in the starboard side. In less than three hours the *Titanic* sank with the loss of 1,500 lives.

△ *Titanic* promotional poster

1910

1911 Norwegian Roald Amundsen becomes the first man to reach the South Pole, beating British Robert Scott

1910 Black American activist William Edward Burghardt Du Bois is one of the founders of the National Association for the Advancement of Colored People

1911 The Inca city of Machu Picchu is rediscovered by US archaeologist Hiram Bingham

1911
QING DYNASTY IS OVERTHROWN

After more than 2,000 years, Imperial China came to an end when nationalist forces overthrew the Manchu-led Qing dynasty. This followed increasing unrest in China as revolutionary and nationalist groups protested Qing corruption, conservatism, and inability to prevent foreign intervention. The nationalist Kuomintang Party, led by Sun Yat-sen, staged an uprising that sparked revolts. The Nationalists declared a republic, the Qing emperor abdicated, and Sun Yat-Sen became provisional president.

◁ **Postcard** depicting revolutionary leaders and scenes

1914
WORLD WAR I BREAKS OUT

On 28 June 1914, Gavrilo Princip, a Serbian nationalist, assassinated Archduke Franz Ferdinand, heir to the Austrian throne. In retaliation, Austria declared war on Serbia. Existing alliances brought other nations into the conflict. Russia mobilized to help Serbia. Germany declared war on Russia and on France, Russia's ally. German troops invaded Belgium. Britain, committed to defending Belgian neutrality, declared war on Austria and Germany on 4 August. World War I had begun. British, French, and German colonies around the world also joined the war.

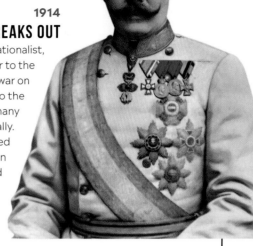

▷ Archduke Franz Ferdinand

1912 The South African Native National Congress, forerunner of the African National Congress (ANC), is founded

1913 Russian women . celebrate International Women's Day on 8 March; it becomes an annual event

1913 Conflict breaks out between the Balkan League (Greece, Serbia, Montenegro, and Bulgaria) and the Ottoman Empire

1914

1914
ALLIES HALT GERMAN ADVANCE

Intending to knock France out of the war quickly, German forces swept through Belgium and into northeastern France. Instead of encircling Paris, they pursued retreating French forces to the River Marne where, in the first major engagement of the war, the French and British mounted a counter-offensive, pushing the Germans back. Both sides started digging trenches and by Christmas stalemate was reached along a line (the Western Front) stretching from the Belgian coast to the Swiss border.

△ German soldiers in a trench

About 65 million men fought during World War I; some 8.5 million of them died and 21.2 million were wounded

1917
OFFENSIVE FAILS AT YPRES

On 31 July, Allied troops began an assault on the German front line around the Ypres salient, with the aim of breaking through to the Belgian ports to capture German U-boats. The offensive was a disaster. Shelling and rain turned the ground into a quagmire with water deep enough to drown a man. In November, Allied forces took Passchendaele, 7 km (5 miles) away, and the offensive was called off. Some 580,000 men died.

▷ **Australian soldiers** cross a devastated landscape at Ypres

"I died in hell, they called it Passchendaele."

POET SIEGFRIED SASSOON, OCTOBER 1918

1915

1915 Six million Black Americans migrate north to work in war industries

1915 The International Women's Peace Conference takes place at The Hague, Netherlands

1915 Italy declares war on Austria-Hungary and enters World War I on the Allied side

1916 Irish republicans rise up against British rule; the rebellion is brutally suppressed

△ The Battle of Verdun

◁ **Maxim 303 MkII,** WWI machine gun

1916
FRENCH AND GERMAN TROOPS BATTLE FOR VERDUN

The longest battle of World War I began on 21 February when German forces bombarded the French fortress town of Verdun. The French were forced back but retaliated: under near constant bombardment and machine gun fire, the battle continued for ten months. In December, when the battle ended, the French held Verdun. More than 700,000 men died in the fighting.

1917
RUSSIAN TSAR OVERTHROWN

Revolution broke out in Russia in February when protesters took to the streets of Petrograd demanding bread and peace. The Russian army, suffering dreadful losses in the war, supported the workers. Tsar Nicholas abdicated and the Mensheviks, a moderate workers party, set up a government. In October, the Bolsheviks, revolutionary Communists, stormed the Winter Palace and seized power. Under Vladimir Lenin, Russia became the Soviet Union, the world's first Communist state.

△ Soviet propaganda poster, 1917

1919
MASSACRE AT AMRITSAR

At least 379 unarmed Indians were killed by British-commanded troops at Jallianwala Bagh, a park in the holy city of Amritsar in the Punjab region. Worried by the rise of nationalism, British authorities had banned public meetings, but unaware of this, thousands of Punjabis had come to the park for a festival. Instructed by Brigadier General Dyer, British troops opened fire. The massacre caused outrage and stirred nationalists' demands for independence for India.

◁ **Memorial to the dead** and wounded, Jallianwala Bagh, India

1917 The US enters World War I, declaring war on Germany and sending troops to France

1919 Benito Mussolini, an Italian journalist and politician, forms the National Fascist Party

1919

1917 The British government declares support for a Jewish homeland in Palestine

1919 In the Red Summer, more than 30 race riots broke out in US cities in response to lynchings and segregationist laws

1918
WORLD WAR I: ARMISTICE

At 11am on 11 November 1918, after more than four years of war and millions of casualties, guns across the world fell silent. By October, Bulgaria, Austria-Hungary, and Turkey had been defeated. Germany fought on but at home anti-war feeling was intense. The Kaiser abdicated, Germany admitted defeat, and on 11 November German and Allied delegations signed an armistice, or cease-fire, at Compiègne, France. News spread worldwide in minutes.

△ **Americans celebrate** the armistice

△ Treaty of Versailles, front cover

1919
PEACE TREATY ENDS WORLD WAR I

The war ended formally with the Versailles Treaty, which was signed on 28 June 1919 and came into effect in January 1920. The treaty was controversial. It was shaped by the "Big Four": Britain, France, Italy, and the US. Germany had to accept blame for the war and was forced to pay huge reparations to the Allies. All Germany's overseas colonies were taken over, and the German army was massively reduced.

1920

PROHIBITION INTRODUCED IN THE US

Following pressure from Christian temperance movements and the Anti-Saloon League, a ban was imposed in the US on the manufacture, sale, and transport of "intoxicating liquors". Prohibition saw a rise in organized crime, which fought over the illegal manufacture and sale of alcohol, and "speakeasies", illicit drinking clubs.

◁ **Police oversee** the disposal of illegal alcohol

1920

1920 Marcus Garvey, a Jamaican activist, launches the Universal Negro Improvement Association (UNIA)

1921 Campaigner Marie Stopes opens Britain's first birth control clinic, in London

1922 Fascist Benito Mussolini marches on Rome and becomes Italy's prime minister

1920 The Council of the League of Nations holds its first meeting in Paris, France

1921 Charlie Chaplin's first full-length film, *The Kid*, opens in the US

1921

FAMINE IN RUSSIA;

A devastating famine hit Soviet Russia, claiming over five million lives. Severe drought had led to food shortages, which were exacerbated by the impact of the 1917 Revolution and subsequent civil war. Facing anti-Bolshevik revolts in Kronstadt and elsewhere, Vladimir Lenin was forced to ask for foreign aid. Backtracking from strict Communist economics, he introduced a New Economic Policy with some free-market elements.

▷ **A Soviet poster** exhorts people to remember the hungry

1870-1924
VLADIMIR ILYICH LENIN

A revolutionary Marxist, Lenin founded the Bolshevik Party. Having seized power in 1917, Lenin ruled as a dictator. He suppressed opposition, nationalized banks and industry, and redistributed land.

"We want to achieve a new and better order of society... there must be neither rich nor poor."

LENIN, TO THE RURAL POOR, COLLECTED WORKS, *1903*

1923
GERMAN MARK COLLAPSES

Harsh reparations were imposed on Germany after World War I. By 1922, the country was unable to meet the payments, prompting French and Belgian forces to occupy the Ruhr, Germany's industrial heartland. The economy collapsed, the Government overprinted money, and the mark plummeted in value, becoming almost worthless.

▷ **100,000 Mark banknote,** printed in 1923

In 1922, a loaf of bread in Germany cost 163 marks; by 1923 it cost 200,000,000

1922 Howard Carter, a British archaeologist, uncovers the tomb of Egyptian pharaoh Tutankhamun

1923 General Primo de Rivera overthrows the Spanish government and takes power as a dictator

1924

1924 The American composer George Gershwin creates *Rhapsody in Blue*

◁ **Mustafa Kemal Ataturk,** first President of Turkey

△ **The signing** of the Anglo-Irish treaty

1923
TURKEY BECOMES A REPUBLIC

Following World War I, the Treaty of Sèvres effectively dismantled the Ottoman Empire, ceding large areas to France, Greece, Italy, and the UK. Led by Mustafa Kemal Ataturk, Turkish nationalists waged a series of wars against the occupiers, particularly the Greeks. The last Ottoman sultan abdicated and, victorious, Kemal declared Turkey a republic, with himself as president.

1922
IRISH FREE STATE FORMS

After years of fighting between the Irish Republican Army (IRA) and British forces, the Anglo-Irish Treaty created the Irish Free State as a self-governing dominion within the British Empire. The six counties of Northern Ireland remained part of the UK. The treaty split the republican movement, leading to civil war.

1925

THE KLAN MARCH ON WASHINGTON

The Ku Klux Klan (KKK) was founded in the late 1860s. Dedicated to white supremacy in the US, it waged a reign of terror against freed black slaves. Outlawed in 1871, the Klan re-emerged in 1915 and grew fast. In August, some 40,000 members, in their distinctive white uniforms, marched on Washington, demanding an all-white, Protestant US.

◁ **KKK march** in Washington DC

1926 In Britain, the Trades Union Congress (TUC) calls for the first general strike in UK history in support of miners. The government breaks the strike after nine days

1925

1926

TELEVISION IS INVENTED

In January 1926, Scottish inventor John Logie Baird gave a demonstration of the world's first working television set. Using a mechanical system with a revolving disk as the scanner, he transmitted recognizable moving images from his laboratory in London to an audience consisting of members of the Royal Institution and a news reporter from *The Times*.

△ John Logie Baird

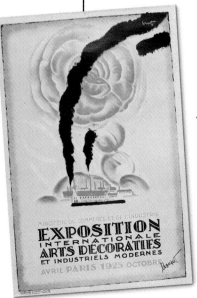

1925

MILLIONS FLOCK TO MODERN ART EXHIBITION

Showcasing modern decorative art from 20 countries, the International Exhibition of Modern Decorative and Industrial Arts opened in Paris. Sixteen million people visited the exhibition, which featured examples of a new design style, Art Deco. Exhibits included fabrics, ceramics, interior designs, architecture, and glass, all of which featured the bold colours and geometric forms of the new style.

◁ **Promotional poster** advertising the 1925 exhibition

▽ The *Spirit of St Louis*,
Charles Lindbergh's aircraft

1927
LINDBERGH MAKES SOLO ATLANTIC FLIGHT

In May, American aviator Charles Lindbergh flew from New York to Paris, becoming the first person to complete a solo non-stop transatlantic flight. His aircraft *Spirit of St Louis* was buffeted by high winds and rain. Lindbergh made the 5,793-km (3,600-mile) journey in 33 hours 30 minutes. More than 100,000 people were waiting to see him land.

1928 American Amelia Earhart becomes the first woman to fly across the Atlantic

1928 Scottish physician Alexander Fleming discovers penicillin

1928 The Kuomintang (Chinese Nationalist Party) led by Chiang Kai-shek take Beijing and set up a national government

1929

1928 In the Soviet Union, Joseph Stalin orders collectivization of agriculture in a programme of radical economic change

▷ Promotional poster for *The Jazz Singer*

1927
THE "TALKIES" ARRIVE

Cinema changed forever when audiences could hear recorded sound along with the images. First seen was a film of Charles Lindbergh taking off on his celebrated flight (*above*), but it was the first talking feature film, *The Jazz Singer* starring Al Jolson, that achieved great popularity.

▷ A stockbroker sells his car

1929
THE WALL STREET CRASH

Following a period of speculation after World War I, share prices faltered. On 24 October – which came to be known as "Black Thursday" – the market plunged; this was followed by a price crash on 29 October, as some 16 million shares were traded. Thousands of investors were ruined as the crash marked the beginning of a worldwide economic depression.

1916-29
THE JAZZ AGE

The decade after the end of World War I is sometimes called the "Jazz Age", or the "Roaring Twenties". It was a period of huge social and cultural change when young people, freed from the troubles of conflict, turned to leisure and enjoyment, adopting new fashions, dances, and music – most particularly jazz. Originating in New Orleans, jazz culture became popular in the US, with London, Paris, Singapore, and other cities following suit. Social restrictions relaxed and a buoyant sense of freedom spread. Women in particular embraced the new era, following increases in social freedoms during World War I and as a result of the suffrage movement. Now they shrugged off old stereotypes of dependency and frailty in favour of independence, public involvement, and sexual freedom. The "new woman" appeared; wearing short skirts, with bobbed hair, and smoking cigarettes, she rejected convention.

In the US, the Jazz Age coincided with prohibition – a nationwide ban on alcohol – and young people flocked to speakeasies and dance halls to drink illegal liquor, allowing gangsters such as Al Capone to make huge profits from bootleg alcohol. Popular entertainment also boomed, fuelled by technological developments in recording, cinema, and radio. The Jazz Age was brought to an end in 1929, when the Wall Street crash heralded a decade of economic depression.

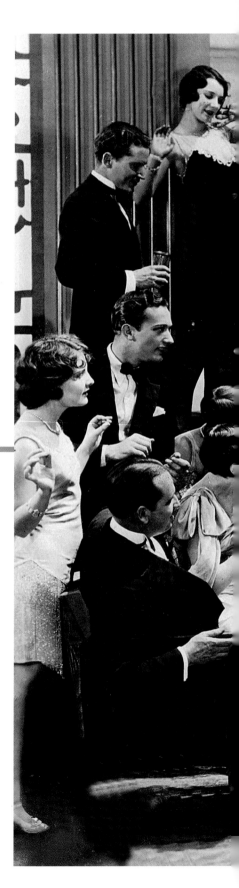

KEY MOMENTS

1916-17 Jazz moves north
Poor economic conditions and discrimination prompted the migration of millions of African Americans from the rural south. Over the following years, musicians such as Louis Armstrong (*left*) brought jazz to Chicago and New York, then to Paris and London.

1918 Harlem Renaissance
From around 1918, Harlem, Manhattan was a focal point of Black American culture. Through literature, music, theatre, and dance, poets such as Langston Hughes and entertainers such as Josephine Baker (*left*) brought Black culture into public consciousness.

1925 The Great Gatsby
With their fast-paced lifestyle, Scott Fitzgerald and his wife Zelda (*left*) epitomized the spirit of the age. Fitzgerald's novel *The Great Gatsby* (1925) portrayed the flamboyance as well as the brittleness of the Jazz Age.

The Charleston became the most popular dance of Jazz Age America. A fast-moving dance, it involved swinging the arms and kicking the legs. Other popular dances were the Lindy Hop and the Black Bottom: all were rooted in music from African-American communities.

> "Victory attained by violence is tantamount to a defeat, for it is momentary."

MOHANDAS GANDHI, SATYAGRAHA LEAFLET NO. 30, 1919

▽ Mohandas Gandhi on the Salt March

1930
GANDHI'S SALT MARCH

Using his strategy of *satyagraha*, or non-violent civil disobedience, Mohandas Gandhi led thousands of Indians in a protest against British rule in India. One campaign was aimed at the "Salt Laws", which imposed a tax on salt and forbade Indians from making it. In his so-called Salt March, Gandhi walked 390 km (240 miles) from Sabarmati Ashram in Gujarat to the coast, where – defying the law – the marchers collected salt from the sea.

1930

1931 Spanish King Alfonso XIII is overthrown and Spain is declared a republic

1931
JAPANESE FORCES INVADE MANCHURIA

Concerned that China was threatening Japan's influence in Manchuria, Japanese forces invaded in September. They justified their action by claiming that Chinese nationalists had blown up the Japanese-owned railway. The Japanese seized the city of Mukden (Shenyang) and occupied Manchuria, ignoring condemnation by the League of Nations, and subsequently set up a puppet government under Pu Yi, China's last emperor.

◁ **Japanese forces** occupying Manchuria

△ Empire State Building, Manhattan, New York City

1931
EMPIRE STATE BUILDING OPENS

Standing 443 m (1,454 ft) tall, the Empire State Building, the world's tallest building at the time, was officially opened on 1 May 1931. It had taken more than 3,500 workers, many of them Irish and Italian immigrants, 18 months to complete. President Herbert Hoover switched on the lights at the opening ceremony.

1933
ADOLF HITLER APPOINTED GERMAN CHANCELLOR

Promising to restore national pride to Germany, the National Socialists (Nazis), led by Adolf Hitler, won seats in government, and Hitler was appointed chancellor. Soon after, the Reichstag building burned down. Blaming Communists, Hitler declared an emergency and imposed a one-party dictatorship. Fuelled by a belief in a pure Aryan race, the Nazis boycotted Jewish businesses, publicly burned books considered "un-German", and violently crushed opposition.

▷ **Adolf Hitler is** greeted by crowds of supporters

1932 The Chaco War, a territorial dispute, breaks out between Bolivia and Paraguay

1933 Spanish anarcho-syndicalists rise up in Madrid, protesting poor living conditions

1933 Franklin D. Roosevelt, the newly elected US president, introduces his New Deal economic relief programme

1934

△ The "Dust Bowl" – the drought-stricken US Midwest

1932
GREAT DEPRESSION INTENSIFIES

By the early 1930s, economic depression had spread worldwide. In the US some 15 million people were out of work and in Germany the figure was about 5 million. Poverty was widespread, soup kitchens were commonplace, and in the US the lack of state welfare meant thousands became homeless. A series of droughts and dust storms in the Midwest drove farmers off their lands, exacerbating the problem.

1934
MAO LEADS THE LONG MARCH

Following attempts by the Kuomintang (the Chinese National Party) to dislodge Chinese Communists from Jiangxi province, Mao Zedong led the Red Army out of the province westwards, hoping to find a safe base. About 100,000 people marched 9,700km (6,027 miles) to Shaanxi province, where Mao set up a Communist base. Only about 7,000 troops of the original force reached Yan'an.

△ The Long March

Die Nürnberger Gesetze

1935
GERMANY INTRODUCES THE NUREMBERG LAWS

At a rally in the city of Nuremberg, the Nazi party announced racist laws restricting citizenship to people "of German or related blood" and forbidding marriage or sexual relations between Germans and Jews, later expanded to apply also to Roma and Black people. Those considered not "of German blood" were deprived of normal citizenship rights. The laws led to widespread persecution of the minority groups both by the state and the population at large, who were discouraged from any social contact.

◁ **Chart defining racial categories** under the laws

1935 Persia formally becomes known as Iran at its ruler's request

1935

1936 Arabs revolt in Palestine against British occupying forces

1935
ITALY INVADES ABYSSINIA (ETHIOPIA)

Italy's Fascist leader Mussolini ordered a force of 200,000 soldiers into what is now Ethiopia in a war of aggression. After 16 months of fighting, the nation's ruler Haile Selassie was forced into exile, and Abyssinia was declared an Italian colony. Hundreds of thousands of Abyssinian civilians were killed.

△ **An Abyssinian warrior**

1936
SPANISH CIVIL WAR BEGINS

Following a Popular Front victory in a general election in Spain, Nationalist forces under General Francisco Franco staged an attempted coup. Republican forces, including Communist and anarchist contingents, took up arms to resist them. The struggle lasted for almost three years, but eventually the Nationalists were able to draw on military support from Nazi Germany and Fascist Italy to achieve a decisive victory. In its wake, Franco would remain in power as Spain's leader until his death in 1975.

△ Republican poster urges a united war effort

△ **Japanese infantry** on campaign in China

1937
WAR BETWEEN CHINA AND JAPAN

After establishing a presence in northern China in 1931, Japan sought to expand its control with a full-scale invasion. Beijing, Shanghai, and Nanjing fell to the Japanese, who committed major atrocities, and China's government was forced to relocate southward to wage a guerrilla resistance campaign that ended only with Japan's defeat in World War II.

1938
GERMANY THREATENS CZECHOSLOVAKIA

German claims on the Sudetenland region of Czechoslovakia, where many German nationals lived, led Hitler to threaten to take the disputed territory by force. The Czech government looked to France and Britain for support, but this was not forthcoming. A general mobilization ensued, attracting over a million volunteers, but Hitler was not deterred.

△ **Adolf Hitler** salutes Sudetenland Germans

△ **Nazi Sudetenland badge of honour**

1938

1937 The Indian National Congress political party wins India's first provincial elections

1937 The first working jet engine is built in England by engineer Frank Whittle

> "I believe it is peace for our time."
>
> *NEVILLE CHAMBERLAIN, 1938*

▽ **Neville Chamberlain** returns from Munich

1938
MUNICH AGREEMENT

Seeking to appease Hitler over his claims in Czechoslovakia, British Prime Minister Neville Chamberlain and France's premier Édouard Daladier flew to Munich to sign an agreement accepting the German occupation of the Sudetenland and establishing a commission to determine the future of other disputed areas. The move led to the dismantling of Czechoslovakia as an independent state.

23 August 1939
NAZI-SOVIET NON-AGGRESSION PACT

An unexpected agreement between the two hostile powers allowed each – at least temporarily – to build up its forces without fear of attack. A secret protocol attached to the treaty defined respective spheres of influence in Poland, the Baltic states, and Finland.

△ Signing of the pact

1889-1945
ADOLF HITLER

After joining the Nazi party in 1919 and pressing for national revolution, Hitler became Chancellor of Germany in 1933. As effective dictator, he pursued a racist agenda and drew the world into war.

1939

September 1939 US President Roosevelt opts for US neutrality in the war while favouring the Allied powers

30 November 1939 The Winter War breaks out when Soviet troops invade neutral Finland

▽ German troops in Warsaw

1 September 1939
GERMAN INVASION OF POLAND

Citing invented provocations, Hitler sent troops into Poland on several fronts, driving the defending forces eastward. Sixteen days later, Soviet forces joined the assault by attacking Poland from the east, catching the defenders in a pincer movement. By early October, formal resistance was overcome and the previously free nation was divided up between the aggressors as agreed in the secret protocol of the Nazi-Soviet Pact.

△ Neville Chamberlain addresses the nation

3 September 1939
DECLARATION OF WAR ON GERMANY

The German invasion of Poland discredited the policy of appeasement by which British and French leaders had hoped to guarantee "peace in our time". British Prime Minister Neville Chamberlain and French premier Édouard Daladier issued an ultimatum that if German troops were not immediately withdrawn, war would be declared. When Hitler's forces instead pressed on with their conquest, the declaration was duly made and World War II began.

April-May 1940
GERMANY LAUNCHES BLITZKRIEG CAMPAIGNS IN WESTERN EUROPE

After seven months of limited activity (later dubbed the "Phoney War"), Hitler ordered the invasion first of Denmark and Norway, which were both overcome within months, and then of Belgium and the Netherlands. From the Low Countries, German forces struck southward into France, capturing Paris by mid-June. An armistice was signed soon after, leaving much of the country in German hands.

▷ **German troops** in Paris

23 March 1940 The All-India Muslim League declares for a separate state of Pakistan

◁ **British Supermarine Spitfire** fighter aircraft

1940

30 March 1940 Japanese invaders set up a puppet Chinese government in Nanjing

27 September 1940 Japan, Germany, and Italy form a military coalition; they are known as the "Axis powers"

"Never in the field of human conflict was so much owed by so many to so few."

WINSTON CHURCHILL, 1940

10 July 1940
THE BATTLE OF BRITAIN BEGINS FOR CONTROL OF THE SKIES

British land forces confronting the German advance in the Low Countries had been made to retreat to Britain from Dunkirk. Now Hitler launched an air campaign to win control of British airspace as a preliminary to a land invasion. Called the "Battle of Britain" by the new Prime Minister, Winston Churchill, the campaign lasted almost a year, during which time London and other cities endured the massive bombing campaign known as the Blitz.

БЯЗЛІТАСНА ЗНІШЧЫМ

фашысцкіх

ЗАХОПНІКАЎ!

22 June 1941

GERMANY INVADES THE USSR

Turning his back on the 1939 Nazi-Soviet Non-Aggression Pact, Hitler ordered a mass assault on the Soviet Union over a front 2,900km (1,800 miles) long and involving almost 3 million men. Despite early successes, the invasion soon became a war of attrition; and by opening this second front and forcing the USSR to link up with the Allied powers, Hitler was soon to find his forces under huge pressure.

◁ Soviet propaganda poster

6 April 1941 Germany invades Yugoslavia, forcing a surrender within 10 days

9 October 1941 The Manhattan Project's atomic research begins in the US

1941

7 December 1941

JAPAN BOMBS PEARL HARBOR

Japan's military leadership launched a surprise air attack on the US naval base at Pearl Harbor in Hawaii, the headquarters of the Pacific Fleet. A dozen warships were destroyed and over 2,400 servicemen killed. The raid brought the US into the war on the Allied side.

▷ US warships under attack at the Pearl Harbor naval base

1941–45
WAR IN THE PACIFIC

The Japanese began their Pacific expansion in 1941, capturing Singapore, Burma's capital Rangoon, and the Dutch East Indies.

April 1942 US troops defending the Philippines surrender to the Japanese on the Bataan Peninsula.

May–June 1942 US naval forces turn the tide of the Pacific conflict by defeating Japanese fleets at the battles of the Coral Sea and Midway.

7 August 1942 Landing on Guadalcanal in the Solomon Islands, US forces start an island-hopping offensive, driving north towards Japan.

21 June 1945 Okinawa, at the southernmost tip of the Japanese archipelago, is captured by US forces after a long struggle.

"Yesterday, December 7th, 1941, a date which will live in infamy…"

FRANKLIN D. ROOSEVELT ON THE DATE OF JAPAN'S ATTACK ON PEARL HARBOUR IN A SPEECH TO THE US CONGRESS, 1941

◁ **British General Bernard Montgomery** at El Alamein

October–November 1942
BATTLE OF EL ALAMEIN

Fighting in North Africa began in 1940 with the entry of Italy into the war. Following early Allied successes, the German Afrika Korps joined the struggle. The tide of battle swung back and forth until Allied troops secured a decisive victory at El Alamein in Egypt. Thereafter, Axis forces were forced to retreat, with the final remnants surrendering in Tunisia in May 1943.

20 January 1942 The Nazi Party commits to the planned genocide of the Jewish people, later known as the Holocaust

1942

8 August 1942 The Indian National Congress launches a "Quit India" campaign against British colonial rule; many arrests follow

1942 Famine hits Henan Province in China, killing 2–5 million

January 1942
BATTLE OF THE ATLANTIC ENTERS A NEW PHASE

From the start of the war, German U-boats attacked supply routes across the Atlantic in an attempt to starve Britain into submission. The campaign entered a new phase with the entry of the US into the war. It only ended with the German surrender in 1945, although by 1943 extended air cover, improved radar, and escorted convoys turned the battle in the Allies' favour.

△ **Allied warships travel in convoy** across the North Atlantic

2 February 1943
DEFEAT AT STALINGRAD

Nazi invasion forces embarked on one of history's most destructive battles in an attempt to take Stalingrad, an important communications centre in the southern USSR. They were forced to surrender after five months' fighting. The loss drained German manpower from other fronts and helped turn the tide of the war.

▷ **Soviet brass medal** for the defence of Stalingrad

▽ **An Allied soldier** comforts an Italian baby

July 1943
ALLIED FORCES INVADE ITALY

Starting with a six-week campaign to capture Sicily, Allied forces fresh from victory in North Africa crossed over to mainland Italy to take the war into the Axis heartland. By early October, they had won control of the south of the country. Their passage northward was bitterly contested, and the final German surrender did not take place until 2 May 1945.

8 February 1943 Indian and British special forces begin a guerrilla campaign against the Japanese in Burma

12 July 1943 German forces retreat at Kursk after the largest tank battle in history

1943

August–September 1944 Advancing Allied forces liberate Paris and Brussels

6 June 1944
OPERATION OVERLORD

As the war swung in favour of the Allies, their commanders ordered the "D-Day" landings on the Normandy coast as the first step in a large-scale offensive to win back German-occupied western Europe. Once successfully established ashore, the Allied forces – eventually some three million strong – drove eastward, crossing the Rhine to enter Germany itself in March 1945.

◁ **Allied forces** establish a beach-head in Normandy

◁ **Soldiers raise the Soviet flag** over Berlin's Reichstag

April–May 1945
FALL OF GERMANY

After the failure of a final offensive in the hilly Ardennes between Belgium and France, Axis forces were in retreat on all fronts. Italy's Fascist leader Mussolini was killed on 28 April, by which time Soviet forces advancing westward were enveloping Berlin. To avoid capture, Hitler took his own life on 30 April, and Germany surrendered unconditionally to the Allies eight days later.

27 January 1945 Soviet troops liberate Auschwitz, the largest Nazi concentration camp complex

12 April 1945 US President Roosevelt dies and is succeeded by Harry Truman

24 October 1945 The United Nations is established with the backing of 50 countries

1945

> "We will accept nothing less than full victory. Good luck!"

US GENERAL DWIGHT EISENHOWER TO TROOPS EMBARKING ON THE D-DAY LANDINGS, 1944

△ **Japanese surrender ceremony** aboard USS *Missouri*

August 1945
DEFEAT OF JAPAN

Once the war in the West had ended, attention swung to the Pacific front, where Japan continued its rearguard action against Allied forces advancing up the Pacific island chain. To break the remaining resistance, the Allies resorted to massive air attacks on the Japanese heartland, culminating in the dropping of atomic bombs on Hiroshima and Nagasaki. The nation's formal surrender followed four weeks later.

1869-1948
MAHATMA GANDHI

The most charismatic of India's independence leaders, Gandhi was imprisoned many times for his campaigns against colonial rule. An advocate of non-violent resistance, he also agitated throughout his life for social justice.

15 August 1947
INDIA WINS INDEPENDENCE

In June 1947, Britain's Viceroy in India announced the forthcoming end of British rule and the creation of two independent entities, India and Pakistan. Once the Indian Independence Act had duly passed through the British Parliament, the two nations achieved full sovereignty. However, sectarian violence claimed more than a million lives.

△ **Indian leaders** accept transfer of power

5 March 1946
Winston Churchill's
"Iron Curtain" speech presages the Cold War

16 August 1946 Rioting breaks out in India following the Muslim League's calls for a separate Pakistani state

1946

June 1946
CIVIL WAR IN CHINA

During World War II, Chinese Nationalist forces under Chiang Kai-shek had struggled for supremacy against Mao Zedong's Communists. After the defeat of Japan, Chiang launched a large-scale assault on Communist positions in the north of China. Despite initial gains, there was no decisive breakthrough in the struggle for dominance.

△ **Chinese Nationalist troops** march out of Canton

14 May 1948
JEWISH LEADERS PROCLAIM THE STATE OF ISRAEL

After World War I, the territory of Palestine was declared a mandate of the British Empire. Zionists had been calling for it to be the Jewish homeland since the 1880s, and Jewish immigration increased after World War II. When the British mandate expired, Israeli leaders proclaimed Israel an independent Jewish state, displacing more than 750,000 Palestinians. Five Arab nations invaded, sparking the first Arab-Israeli war.

◁ **Jerusalem** in the first Arab-Israeli War

30 January 1948
Mahatma Gandhi is assassinated by a Hindu nationalist

3 April 1948 US congress passes the Marshall Plan to rebuild European economies

1948

▽ **Facsimile of a section** of the Dead Sea scrolls

◁ **Daniel Malan** depicted on a South African stamp

1947
DEAD SEA SCROLLS DISCOVERED

Hidden for centuries in the Judaean Desert, the first scrolls were discovered by chance by Bedouin shepherds. Once scholars had realized their importance as some of the earliest known Biblical manuscripts, researchers set out to find and preserve additional texts.

26 May 1948
DANIEL MALAN'S NATIONALIST PARTY WINS POWER IN SOUTH AFRICA

Taking its support from South Africa's Afrikaner community of white settlers, the National Party adopted racial segregation – apartheid – as its signature policy. Interracial marriage was banned, and non-whites, who were already denied voting rights, were now also forbidden to enter white-only areas without passes permitting them to do so.

1941–1952
THE NUCLEAR ARMS RACE

Nuclear weapons technology was first developed in 1941 under the US Manhattan Project. This resulted in the creation of a fission weapon which was tested in New Mexico and used to devastating effect on the Japanese cities of Hiroshima and Nagasaki in August 1945. US authorities kept the nuclear programme secret from the USSR, its wartime ally, but information leaked to the Soviets via a network of spies. The Soviets worked clandestinely to develop their own bomb, surprising Western experts by successfully testing it before the end of the decade. Meanwhile other nations were also working on nuclear projects of their own: Britain conducted its first nuclear test in 1952, France in 1960, and China in 1964.

The two superpowers raced to upgrade their nuclear arsenals through the development of far more powerful fusion weapons. US scientists led the way, exploding a thermonuclear device at Enewetak Atoll in 1952, but the Soviets were not far behind, testing a less sophisticated device just nine months later. Their rivalry made the world a much more dangerous place for future generations.

KEY MOMENTS

29 August 1949 First Soviet atomic test
US authorities were taken by surprise when a plane conducting a weather reconnaissance flight in the northern Pacific detected traces of radioactivity in the atmosphere off Russia's Kamchatka Peninsula. To their alarm, their Cold War opponents had successfully tested a bomb, dubbed "First Lightning" (*left*). The Soviets devoted vast resources – including the use of forced labour from the Gulags – to mine the uranium needed to produce their weapons.

January 1950 Soviet spy arrested
One reason for the Soviet success, besides the discovery of new uranium sources in eastern Europe, was technical information passed clandestinely by Klaus Fuchs (*left*), a German physicist who carried out nuclear research in the US from 1944 to 1946 and then in Britain. In secret a committed Communist, Fuchs confessed and received a 14-year jail sentence.

A mushroom cloud forms above Enewetak Atoll in the Marshall Islands after the detonation of the world's first hydrogen bomb. Over 450 times more powerful than the bomb dropped on Nagasaki, the device vaporized the islet of Elugelab, which disappeared into a sea-filled crater.

1949

February 1950 The persecution of suspected Communists for "un-American activities" in the US reaches a peak under the influence of Senator Joe McCarthy

△ **NATO treaty,** original

4 April 1949
NORTH ATLANTIC TREATY SIGNED

Designed to confront the threat of Soviet intervention in western Europe, the document establishing the North Atlantic Treaty Organization was initially signed by the US, Canada, and ten European nations including Britain, France, and the Low Countries. Since that time a further 18 have joined. The only time the treaty has so far been invoked was in response to the terrorist attacks on the US on 11 September 2001.

◁ **United Nations Korean War** service medal

25 June 1950
START OF THE KOREAN WAR

After World War II, the Korean peninsula was divided between a Communist north and a capitalist south, both claiming to be the true government of a united Korea. In 1950, North Korean forces invaded the south before being driven back by United Nations forces. The UN advance in turn triggered a Chinese counter-attack. The two sides eventually agreed an armistice in 1953.

▷ **Civilians** during the Korean War

1 October 1949
PEOPLE'S REPUBLIC OF CHINA IS ESTABLISHED

In the four years after World War II, the long-running conflict between Nationalists and Communists for control of China swung in favour of Mao Zedong's Communists. From late 1948, the Nationalist leader Chiang Kai-shek started withdrawing his forces to the island of Taiwan, ceding control of the mainland. Following several decisive victories, including the capture of the Nationalist capital Nanjing, Mao officially proclaimed the establishment of the People's Republic in Beijing's Tiananmen Square.

◁ **Propaganda poster** featuring Mao Zedong

1893-1976
MAO ZEDONG

A Marxist-Leninist, Mao helped found the Red Army and became head of the Communist Party, leading the struggle against the Nationalists for control of China. After proclaiming the People's Republic of China, he was the nation's leader until his death.

1 September 1951 Australia, New Zealand, and the US sign the ANZUS Pacific Security Treaty

8 September 1951 The Allied military occupation of Japan ends when a treaty signed in San Francisco hands back sovereignty

4 November 1952 Dwight D. Eisenhower is elected 34th President of the US

1952

18 April 1951
TREATY OF PARIS

Scarred by the horrors of war, leaders from France, Germany, Italy, and the Benelux countries determined to co-operate on a supranational level. A treaty, championed by the French diplomat Jean Monnet, set up the European Coal and Steel Community, which in time would evolve into first the European Economic Community (EEC) and later the European Union (EU).

◁ **European Coal and Steel Community** poster

▷ **Rebel suspects** under guard

3 October 1952
MAU MAU REBELLION

Amid resentment at British rule in Kenya, militants of the clandestine Kenya Land and Freedom Army – also known as the Mau Mau – launched an uprising against white settlers and the colonial authorities. The revolt was put down with great brutality, but the drive for majority rule continued and, in December 1963, Kenya became an independent nation.

"There is no future for the people of Europe other than in union."

JEAN MONNET, 1950

5 March 1953

DEATH OF STALIN

The Soviet Union's autocratic ruler died four days after suffering a cerebral haemorrhage, unleashing a struggle for power among his subordinates in the Central Committee of the Communist Party of the Soviet Union. Eventually, Nikita Khrushchev emerged victorious. In 1956, he denounced Stalin's crimes, attacking the personality cult that until that time had surrounded the dictator, particularly after his success in leading the USSR to victory in World War II.

◁ **Stalin memorial** rally in Bucharest

1953

27 July 1953 The Korean War ends with a ceasefire agreement

19 August 1953 Iran's Prime Minister Mohammad Mosaddegh is overthrown in a US-backed coup

7 May 1954 French forces surrender to Vietnamese insurgents at Dien Bien Phu: it is the end of French colonial rule in Indochina

◁ **Muhammad Naguib,** the first President of Egypt

18 June 1953

EGYPT BECOMES A REPUBLIC

In the wake of a military coup that had overthrown the reigning monarch King Farouk in August 1952, leaders of the revolutionary Free Officers Movement abolished the monarchy and declared Egypt to be a republic with Muhammad Naguib as President and Gamal Abdel Nasser as his deputy.

△ Crowds celebrate in Cairo

1 November 1954

ALGERIA'S WAR OF INDEPENDENCE BREAKS OUT

The war was one of the longest and bloodiest independence struggles that marked the end of the colonial era. It started when members of the FLN (National Liberation Front) launched a series of attacks on French targets and called on the Algerian people to rise up against the colonial authorities. The conflict, which also caused major political upheavals in France, only ended with the granting of independence in July 1962.

△ **French mounted servicemen** in Algeria

1878–1953
JOSEPH STALIN

Josef Stalin ruled the Soviet Union for 30 years, first as part of a leadership team, later with dictatorial powers. His brutal rule came to overshadow his role in defeating Nazi Germany in World War II.

1955
TELEVISION REACHES A MASS AUDIENCE

Black-and-white television sets made their first appearance in the 1920s, but it was only after World War II that they became a regular feature of middle-class homes. In 1950, only 9 per cent of US households had one, but by 1959 the figure was over 80 per cent; colour television followed in the 1960s.

△ Graetz tabletop television set, 1953

14 May 1955 The Warsaw Pact links the Communist nations of Eastern Europe in a defensive alliance

21 September 1955
Military leaders topple Juan Perón from his post as President of Argentina

1955

"The enemy has overrun us. We are blowing up everything. Vive la France."

THE LAST FRENCH RADIO COMMUNICATION FROM DIEN BIEN PHU, 7TH MAY 1954

1954–1968
THE US CIVIL RIGHTS MOVEMENT

The fight for social justice and racial equality in the US gained huge momentum in the 1950s. Grass-roots groups fought inequality and forced changes in state and federal laws.

1955 Rosa Parks refuses to give up her seat to a white man on an Alabama bus, inspiring a boycott of the bus company.

1962 James Meredith becomes the first black student to attend the University of Mississippi, despite attempts to bar him.

1963 Martin Luther King gives his "I Have a Dream" speech; Medgar Evers, civil rights activist, is assassinated.

1964 The Civil Rights Act is signed into law, prohibiting employment discrimination. A second act follows in 1968.

29 October 1956
START OF SUEZ CRISIS

After President Nasser of Egypt announced the nationalization of the Suez Canal, Britain and France responded by colluding with Israel to invade Egypt. In the face of US hostility, the European nations had to back down and withdraw their forces.

▽ **Ships block the Suez canal**

4 October 1957
LAUNCH OF SPUTNIK 1

Launched by Soviet scientists into low Earth orbit, Sputnik was the first artificial satellite to circle the planet beyond the limits of its atmosphere. Its success caught the US by surprise, triggering a Space Race between the two superpowers. Travelling at a speed of 29,000 km/h (18,000 mph), Sputnik sent back signals for three weeks before its batteries died. It finally fell back into the atmosphere early in 1958.

▷ **Monument near Rizhskaya Metro station in Moscow** celebrating Sputnik 1

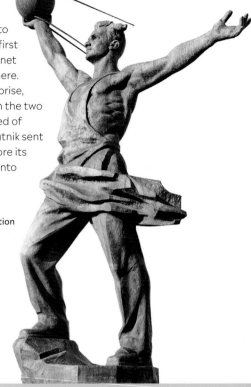

1956

6 March 1957 Ghana, under Kwame Nkrumah, is the first former colony in sub-Saharan Africa to gain independence

June 1956 Egypt's President Nasser accepts Soviet aid to build the Aswan Dam

25 March 1957
THE TREATY OF ROME

Building on the success of the European Coal and Steel Community (1951), the six founder members – France, West Germany, Italy, Belgium, the Netherlands, and Luxembourg – broadened their alliance, creating a single market for goods and services. The result was the European Economic Community (EEC), which formed the basis of the later European Union (EU).

△ **Ministers** sign the treaty creating the EEC

January 1958
THE GREAT LEAP FORWARD

China's Mao Zedong launched a programme of reform, known as the "Great Leap Forward", intending to make China an industrial power that could match Britain and the United States. The people of rural China lived in massive communes where labour was pooled and many goods and services became free. The resulting policy distortions, combined with droughts and floods, brought about famine on a massive scale. Initially planned to last for five years, the campaign was abandoned after three.

2 January 1959

FIDEL CASTRO TAKES POWER IN CUBA

Taking advantage of popular discontent with the corrupt rule of President Fulgencio Batista, guerrilla forces led by Fidel Castro and Che Guevara took up arms in 1953 and gradually gained support despite setbacks including defeat, imprisonment, and exile. From a base in the Sierra Maestra mountains, they wore down government troops sent against them until they were finally able to take the offensive and make a triumphal entry into the capital, Havana.

> ## "A revolution is a fight to the death between the future and the past."
>
> *FIDEL CASTRO, SPEECH, 1961*

△ **Cuban banknote** celebrating the 1959 revolution

29 July 1958 The National Aeronautics and Space Administration(NASA) is established in the US

1959

4 October 1958 The Fifth Republic is established in France, with Charles de Gaulle as its first president

△ Poster promoting the Great Leap Forward

1926–2016
FIDEL CASTRO

After leading his guerrilla army to victory, Castro served as Cuba's prime minister until 1976 and then as President until 2008. He turned Cuba into a one-party Communist state.

1960-70
COUNTERCULTURE

In the mid-1960s, increasing prosperity and full employment fuelled a growing middle-class youth counterculture in Britain and the US. Young people questioned the values of mainstream society and drew together in an anti-establishment movement that sought to create an alternative society based on ideals of love, peace, and communal values. Known variously as "freaks", "hippies", or the "underground", many experimented with psychedelic drugs, such as LSD, alternative religions, and sexual freedom as they sought to expand human consciousness and break down societal boundaries. This experimental culture was reflected in music, literature, and film-making.

Writers such as Jack Kerouac, Tom Wolfe, and Hunter S. Thompson explored new freedoms and themes including sex, drugs, and life on the road, while musicians blended folk, rock, and psychedelic styles to provide a soundtrack for the new culture.

The counterculture spawned some of the largest protests seen in America, as hundreds of thousands campaigned to "make love not war", hoping to bring about nuclear disarmament and an end to the Vietnam War (1955–75). The new freedoms of the 1960s also fed into the US Civil Rights Movement, resulting in a series of important legal rulings that outlawed some forms of discrimination against women and African Americans.

KEY MOMENTS

1966 *Turn On, Tune In, Drop Out*
American psychologist Timothy Leary (*left*) released a spoken word album exploring his views on the meaning of inner life, LSD, and peace, among many other issues. It sparked San Francisco's Summer of Love in 1967.

1967 *Sgt Pepper's Lonely Hearts Club Band*
British band The Beatles embraced the counterculture, releasing an album about drugs, expanding the mind, and dropping out. They were the most popular band in the world at the time, so *Sgt Pepper* (*left*) exposed millions of listeners to hippy values.

1969 Anti-war protests
More than 500,000 people gathered in Washington D.C. on 15 November 1969 (*left*) to demand that US forces withdraw from Vietnam. Although it was a largely peaceful demonstration, the police attacked the crowd with tear gas; President Nixon refused to be moved by the protests.

The Woodstock festival on 15–18 August 1969 drew 400,000 people to a dairy farm in Bethel, New York, to watch 32 acts take to the stage for "3 days of Peace & Music". A 1970 documentary film and the festival soundtrack album helped secure Woodstock's legendary status.

1 May 1960
THE U-2 INCIDENT

An American U-2 spyplane piloted by Gary Powers was shot down deep inside the Soviet Union by a Russian surface-to-air missile. Previous successful missions had made US authorities confident that the high altitude at which the U-2s flew put them outside enemy range. Powers survived and was taken prisoner. The incident increased Cold War tensions and helped derail a four-power summit held in Paris a fortnight later.

▷ **Gary Powers**, U2 pilot

1960

8 November 1960 John F. Kennedy is elected 35th President of the US

5 July 1962 Algeria wins independence from France after a bitter eight-year war

1917–63
JOHN F. KENNEDY

As the youngest candidate elected to the US presidency, Kennedy brought charm and good looks to the office. The hopes raised by his tenure were brutally dashed by his assassination.

12 April 1961
FIRST MAN IN SPACE

Soviet cosmonaut Yuri Gagarin became the first human to enter outer space when he travelled as the lone passenger on the first flight of the Vostok 3KA spacecraft, launched from the Baikonur Cosmodrome in southern Kazakhstan. The capsule he flew in completed one full orbit of the Earth after separating from its booster rockets. As it fell back to Earth, Gagarin ejected and landed successfully by parachute. The event was seen as another triumph for the ongoing Soviet space programme.

△ **Vostok** capsule

"I see Earth! It is so beautiful!"

YURI GAGARIN, ON THE VIEW FROM THE VOSTOK CRAFT, 1961

16–29 October 1962

THE CUBAN MISSILE CRISIS

Responding to US deployments in Turkey and Italy, Soviet premier Nikita Khrushchev sought to site missiles in Cuba, near the US mainland. The US demanded the weapons' removal under threat of military reprisal. A potential nuclear confrontation was avoided when Khrushchev withdrew the missiles.

▽ **US and Russian naval ships meet** off Puerto Rico

25 May 1963

ORGANISATION OF AFRICAN UNITY (OAU) FORMED

At a gathering in the Ethiopian capital Addis Ababa, representatives of 32 African nations came together to form a body dedicated to improving political and economic co-operation and confronting colonialism. The lack of any military wing limited the ability of the organization to enforce its decisions, and in 2002 it was replaced by the 55-member African Union.

◁ **Delegates** attend the first session of the OAU

5 August 1963 A partial Nuclear Test Ban Treaty is signed by the Soviet Union, the US, and the UK

1963

1962 US troops are sent to Vietnam to support South Vietnamese forces against North Vietnamese insurgents

20 October 1962 Military conflict breaks out between China and India

July 1963 Links between the Chinese and Soviet Communist parties are formally severed

22 November 1963

US PRESIDENT JOHN F. KENNEDY IS ASSASSINATED

Almost three years into his term of office, Kennedy travelled to Dallas, Texas, on a political mission. While riding in a motorcade through the streets, he was shot twice by an assassin stationed on the sixth floor of a roadside building. The killing had a profound effect on the nation, and conspiracy theories about the motives behind the assassination spread for many years afterwards. In its wake, Vice President Lyndon B. Johnson took office as the 36th US President.

△ **John F. Kennedy in the presidential motorcade** moments before his assassination

"Revolution is not a crime! Rebellion is justified!"

CULTURAL REVOLUTION SLOGAN IN CHINA, 1966-76

△ Mao's "little red book"

1964

14 October 1964 **Leonid Brezhnev** succeeds Nikita Khrushchev as leader of the Soviet Union

21 February 1965 **Malcolm X, a Black Muslim** minister, human rights activist, and prominent leader in the Nation of Islam is assassinated in New York, US

▽ **Chinese poster** in support of North Vietnam

2 August 1964
THE GULF OF TONKIN INCIDENT

When torpedo boats fired on a US ship off the North Vietnamese coast, the US State Department used the incident – and an invented second attack – to justify passing the Gulf of Tonkin Resolution through Congress. This gave the US President a free hand to resist Communist aggression and so fuelled US involvement in the Vietnam War.

August 1965
CONFLICT BREAKS OUT IN KASHMIR

The region of Kashmir had been forcibly divided between India and Pakistan during the 1947 partition of those nations, but both sides continued to claim it as their own. Under "Operation Gibraltar", Pakistan launched a guerrilla insurgency, backed by army special forces. The population failed to rise in support, and after battles with the Indian army, both sides fell back to their previous borders.

△ **Waziristan tribesmen** who fought against India

16 May 1966
CULTURAL REVOLUTION IN CHINA

After the failure of his "Great Leap Forward" initiative, China's leader Mao Zedong moved to regain control by proclaiming a purge of revisionist elements and a return to hardline Communist doctrines as in the "little red book" of Maoist thought. Intellectuals and cultural artefacts were attacked, economic activity slowed, and hundreds of thousands of suspected opponents were killed by his youthful Red Guard supporters. Many significant ancient structures and customs were destroyed because traditional culture was seen as preventing a true Communist revolution.

◁ **Chairman Mao's backers** show their support at a mass rally

24 November 1965 General Mobutu stages a coup that puts an end to five years of civil war in the former Belgian Congo

21 April 1967 A military junta seizes power in Greece, ending 23 years of democratic government

1967

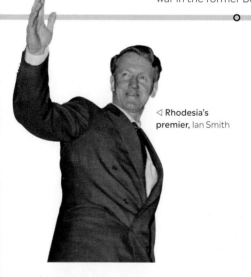

◁ Rhodesia's premier, Ian Smith

11 November 1965
RHODESIA PROCLAIMS UDI

Britain refused to hand power to its colony Rhodesia unless it introduced majority rule. The white-dominated government of the colony announced a Unilateral Declaration of Independence (UDI), declaring itself a sovereign state. Fifteen years of conflict followed before white rule ended and the state of Zimbabwe came into being in 1980.

▽ Israeli tanks moving into the Gaza Strip

5–10 June 1967
THE SIX DAY WAR

Following increased tensions between Israel and Egypt, the Israeli military launched pre-emptive strikes against Egyptian airfields. Israeli forces dominated the ensuing land battle against Egypt and its allies Jordan and Syria. By the time a ceasefire was declared it had won control of East Jerusalem, the Golan Heights, the Sinai Peninsula, and the Gaza Strip.

▷ **Protesters** surround Soviet tanks entering Prague

August 1968
CZECHOSLOVAKIA'S PRAGUE SPRING CRUSHED

The election of Alexander Dubček as head of the Czech Communist Party in January 1968 began a time of liberalization that soon attracted the hostility of the USSR. After seven months of mounting frustration the USSR took action, sending half a million troops into the country to restore the status quo. The action attracted worldwide criticism as well as fierce opposition within Czechoslovakia itself.

1968

△ **Martin Luther King's funeral**, Atlanta

2 March 1969
Chinese and Soviet troops clash on the Ussuri River border

▷ **Apollo 11** mission patch

1930–2012
NEIL ARMSTRONG

A one-time test pilot, Armstrong joined NASA's astronaut training programme in 1962. Four years later, he made his first spaceflight in the Gemini programme preceding Apollo. He retired from NASA in 1971 to take up a post teaching engineering.

4 April 1968
MARTIN LUTHER KING ASSASSINATED

As the most prominent leader of the US Civil Rights movement, Baptist minister Rev. Dr Martin Luther King Jr was a target for racist hostility. While visiting Memphis to support a local strike, he was killed by a single bullet fired by James Earl Ray, a career criminal with previous convictions for burglary and armed robbery. His death caused widespread shock and grief, and rioting broke out in many cities.

▷ **Neil Armstrong** walks on the lunar surface

August 1969
THE TROUBLES IN NORTHERN IRELAND
The division of Ireland in 1921 left Catholics in Northern Ireland as a minority. When the Northern Ireland Civil Rights Association protested against unfair treatment by the majority Protestant government, Ulster Loyalists resisted their demands. Violence erupted and British troops were deployed. The Troubles only ended with the Good Friday peace agreement of 1998.

△ Ulster police fire tear gas

△ Biafran demonstration

14 January 1970
THE BIAFRAN WAR COMES TO AN END
Nigeria's province of Biafra declared independence in 1967. The Nigerian government responded with a blockade, causing mass starvation. A final offensive in December 1969 forced the Biafran leadership to surrender, by which time an estimated two million civilians were dead.

October 1969 West Germany's Chancellor Willy Brandt adopts a new "Ostpolitik" – a policy of détente with Soviet-bloc countries

28 September 1970 President Nasser of Egypt dies and is succeeded by Anwar Sadat

1970

1 May 1970 US troops invade Cambodia

10 October 1970 The Fiji Islands in the Pacific gain full independence from Britain

"That's one small step for [a] man, one giant leap for mankind."

NEIL ARMSTRONG ON FIRST STEPPING ONTO THE LUNAR SURFACE, 1969

20 July 1969
MOON LANDING
Shaken by Soviet advances in space exploration, US President John F. Kennedy announced in 1961 the goal of landing a man on the Moon by the end of the decade. That ambition was realized when astronauts Neil Armstrong and Buzz Aldrin stepped onto the lunar surface following a successful touchdown by their landing module. The feat marked the climax of NASA's Apollo 11 mission.

16 December 1971
BIRTH OF BANGLADESH

At independence, Pakistan was split into two halves, West and East, about 1,600 km (1,000 miles) apart. Bengali nationalists in the East came to resent the West's dominance. Tensions boiled over in a liberation war, won by the Bengalis with Indian military assistance, that ended with the establishment of Bangladesh as an independent nation.

◁ **Bangladesh's** first newspaper

October 1973
OPEC OIL CRISIS

In the wake of the Yom Kippur War, the Organization of Petroleum Exporting Countries (OPEC) led by Saudi Arabia imposed an oil embargo on countries supporting Israel. The move tripled the price of oil worldwide, forcing affected nations to impose extreme conservation measures including rationing. This drove up the cost of fuel, leading to long queues at petrol stations, and increased inflation.

26 May 1972 The Strategic Arms Limitation Treaty (SALT) is signed by President Nixon and the Soviet leader Leonid Brezhnev

▷ **Pump prices** rise by almost one half

1971

21 February 1972 US President Nixon visits China, initiating friendlier relations

1 January 1973 Britain, Ireland, and Denmark join the European Economic Community

"Today Bangladesh is a sovereign and independent country."

DECLARATION RELEASED BY SHEIKH MUJIBUR RAHMAN, 1971

6–25 October 1973
YOM KIPPUR WAR

Learning from Israel's surprise attack at the start of the 1967 Six-Day War, Egypt's President Sadat and his allies in Syria chose the Jewish holy day of Yom Kippur to send troops across the ceasefire lines into territories previously taken by Israel. After initial gains the allies were driven back, and the fighting ended without major gains on either side but with Israel's confidence in its security shaken.

▷ **Israeli armoured vehicles** in the Sinai Peninsula

30 April 1975
PEACE IN VIETNAM

When the US pulled its forces out of Vietnam in 1973, the South Vietnamese army was left to resist the Communist People's Army of North Vietnam (PAVN) on its own. The war continued for two more years after an initial peace deal was broken, only ending when a PAVN spring offensive finally broke southern resistance by capturing Saigon. The two halves of the country finally reunited in July 1976.

▷ Citizens wave Viet Cong flags to celebrate the fall of Saigon

13 April 1975 Civil war breaks out in Lebanon, setting pro-Palestinian Muslims against Christian forces backed by Israel

1975

11 November 1975 Angola wins independence from Portugal six months after Mozambique

20 November 1975 Spain's dictator General Franco dies, paving the way for the restoration of democracy

△ **Nixon** announces his resignation

9 August 1974
WATERGATE SCANDAL

After US police arrested five men trying to steal information from the Democratic Party HQ in Washington's Watergate complex, the Republican government denied any involvement. When the cover-up eventually unravelled, President Richard M. Nixon was forced to resign from office under threat of impeachment.

1892–1975
GENERAL FRANCISCO FRANCO

After leading Nationalist forces to victory in the Spanish Civil War, Franco ruled Spain until his death. Latterly he re-established the monarchy and was succeeded as head of state by King Juan Carlos I.

8 March 1978
CHINA CHANGES COURSE

In the vacuum following Mao Zedong's death, the moderate Deng Xiaoping emerged as China's leader. He used his position to introduce limited free-market reforms and greater personal freedoms. The changes spurred rapid economic growth. This marked the beginning of China's "Reform and Opening Up".

▷ **Mural** showing China's "Four Modernizations"

1976

9 September 1976 Mao Zedong dies; his wife and other powerful officials (the Gang of Four) are arrested

13 July 1977 Somali forces invade Ethiopia, starting the Ogaden War

17 September 1978
CAMP DAVID ACCORDS

In the wake of the Yom Kippur War, US President Jimmy Carter sought to revive the Middle East peace process. He eventually succeeded in bringing Israel's premier Menachem Begin and Egypt's Anwar Sadat together at Camp David in Maryland. The men signed a framework agreement that led six months later to a peace treaty between the two nations.

△ **Sadat and Begin embrace** as Carter applauds

1976-2007
THE COMPUTER REVOLUTION

Once the preserve of large companies, institutions, and universities, computers became available to consumers in the 1970s.

1976 Steve Jobs and Steve Wozniak found the Apple Computer Company introducing the Apple 1, with its single circuit board.

1981 IBM unveils the Acorn, the first Personal Computer (PC) to use the MS-DOS operating system developed by Microsoft.

1990 Tim Berners-Lee develops HyperText Mark-up Language (HTML), paving the way for the World Wide Web.

2007 The introduction of the iPhone and other smartphones places computing power into consumer's pockets.

11 February 1979
THE IRANIAN REVOLUTION

The Shah of Iran was forced to depart amid dissatisfaction with his regime. Sixteen days later, the exiled opposition leader Ayatollah Khomeini returned to Tehran to a hero's welcome. Following large-scale demonstrations and some fighting, the Shah's last prime minister fled the country, leaving Iran in the hands of the revolutionaries.

▷ Ayatollah Khomeini

> "We have set as our goal the worldwide spread of the influence of Islam."

*AYATOLLAH KHOMEINI,
FROM HIS BOOK* COMMENTARIES
ON THE MEANS OF SALVATION, *1986*

1 January 1979 The US and People's Republic of China establish full diplomatic relations

1979

4 May 1979 Margaret Thatcher becomes Prime Minister of Britain, bringing a free-market ideology to power

17 July 1979
REVOLUTION IN NICARAGUA

Reflecting growing opposition to the Somoza dynasty that had ruled Nicaragua for 42 years, Sandinista rebels launched a guerrilla campaign. The oppressive measures the government adopted to suppress the rising eventually led it to lose US support. Amid renewed unrest after the murder of a leading newspaper editor, the revolutionary forces gradually spread their hold across the country and on 17 July entered the capital, Managua. President Somoza resigned and went into exile, leaving the country in Sandinista hands.

Bajo las banderas de Carlos Fonseca venceremos al... IMPERIALISMO

△ Sandinista National Liberation Front propaganda poster

31 August 1980
POLAND'S SOLIDARITY TRADE UNION FOUNDED

Emerging from the Lenin Shipyards in Gdańsk, Solidarity became the focus for agitation for improved workers' rights and opposition to the country's Soviet-backed government. Within a year it had won the support of a third of the nation's working population. Despite attempts to close it down, including the imposition of martial law, it survived to play a decisive part in the ending of Communist rule.

▷ **Lech Wałęsa,** Solidarity's co-founder, addresses a crowd

1980
CHINA INTRODUCES THE ONE-CHILD POLICY

Faced with a rising population, China had – from 1970 on – introduced a recommended maximum of two children per family. Now most parents were restricted to a single child, and the policy was enforced through cash inducements for those who complied and heavy fines for offenders. In practice the population continued to grow, though at a reduced rate.

▷ **Poster** promoting the policy

1980

4 November 1980
Ronald Reagan is elected 40th US president

19 April 1980 **Robert Mugabe** becomes the first prime minister of an independent Zimbabwe

"Practise birth control for the revolution."

SLOGAN TO PROMOTE THE ONE-CHILD POLICY IN CHINA, 1980

22 September 1980
THE IRAN–IRAQ WAR BREAKS OUT

Seeking to establish supremacy in the oil-rich Persian Gulf region, Iraqi leader Saddam Hussein sent troops into neighbouring Iran, still shaken by the 1979 Islamic revolution. The invasion stalled after three months, following which the conflict bogged down into eight years of lethal stalemate that left more than half a million soldiers and civilians dead.

▷ **Iraqi soldiers** celebrate a victory

▷ **Columbia blasts off** from the Kennedy Space Center

12 April 1981

FIRST SPACE SHUTTLE MISSION LAUNCHED BY THE US

Launched from the Kennedy Space Center, Florida, the Shuttle *Columbia*, carrying a two-man crew, pioneered a programme of reusable craft able to return to Earth after completing space flights. Over the next three decades, five such craft made a total of 135 missions, two of which ended in disaster.

◁ Columbia mission badge

1983

6 October 1981 Egypt's President Sadat is assassinated at a military parade

6 June 1982 Israel invades Lebanon, laying siege to the capital, Beirut

23 March 1983 Ronald Reagan announces the "Star Wars" Strategic Defense Initiative

1911–2004
RONALD REAGAN

Famed as a film star, Reagan served as governor of California before becoming US president. A committed conservative, he played a major role in bringing on the collapse of the Soviet Union.

△ British troops "yomp" towards Port Stanley

April–June 1982

FALKLANDS WAR BETWEEN BRITAIN AND ARGENTINA

Following Argentina's invasion of the Falkland Islands, a British dependency in the South Atlantic since 1833, Margaret Thatcher's Conservative government dispatched a naval task force to reassert control. The conflict ended 10 weeks later with an Argentine surrender and the re-establishment of British sovereignty.

> ## "The Soviet people want full-blooded and unconditional democracy."
>
> *MIKHAIL GORBACHEV IN A JULY 1988 SPEECH*

11 March 1985
MIKHAIL GORBACHEV LEADS THE USSR

On the death of Konstantin Chernenko, the USSR's governing Politburo turned to the reformer Gorbachev to fill the role of General Secretary of the ruling Communist Party. The choice was to have dramatic results, as Gorbachev's policy of *glasnost* or openness encouraged debate, whittling away the power of the Party and hastening the break-up of the Soviet Union.

△ Mikhail Gorbachev

31 October 1984 Indira Gandhi, India's first female prime minister, is assassinated by her own bodyguards

1984

△ Refugees fleeing Ethiopia

1984
FAMINE STRIKES IN ETHIOPIA

With three-quarters of the population living as subsistence farmers, famine was a constant risk in Ethiopia. In the early 1980s, a bitter civil war and the repressive policies of the ruling military junta made life even more precarious. In 1984, the failure of the spring rains caused widespread starvation, particularly in the rebel northern province of Tigray. Despite international aid efforts, including the Live Aid fundraising campaign, half a million people are thought to have died.

△ Corazon Aquino at a victory rally

25 February 1986
PRESIDENT MARCOS OF THE PHILIPPINES IS TOPPLED

Ferdinand Marcos had ruled the Philippines for over 20 years, but when the economy declined from 1983, attention turned to the corruption underlying his rule. After opposition leader Benigno Aquino was assassinated later that year, his widow, Corazon, became the focus for a resistance movement. This culminated in the People Power Revolution that drove Marcos into exile and established Corazon as president.

26 April 1986
EXPLOSION AT CHERNOBYL
The world's worst nuclear disaster occurred when a safety test on a reactor at a power plant in Ukraine (then part of the USSR) went wrong, causing an uncontrolled chain reaction. The resulting explosion and fire released radioactivity that spread across large areas of western Europe. A 10 km (6 mile) exclusion zone was set up around the site, but even so some 60 individuals are reckoned to have died as a direct result of the accident, with estimates of long-term increased mortality ranging into the thousands.

◁ **Chernobyl** after the explosion

9 November 1989 The Berlin Wall falls in the first step to German reunification

1989

15 April 1986 The US bombs "terrorist-related" targets in Libya, striking at the ports of Tripoli and Benghazi

20 August 1988 The war between Iran and Iraq ends after almost eight years

8 December 1987
INF TREATY SIGNED
Negotiated between the US and the USSR, the Intermediate-Range Nuclear Forces (INF) Treaty was signed by presidents Reagan and Gorbachev and ratified the following June. It banned short- and medium-range land-based missiles, leading to the elimination of over 2,500 weapons and a 10-year programme of on-site verification inspections. In 2019, US President Donald Trump first suspended and then withdrew from the treaty, citing claimed Russian non-compliance.

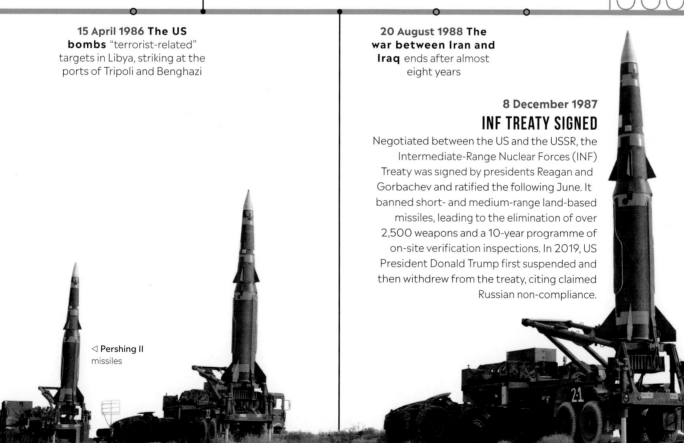

◁ **Pershing II** missiles

1980–1991
THE COLLAPSE OF THE SOVIET EMPIRE

The "iron curtain" – an ideological and military barrier established by the Soviet Union – had separated Europe's Communist and non-Communist states since the end of World War II. By the early 1980s, however, the Soviet economy was failing and the urgent need for reform drove the Politburo to appoint Mikhail Gorbachev as its new leader in 1985. His policy of *glasnost* or openness only served to expose deep veins of resentment at the system and its failings. Ungagged by the lifting of censorship, liberals in the USSR's satellites began to speak out for greater freedom. First,

Poland's Solidarity trade union gained public support, then the Baltic republics demanded self-government, and in January 1989 the Hungarian parliament allowed the formation of opposition parties.

In November of that year, the Berlin Wall fell, followed by Communist regimes in Romania and the Czech Republic. By the end of 1989, Lithuania, Poland, and East Germany had taken the same route. In 1991, the liberal nationalist Boris Yeltsin became president of Russia, and in December that year the Soviet Union was formally dissolved.

KEY MOMENTS

22 December 1989 Fall of Ceauşescu
Nicolai Ceauşescu was Romania's Soviet-backed head of state for two decades, presiding over an increasingly repressive regime and a steadily worsening economy. On 17 December 1989, he ordered police to open fire on demonstrators in western Romania; protest and unrest (*left*) followed in the capital Bucharest. Ceauşescu tried to flee the country, but was arrested and executed.

29 December 1989 The Velvet Revolution
In the Czech Republic, a non-violent protest movement that came to be known as the Velvet Revolution overthrew the old Soviet-backed regime. Its figurehead was the playwright Václav Havel (*left*), who had spent lengthy terms in prison under Communist rule. Havel took over the nation's presidency, negotiating the removal of Soviet troops from the country and organizing free elections for 1990.

The Berlin Wall was built to prevent East German citizens from defecting to the West. After a mistaken report on 9 November 1989 that border restrictions were being removed, demonstrators flocked to the wall and soon began knocking down this symbol of oppression.

"Our struggle has reached a decisive stage. Our march to freedom is irreversible."

NELSON MANDELA ON HIS RELEASE FROM PRISON, 1990

2 February 1990
SOUTH AFRICAN GOVERNMENT ANNOUNCES AN END TO APARTHEID

After years of international pressure, South Africa's new president, F. W. de Klerk, announced an end to discriminatory laws and to the ban on the African National Congress (ANC) and other groups fighting apartheid. Nine days later, the leading anti-apartheid campaigner and ANC leader Nelson Mandela, who had been imprisoned for 27 years, was released from jail. Negotiations between the government and the ANC began that led to the nation's first universal-suffrage general election four years later.

◁ Nelson Mandela

4 October 1991 The Madrid Protocol on the preservation of Antarctica is agreed

1990

1 October 1990 The Human Genome Project to read the entire human DNA code sequence is launched

3 October 1990 Germany is reunified after 45 years of division

3 November 1992 Bill Clinton is elected 42nd President of the United States

△ **Iraqi soldiers** confident of victory

2 August 1990
IRAQ'S INVASION OF KUWAIT TRIGGERS THE GULF WAR

In a dispute over oil production, Iraq's leader Saddam Hussein ordered his troops to invade neighbouring Kuwait. US President George H. W. Bush set about organizing a multinational force to liberate the country. Eventually 35 nations joined this "coalition of the willing", with most troops coming from the US, Saudi Arabia, the UK, and Egypt. After six weeks' fighting early in 1991, Kuwait's independence was restored.

1 November 1993

THE EUROPEAN COMMUNITY BECOMES THE EUROPEAN UNION

The European Economic Community (EEC) became the European Union (EU) when the Maastricht Treaty, signed by its 12 existing member states in February 1992, came into force. The treaty introduced new pillars of co-operation covering security and home affairs, and gave citizens of any one EU country the right to live and work in any other. Passport-free travel and a common currency would follow in future years for states that signed up to them.

◁ **Flags of the EU** and member states

1 January 1994 The NAFTA agreement comes into effect, creating a free-trade zone between the US, Canada, and Mexico

11 December 1994 Russian forces enter the breakaway province of Chechnya, starting the First Chechen War

1994

13 September 1993 Israel and the Palestine Liberation Organisation sign up to the first Oslo Accord

1994

THOUSANDS MASSACRED IN RWANDA

The worst genocide since the Holocaust occurred when militias from Rwanda's majority Hutu community turned on the minority Tutsi who had long dominated the country. The killing was triggered by the assassination of the nation's Hutu president, who had earlier negotiated a truce with Tutsi rebels. Up to a million people are thought to have died.

▷ **Memorial** to the Rwandan genocide

1991-1998 THE BALKAN WARS

The socialist state of Yugoslavia was created after World War II as a federation of six republics. Tensions between the groups exploded into conflict.

25 June 1991 Croatia declares independence from Yugoslavia, triggering four years of war with Serbia at a cost of 20,000 dead.

2 April 1992 Sarajevo endures what will be almost four years of siege as civil war breaks out between ethnic groups in Bosnia.

14 December 1995 The Dayton Agreement splits Bosnia-Herzogovina into Serb-dominated and Bosnian-Croat entities.

28 February 1998 War starts in Kosovo between Albanian separatists and the Serb-dominated Federal Republic of Yugoslavia.

"The Court has jurisdiction... with respect to the following crimes: (a) genocide; (b) crimes against humanity; (c) war crimes; (d) the crime of aggression."

STATUTE ESTABLISHING THE INTERNATIONAL CRIMINAL COURT, 1998

27 September 1996

THE TALIBAN SEIZE CONTROL OF AFGHANISTAN

Political instability followed the overthrow of the last Afghan king in 1973. Ten years of Soviet occupation saw the rise of US-backed Islamic militias opposed to the Communists' anti-religious agenda. Following Soviet withdrawal in 1989, rival warlords fought for power until the militant Islamists of the Taliban took control of the capital, Kabul, and with it the greater part of the country.

◁ Taliban soldier

10 April 1998 The Good Friday Agreement brings 30 years of the Troubles in Northern Ireland to an end

1995

26 March 1995 The Schengen Agreement comes into effect, removing internal borders between most European Union states

10 September 1996 The Comprehensive Nuclear Test Ban Treaty is signed; it is later ratified by 170 states

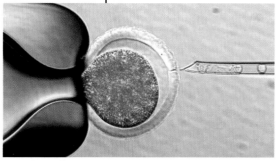
△ The cloning process

5 July 1996

DOLLY THE SHEEP IS CLONED

Dolly the sheep became the first mammal to be successfully cloned. British scientists working at the Roslin Institute of Edinburgh University were able to transfer a cell nucleus into a separate unfertilized egg cell, and then implant this in a surrogate mother to bear the embryo to term. Dolly lived to the age of six and bore six lambs.

△ Vladimir Putin (left) shakes the hand of Boris Yeltsin

31 December 1999
VLADIMIR PUTIN BECOMES ACTING PRESIDENT OF THE RUSSIAN FEDERATION

Putin took over from his predecessor Boris Yeltsin at a time of deep economic crisis. He cemented his position the following year by defeating his opponents in a presidential election, winning more than 50 per cent of the vote. Buoyed by high oil prices, the first years of his rule were a time of uninterrupted economic growth, with real incomes across the nation more than doubling. Standing again for election in 2004, Putin saw his share of the vote rise to 71 per cent.

17 July 1998 The International Criminal Court is established to prosecute crimes against humanity

26 August 1999 The Second Chechen War breaks out; it will end in a Russian victory

1999

24 March 1999 NATO airstrikes force the Yugoslav government to relinquish its attempts to enforce its control over Kosovo

1 July 1997
HONG KONG RETURNS TO CHINESE RULE

Hong Kong had been under British rule since 1841, with much of the territory held on a 99-year lease signed by China's imperial government in 1898. On its expiration, Britain ceded sovereignty of all Hong Kong to the People's Republic in return for a guarantee that its existing political and economic structure would be retained for 50 years. By the time of the transfer, the territory had already become a global financial hub.

◁ **Hong Kong** celebrates British withdrawal

1973-2021
CLIMATE CRISIS

The idea that agricultural practices such as farming, irrigation, and forest clearance could affect local patterns of temperature and rainfall dates back to the ancient world. However, the notion that global climate can be affected by human activity emerged only in the 19th century. Scientists including Joseph Fourier and John Tyndall realized that certain gases in Earth's atmosphere – notably carbon dioxide and methane – absorbed heat from the Sun and warmed the atmosphere, a phenomenon that became known as the "greenhouse effect". By the mid-20th century, research had established a link between increasing amounts of carbon dioxide in the atmosphere – the result of burning fossil fuels – and rising global temperatures. These findings led US oceanographer Roger Revelle to write: "Human beings are now carrying out a large scale geophysical experiment…".

Atmospheric monitoring by the US geochemist Charles Keeling in the 1950s showed a clear pattern of rising carbon dioxide concentrations, and the new science of computer modelling used such data to predict future climate scenarios; these included higher global temperatures, droughts, melting glaciers and ice caps, and rising sea levels. In 1965, climate change appeared on the political agenda as a US Presidential Advisory Committee called the greenhouse effect a matter of "real concern".

KEY MOMENTS

1973 UN Conference on the Environment
Stockholm in Sweden hosted the world's first conference to address global environmental issues. Commitments were made to study the links between growth and environmental damage such as deforestation (*left*).

1989 IPCC assessments
The first report of the Intergovernmental Panel on Climate Change (IPCC) showed that temperatures had risen by 0.3–0.6°C (0.5–1.1°F) over the last 100 years. Its fifth report stated with 95 per cent certainty that humans were the "dominant cause" of global warming and climate change (*left*) since the 1950s.

1997-2021 Agreements and disagreements
International treaties such as the Kyoto Protocol (1997) and the 2015 Paris Agreement (*left*) sought commitment to reduce the output of greenhouse gases. Many countries failed to meet their targets; some, such as the US, withdrew for political reasons.

Millions of young people have demanded climate action from their political leaders. Protests such as Extinction Rebellion and school strikes have given voice to the issue of climate change, which continues to be one of the most prominent concerns of the 21st century.

11 September 2001
TERRORIST ATTACKS ON THE US

Four commercial flights from US airports were hijacked by terrorists posing as normal passengers in a co-ordinated series of attacks on the US. The Al-Qaeda radical Islamist group responsible had been founded by Osama bin Laden, a Saudi-born citizen who had earlier fought with Mujahideen guerrillas against the Soviets in Afghanistan. Two planes brought down the Twin Towers of New York's World Trade Center. A third struck the Pentagon, while the fourth crashed in Pennsylvania following an onboard fight between passengers and hijackers. Together, the attacks constituted the deadliest terrorist incident to that date, causing almost 3,000 deaths.

△ **The Twin Towers collapse** after being attacked

2000

13 December 2001 A Kashmiri insurgent group launches a suicide attack on the Indian Parliament

8 February 2002 A decade of civil war ends in Algeria as Islamic fighters surrender to government forces

7 October 2001
US-LED "WAR ON TERROR" BEGINS

In response to the terrorist attacks on the United States of 11 September, the US launched its "war on terror" by bombing strongholds of the Taliban – Afghanistan's fundamentalist government. This was followed by "Operation Enduring Freedom", the invasion of Afghanistan by US and allied forces, which was to last for 20 years.

◁ **US soldiers** board a Chinook helicopter in Afghanistan

"The United States of America will not permit the world's most dangerous regimes to threaten us with the world's most destructive weapons."

PRESIDENT GEORGE W. BUSH, STATE OF THE NATION ADDRESS, 29 JANUARY 2002

4 January 2004

NASA ROVERS LAND ON MARS

The US National Aeronautics and Space Administration (NASA) succeeded in landing the powered robot rover *Spirit* on the surface of Mars. It was followed three weeks later by its companion, *Opportunity*, which landed on the other side of the planet. Over the following years (*Opportunity* remained active until 2018) the rovers gathered data about Martian rocks and soils and searched for evidence of water.

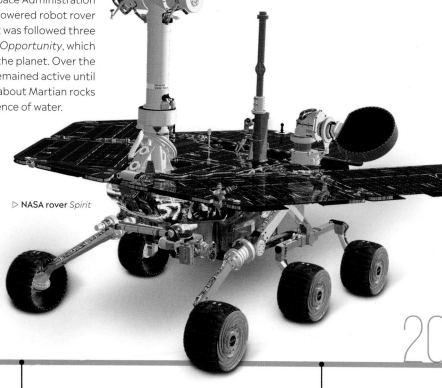

▷ **NASA rover** *Spirit*

26 February 2003
Conflict breaks out in the Darfur region of western Sudan

2004

▷ **US tanks** in Iraq

20 March 2003

US-LED FORCES INVADE IRAQ

Claiming that Iraq's dictator Saddam Hussein possessed weapons of mass destruction which posed a threat to the West, US President George W. Bush assembled a group of allied powers to effect regime change. The military campaign was successful and Saddam was overthrown. However, civil strife spread in the power vacuum following his removal and dissidents launched a long-running insurgency against the occupying forces.

▷ **Banda Aceh**, Sumatra, after the tsunami

26 December 2004

INDIAN OCEAN TSUNAMI

Triggered by an undersea earthquake, the tsunami was the third-largest ever recorded, driving waves up to 30 m (100 ft) high onto coastal locations in Indonesia, Thailand, Sri Lanka, and southern India, as well as at least 10 other countries. In its wake it left an estimated 227,000 people dead, making it the most lethal such event so far recorded.

"What we know about the global financial crisis is that we don't know very much."

ECONOMIST PAUL SAMUELSON, 2008

25 August 2005
HURRICANE KATRINA

This powerful storm first made landfall in southern Florida, but gathered force as it travelled west across the Gulf of Mexico. When it hit land again in southern Louisiana and Mississippi, it caused massive devastation, particularly in New Orleans, much of which was flooded for weeks. In all, Katrina caused over 1,800 deaths and US$125 billion of damage.

△ **Devastation** in the wake of Hurricane Katrina

12 July 2006 War breaks out in Lebanon between Israeli forces and Hezbollah paramilitaries

2005

30 January 2005
Elections are held in Iraq, but violence continues to trouble the country

▽ A coal-fired power station producing polluting gases and steam

16 February 2005
KYOTO PROTOCOL COMES INTO FORCE

Adopted in 1997 and signed initially by 84 countries, the Protocol entered into force after an agreed percentage of major polluters had signed up to its terms. The accord commits signatories to accept agreed targets for reducing greenhouse gas emissions. Currently 192 parties have put their name to it.

△ Mourning wreaths for Benazir Bhutto

27 December 2007
BENAZIR BHUTTO ASSASSINATED

Benazir Bhutto served two terms as prime minister of Pakistan (in 1988-90 and 1993-96) before being driven from office on corruption charges. After nine years in exile, she returned to Pakistan to stand in a general election, but was killed when leaving a political rally. It is uncertain who was responsible for the attack, but in Pakistan itself, the former President Musharaf, then in exile, was indicted for the murder.

2008
GLOBAL ECONOMIC CRISIS

Triggered initially by a collapse in the US housing market, the crisis saw banks and financial houses around the developed world unable to meet their commitments. Starting in late 2007, the panic crescendoed with the failure of the Lehman Brothers investment bank the following September, and then spread across much of North America and Europe, causing the most severe economic recession since the Great Depression of the 1930s.

◁ **Traders watch** as markets tumble

1961–
BARACK OBAMA

Born in Hawaii, Obama spent almost four years as a US Senator before winning the Democratic Party nomination for the 2008 Presidential Election. He served two terms in office.

1 August 2008 The South Ossetia War breaks out between Russia and Georgia

8 August 2008 China hosts its first Olympic Games in Beijing

4 November 2008 Barack Obama wins the US Presidential election, becoming the nation's first African-American president

2009

18 May 2009 In Sri Lanka, 26 years of civil conflict comes to an end with the final defeat of Tamil Tiger guerrillas

10 September 2008
LARGE HADRON COLLIDER (LHC) COMMISSIONED

CERN's LHC – the world's largest particle collider – was started up on 10 September 2008. The machine occupies a tunnel 27 km (17 miles) long below the French–Swiss border and allows scientists to accelerate particles to near the speed of light and study the effect of collisions, providing information on the behaviour of the basic building-blocks of the universe.

▷ The Large Hadron Collider

4 January 2011
THE ARAB SPRING BEGINS

Discontent with poor living conditions and repressive regimes spread across North Africa into the Middle East. It reached new heights when the self-immolation of a street trader triggered protests in Tunisia. In the ensuing power struggles, existing regimes were brought down in Libya, Egypt, and Yemen, as well as in Tunisia itself, while large-scale demonstrations rocked Algeria, Morocco, Syria, Iraq, Lebanon, Jordan, and Oman, among other countries.

△ Tunisian protesters

25 August 2012
VOYAGER 1 ENTERS INTERSTELLAR SPACE

Launched in 1977, the Voyager space probe made successful flybys of Jupiter, Saturn, and Saturn's largest moon Titan before heading into the further reaches of the Solar System. It became the first spacecraft to enter interstellar space when it crossed the heliosphere – the boundary beyond which our Sun's influence is no longer the dominant one. It continues to collect data that it communicates to NASA's Deep Space Network.

◁ Voyager 1

2010

31 October 2011 The UN officially declares the population of the planet to have exceeded 7 billion people

2013 China launches the Belt-and-Road Initiative of global infrastructure development

March 2010 Eyjafjallajökull, an Icelandic volcano, erupts, disrupting air travel across northern Europe

5 March 2013 Hugo Chávez, president of Venezuela since 2002, dies at the start of a fourth term in office

3 July 2013
EGYPT'S PRESIDENT MORSI IS FORCED FROM POWER

Mohamed Morsi came to power in the wake of the Arab Spring demonstrations that forced the resignation of his predecessor, Hosni Mubarak. A former leader of the Islamist Freedom and Justice Party, Morsi stirred protests in their turn from anti-Islamist demonstrators. In response, the military staged a coup that removed Morsi from power, replacing him with General Abdel Fattah al-Sisi.

1954–2013
HUGO CHAVEZ

After becoming Venezuela's President in 1998, Chávez went on to win three further elections. Buoyed by record oil revenues, he pursued a programme of social reforms designed to help the poor.

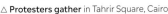
△ **Protesters gather** in Tahrir Square, Cairo

2014–15
THE EUROPEAN UNION FACES AN UNPRECEDENTED MIGRANT CRISIS

The EU had long been a destination of choice for people fleeing war and persecution, but in 2014–15, numbers increased dramatically. Refugees from wars in Syria and Afghanistan sought to cross EU borders from Turkey, while many thousands more risked their lives by sailing over the Mediterranean in small boats from North Africa. By the end of the year almost a million people had applied for asylum in Germany, the most welcoming host country.

▷ **Refugees disembarking** onto the Greek Island of Lesbos, 2015

16 September 2014 Civil war breaks out in Yemen between the government and Houthi rebels

2014

△ "Crimea is Ukraine" graffiti

27 February 2014
RUSSIA ANNEXES CRIMEA

Russia's President Putin reacted to the deposing of Ukraine's pro-Russian President Viktor Yanukovych by reviving Russian claims to Crimea, a territory that had been transferred from Russia to Ukraine in 1954. Russian troops were dispatched to install a pro-Russian government that, following a referendum and a declaration of independence, accepted the status of a republic of the Russian Federation.

△ Islamic State supporters celebrate

10 June 2014
ISLAMIC STATE TERRORISTS CAPTURE THE IRAQI CITY OF MOSUL

In the chaotic aftermath of the Iraq War, supporters of the Islamic State of Iraq and the Levant (ISIL), a Sunni insurgent group, took control of Mosul, the most important city in the north of the country, after the government troops defending it fled. The terrorists held it for three years, during which minority groups were brutally oppressed and more than 2,000 people were summarily executed. The Iraqi military, backed by international forces, retook the city after a nine-month campaign .

1924–2019
ROBERT MUGABE

Hailed as the father of his country when elected Prime Minister of an independent Zimbabwe in 1980, Mugabe clung on to power for 37 years, despite claims of corruption and human rights abuses.

4 November 2016

PARIS CLIMATE AGREEMENT COMES INTO FORCE

Initially signed in April 2016, the agreement came into force once 55 nations responsible for at least 55 per cent of global greenhouse gas emissions had signed up. The accord aims to limit global warming to below a 2 per cent increase on pre-industrial levels, and commits signatories to report regularly on the steps taken to meet that goal. So far 191 states and the European Union have ratified the agreement.

△ Signatories celebrate

▷ COVID-19 patients undergoing treatment

21 November 2017 Robert Mugabe is ousted as President of Zimbabwe after almost four decades in power

2015

23 June 2016 The United Kingdom votes to leave the European Union after 43 years in its "Brexit" referendum

8 November 2016 Donald Trump is elected 45th President of the United States

"From this day forward it's going to be only America first. America first."

DONALD TRUMP, PRESIDENTIAL INAUGURATION ADDRESS, JANUARY 2017

▷ Rohingya Muslims flee persecution

9 October 2016

MYANMAR'S ARMED FORCES TARGET ROHINGYA MUSLIMS

Following violence between Rohingya Muslims and Rakhine Buddhists and attacks on Myanmar's border posts, the Myanmar military launched a brutal crackdown on Rohingya villages in the northern state of Rakhine, bordering on Bangladesh. The repression left more than 20,000 civilians dead, and displaced a million more.

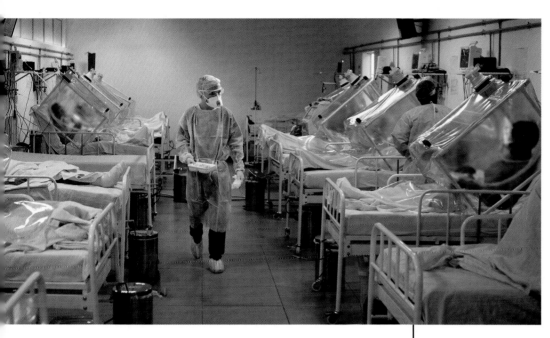

March 2020
COVID-19 PANDEMIC

Originating in Wuhan, China, in late 2019, the coronavirus outbreak was classed as a pandemic by the World Health Organization the following March. In the months that followed, it spread around the world, infecting more than 200 million people and causing over 4.25 million deaths by the autumn of 2021.

22 March 2018 President Trump announces tariffs that prompt a US–Chinese trade war

25 May 2020 George Floyd, a Black man, is killed by a white police officer in the US, triggering protests in many countries

2021

15 March 2019 Mass pro-democracy protests break out in China's Special Administrative Region of Hong Kong

▷ Yellow vest protester

November 2018
GILETS JAUNES PROTEST IN FRANCE

Motivated initially by discontent over carbon taxes and rising fuel prices, the *gilets jaunes* – so called from the high-visibility yellow vests they chose to wear – expanded their demonstrations to protest about rising economic inequality and inadequate public services in rural areas. About 3 million people are thought to have been involved in all. The protests were stopped only by the arrival of the COVID-19 pandemic.

▷ Trump supporters besiege the US Capitol

6 January 2021
PRO-TRUMP PROTESTERS STORM THE US CAPITOL

Responding to false claims by Donald Trump that the 2020 presidential election was being stolen by the Democrats, supporters broke into the Capitol building in Washington DC. The ensuing violence left five people dead. Joe Biden was declared the 46th President the following day.

INDEX

Bold text indicates a main entry
for the subject.

ACKNOWLEDGMENTS

The publisher would like to thank Diana Vowles for proofreading.

The publisher would like to thank the following for their kind permission to reproduce their photographs:
(Key: a-above; b-below/bottom; c-centre; f-far; l-left; r-right; t-top)

1 Alamy Stock Photo: blickwinkel (c). 2 Alamy Stock Photo: Historic Images (c). 4-5 Shutterstock: Dima Moroz (c). 6 Alamy Stock Photo: The Picture Art Collection (cl); IanDagnall Computing (c1); CPA Media Pte Ltd (c2); Pictorial Press Ltd (c3); De Luan (cr). 7 Alamy Stock Photo: Nick Higham (cl). Getty Images: Photo Josse/Leemage (c1). Alamy Stock Photo: Heritage Image Partnership (c2). NASA: (c3). Alamy Stock Photo: REUTERS (cr). 8-9 Alamy Stock Photo: Michele Falzone (c). 10-11 Alamy Stock Photo: Andia (t). 10 Alamy Stock Photo: blickwinkel (tl); HeritagePics (c). Dorling Kindersley: Harry Taylor / Natural History Museum, London (bl). 11 Dorling Kindersley: Colorado Plateau Geosystems Inc / NASA (cl). British Museum: Trustees of the British Museum (br). 12-13 akg-images: Balage Balogh (t). 12 Shutterstock: omurbilgili (b). 13 Getty Images: Heritage Images (tr). Alamy Stock Photo: www.BibleLandPictures.com (cr). Dorling Kindersley: Geoff Brightling / Butser Ancient Farm, Hampshire (bl). Shutterstock: Lubo Ivanko (bc1); Xidong Luo (bc2). Wikimedia Commons: Osado (br). 14 Alamy Stock Photo: Granger Historical Picture Archive (tl); Elitsa Lambova (cl). Getty Images: DEA PICTURE LIBRARY (br). 15 Shutterstock: Simon Edge (t). Alamy Stock Photo: Suzuki Kaku (bl); Granger Historical Picture Archive (br). 16-17 Getty Images: Roland Birke (r). 16 Getty Images: Giampaolo Cianella (cl). Shutterstock: Gurgen Bakhshetyan (clb); Benvenuto Cellini (bl). 18 Dorling Kindersley: Dreamstime.com (t). Alamy Stock Photo: Adam Eastland Art + Architecture (tr). Shutterstock: iuliia_n (br). 19 Getty Images: DEA / G. DAGLI ORTI (tc); Photo 12 (bl). Alamy Stock Photo: CPA Media Pte Ltd (br). 20-21 Alamy Stock Photo: Artokoloro (br). 20 Alamy Stock Photo: CPA Media Pte Ltd (tl). Metropolitan Museum of Art: Gift of Nanette B. Kelekian, in memory of Charles Dikran and Beatrice Kelekian, 1999 (c1). Alamy Stock Photo: INTERFOTO (bl). Shutterstock: Donna Carpenter (bc). 21 Getty Images: Universal History Archive (t). Alamy Stock Photo: Richard Ellis (b). 22 Alamy Stock Photo: CPA Media Pte Ltd (tl); Peter Horree (cr). Getty Images: DEA / M. SEEMULLER (bl). Shutterstock: Only Fabrizio (br). 23 Shutterstock: Dima Moroz (tl). Getty Images: Buyenlarge (br). 24-25 Alamy Stock Photo: Danita Delimont (c). 24 Getty Images: Heritage Images (tl). Alamy Stock Photo: funkyfood London - Paul Williams (tr). Metropolitan Museum of Art: Jan Mitchell and Sons Collection, Gift of Jan Mitchell, 1999 (br). 25 Alamy Stock Photo: World History Archive (t); Album (br). 26 Alamy Stock Photo: The Picture Art Collection (tl). Metropolitan Museum of Art: Rogers Fund, 1914 (bc). Getty Images: Zhang Peng (br). 27 Shutterstock: maratr (t); Kamira (bl). Alamy Stock Photo: AGF Srl (br). 28-29 Alamy Stock Photo: MeijiShowa (t). 28 Bridgeman Images: Boltin Picture Library (c). Getty Images: Heritage Images (b). 29 Getty Images: Heritage Images (t). Alamy Stock Photo: www.BibleLandPictures.com (bl). 30 Alamy Stock Photo: HeritagePics (tl); www.BibleLandPictures.com (cr); Science History Images (bl); Lanmas (bc1). 30 Getty Images: UniversalImagesGroup (c). 31 Alamy Stock Photo: Giannis Katsaros (ca); CPA Media Pte Ltd (cra). Getty Images: DEA PICTURE LIBRARY (bl). Alamy Stock Photo: robertharding (br). 32-33 Metropolitan Museum of Art: Gift of Mrs. Heyward Cutting, 1942 (t). 32 Shutterstock: wayak (tl). Alamy Stock Photo: Nick Bobroff (cr); Gina Rodgers (bc). 33 Alamy Stock Photo: adam eastland (tr). Getty Images: Heritage Images (bc). 34 Getty Images: Heritage Images (tr). Alamy Stock Photo: www.BibleLandPictures.com (bl); Reciprocity Images Editorial (br). 35 Alamy Stock Photo: Chronicle (tr); Heritage Image Partnership Ltd (c); Heritage Image Partnership Ltd (bl); INTERFOTO (bc1). 35 Getty Images: DEA / G. DAGLI ORTI (bc2). Shutterstock: Gilmanshin (b). 36-37 Shutterstock: Hung Chung Chih (r). 36 Alamy Stock Photo: incamerastock (cl); Science History Images (bl). 38-39 Getty Images: Sepia Times (cb). 38 Alamy Stock Photo: Dinodia Photos (tc); agefotostock (bl). 39 Alamy Stock Photo: colaimages (tl). Getty Images: ullstein bild Dtl. (ca). Alamy Stock Photo: Leonardo Lazo (b). 40-41 Alamy Stock Photo: Granger Historical Picture Archive (b). 40 Alamy Stock Photo: Historic Images (tl); www.BibleLandPictures.com (tc); The Artchives (tr). 41 Getty Images: Richard I'Anson (tr). Alamy Stock Photo: Erin Babnik (br). 42-43 Alamy Stock Photo: PRISMA ARCHIVO (ca). 42 Alamy Stock Photo: Album (tl). Bridgeman Images: Ashmolean Museum (c). Alamy Stock Photo: Peter Horree (bc). 43 Getty Images: PHAS (tr). Alamy Stock Photo: Artefact (br). 44-45 Alamy Stock Photo: IanDagnall Computing (t). 44 Alamy Stock Photo: Cristiano Fronteddu (bl). 45 Alamy Stock Photo: Jon G. Fuller, Jr. (tc); Jose Lucas (cr). Getty Images: Fototeca Storica Nazionale (bl). Alamy Stock Photo: Russell Mountford (bc1); Album (bc2); imageBROKER (br). 46 Alamy Stock Photo: Erin Babnik (tc); World Religions Photo Library (br). 47 Alamy Stock Photo: Adam Ján Figeľ (tr). Getty Images: flik47 (bl).

Alamy Stock Photo: Heritage Image Partnership Ltd (br). 48-49 Shutterstock: kavram (r). 48 Alamy Stock Photo: Granger Historical Picture Archive (cl); Ivan Vdovin (bl). 50 Alamy Stock Photo: Science History Images (tl); GL Archive (bl). Heritage Image Partnership Ltd (br). 51 Alamy Stock Photo: IanDagnall Computing (tr). Metropolitan Museum of Art: Gift of J. Pierpont Morgan, 1917 (bl). 52-53 Alamy Stock Photo: Independent Picture Service (t). 52 Getty Images: AGF (tl); Dreamframer (b). 53 Shutterstock: Gilmanshin (tr). Alamy Stock Photo: Anita Nicholson (cl); CPA Media Pte Ltd (bl); The Picture Art Collection (bc1); World History Archive (bc2). 54-55 Alamy Stock Photo: Lanmas (t). 54 Alamy Stock Photo: Artokoloro (bl). Getty Images: DE AGOSTINI PICTURE LIBRARY (br). 55 Alamy Stock Photo: INTERFOTO (tr). Bridgeman Images: Stefano Baldini (bc). 56-57 Alamy Stock Photo: Brian Overcast (c). 56 Alamy Stock Photo: Kevin Schafer (bl1); Design Pics Inc (bl2); Juan Vilata (bl3). 58 Getty Images: Sepia Times (tl). Metropolitan Museum of Art: Rogers Fund, 1923 (tr). Alamy Stock Photo: Kevin Archive (bc); David Lyons (br). 59 Alamy Stock Photo: CPA Media Pte Ltd (tc); Richard Slater (cl); adam eastland (bc). 60-61 Getty Images: Heritage Images (t). 60 Getty Images: Sepia Times (tl). Shutterstock: Alexandre Laprise (bl). 61 Alamy Stock Photo: CPA Media Pte Ltd (cl). Shutterstock: ansharphoto (br). 62-63 Getty Images: Godong (tl). 62 Alamy Stock Photo: Heritage Image Partnership Ltd (c); Peter Horree (br). 63 akg-images: Cameraphoto (tc). Alamy Stock Photo: imageBROKER (bl). Shutterstock: Lefteris Papaulakis (bc1). Alamy Stock Photo: Granger Historical Picture Archive (bc2); GL Archive (br). 64-65 Alamy Stock Photo: Azoor Photo (r). 64 Alamy Stock Photo: Peter Cripps (cl); North Wind Picture Archives (clb); Peter Horree (bl). 66 Bridgeman Images: The Holbarn Archive (t); THP Creative (b). 67 Alamy Stock Photo: Heritage Image Partnership Ltd (tl). Getty Images: UniversalImagesGroup (cr). Alamy Stock Photo: Imaginechina Limited (bl); CPA Media Pte Ltd (bc1); Album (bc2); Niday Picture Library (br). 68-69 Alamy Stock Photo: Album (t). 68 Alamy Stock Photo: Panther Media GmbH (tc). Getty Images: Heritage Images (bl). 69 akg-images: Eric Vandeville (c). Alamy Stock Photo: Stefano Ravera (b). 70 Alamy Stock Photo: INTERFOTO (tl); The Print Collector (cl); Suzuki Kaku (br). 71 Alamy Stock Photo: Album (tl); Chronicle (tr); World Discovery (br). 72 Alamy Stock Photo: Matteo Omied (tl); Granger Historical Picture Archive (br). 73 Alamy Stock Photo: Granger Historical Picture Archive (cl); agefotostock (cr); Granger Historical Picture Archive (br). 74 Bridgeman Images: Leonard de Selva (c). Alamy Stock Photo: Album (b). 75 Alamy Stock Photo: Maidun Collection (tl); Jonathan Orourke (c); Rapp Halour (b). 76-77 Alamy Stock Photo: Album (tc). 76 Alamy Stock Photo: Granger Historical Picture Archive (bl). 77 Bridgeman Images: Photo Josse (tl). Alamy Stock Photo: The Print Collector (cl); Album (bl). 77 Getty Images: The Print Collector (bc1). Alamy Stock Photo: Heritage Image Partnership Ltd (bc2); Peter Righteous (br). 78-79 Alamy Stock Photo: Fedor Selivanov (c). 78 Bridgeman Images: Photo Josse (tl). Alamy Stock Photo: The Print Collector (bl). Dorling Kindersley: iStock: duncan1890 (br). 79 Alamy Stock Photo: Stephen Coyne (tr); Granger Historical Picture Archive (b). 80-81 Alamy Stock Photo: Album (c). 80 Alamy Stock Photo: Science History Images (bl1). Getty Images: Universal History Archive (bl2). Alamy Stock Photo: Science History Images (bl3). 82-83 Alamy Stock Photo: PRISMA ARCHIVO (c). 82 Alamy Stock Photo: Science History Images (tl); The Picture Art Collection (b). 83 Alamy Stock Photo: Historic Collection (tr); HeritagePics (bl); CPA Media Pte Ltd (br). 84 Alamy Stock Photo: Heritage Image Partnership Ltd (tl); Heritage Image Partnership Ltd (tr); MichaelGrant (bl). 85 Alamy Stock Photo: Peter Horree (tl); Wolfgang Kaehler (br). 86-87 Alamy Stock Photo: CPA Media Pte Ltd (c). 86 Alamy Stock Photo: Scott Hortop Images (tl); CPA Media Pte Ltd (b). 87 Alamy Stock Photo: Ancient Art and Architecture (cr); History and Art Collection (bl); Stefano Politi Markovina (bc1); Michael Foley (bc2); Everett Collection Inc (br). 88 Getty Images: Heritage Images (tr). Alamy Stock Photo: Chronicle (cl); Natalia Lukiianova (br). 89 Alamy Stock Photo: Heritage Image Partnership Ltd (tr); CPA Media Pte Ltd (br). 90-91 Getty Images: Sepia Times (tc). 90 Shutterstock: Fotowan (bl). Alamy Stock Photo: Album (br). 91 Alamy Stock Photo: Shelly Rivoli (c); Yogi Black (bl); Konstantin Kalishko (br). 92-93 Alamy Stock Photo: The Picture Art Collection (c). 92 Alamy Stock Photo: CPA Media Pte Ltd (bl1). akg-images: Pictures from History (bl2); Ronald and Sabrina Michaud (bl3). 94-95 Alamy Stock Photo: funkyfood London - Paul Williams (d). 94 Alamy Stock Photo: Granger Historical Picture Archive (tl); Album (cr). 95 Alamy Stock Photo: The Picture Art Collection (tl); Artokoloro (br). 96 Alamy Stock Photo: The Picture Art Collection (tl). akg-images: ROLAND & SABRINA MICHAUD (cl). Alamy Stock Photo: PA Images (bl). 97 Alamy Stock Photo: Science History Images (t). Getty Images: Werner Forman (cr). Alamy Stock Photo: Nature Picture Library (bl). 98 Alamy Stock Photo: Science History Images (t); imageBROKER (b). 99 Alamy Stock Photo: Joris Van Ostaeyen (tl); PRISMA ARCHIVO (tr). Metropolitan Museum of Art: Edward Elliott Family Collection, Purchase, The Dillon Fund Gift, 1982 (br). 100

Shutterstock: Uwe Aranas (tl). **Alamy Stock Photo:** World History Archive (c). **Bridgeman Images:** St. Louis Museum of Science & Natural History, Missouri, US (br). **101 Alamy Stock Photo:** World History Archive (tl); The Picture Art Collection (br). **102 Alamy Stock Photo:** World History Archive (tl); Dinodia Photos (tr); The Picture Art Collection (b). **103 Alamy Stock Photo:** Album (tl). **Getty Images:** The Print Collector (br). **104 Getty Images:** Heritage Images (tr); DEA / A. DAGLI ORTI (c); Heritage Images (br). **105 Dorling Kindersley:** Richard Leeney / Faversham Town Council (tl). **Alamy Stock Photo:** Peter Horree (tc). **Getty Images:** UniversalImagesGroup (br). **106 Alamy Stock Photo:** The Picture Art Collection (tr). **Shutterstock:** ppl (bl). **107 akg-images:** (br). **Alamy Stock Photo:** The Picture Art Collection (tl); Science History Images (tr). **akg-images:** (bc). **Getty Images:** Universal History Archive (br). **108-109 Alamy Stock Photo:** CPA Media Pte Ltd (b). **108 Alamy Stock Photo:** HeritagePics (tl); CPA Media Pte Ltd (tr). **Wikimedia Commons:** Gary Todd (bc). **109 Alamy Stock Photo:** Heritage Image Partnership Ltd (tr). **110 Alamy Stock Photo:** Dietmar Rauscher (tl). **Getty Images:** Heritage Images (br). **111 Shutterstock:** Rachelle Burnside (tl). **Alamy Stock Photo:** Science History Images (tr). **Getty Images:** Werner Forman (cl). **Alamy Stock Photo:** The Granger Collection (br). **112-113 Alamy Stock Photo:** Aliaksandr Mazurkevich (b). **112 Alamy Stock Photo:** Heritage Image Partnership Ltd (tr). **Dorling Kindersley:** Gary Ombler / University of Aberdeen (cla). **Shutterstock:** Everett Collection (cl). **Getty Images:** Heritage Images (clb). **113 Alamy Stock Photo:** Niday Picture Library (tc). **114 Getty Images:** Photo Josse/Leemage (cl). **Alamy Stock Photo:** Pictorial Press Ltd (clb). **Getty Images:** Heritage Images (bl). **115 Alamy Stock Photo:** Pictorial Press Ltd (r). **116-117 Getty Images:** Angelo Hornak (t). **116 Getty Images:** Sepia Times (tl). **Alamy Stock Photo:** CPA Media Pte Ltd (bl); Robert Kawka (c). **117 Getty Images:** UniversalImagesGroup (tr). **Alamy Stock Photo:** Album (bl); PRISMA ARCHIVO (bc1); The History Collection (bc2); Album (br). **118-119 Getty Images:** Photo 12 (t). **118 Metropolitan Museum of Art:** Gift of Florence and Herbert Irving, 2015 (tl). **Alamy Stock Photo:** CPA Media Pte Ltd (bc). **119 Shutterstock:** neftali (tr). **Getty Images:** Carl Court / Staff (bl). **Alamy Stock Photo:** Niday Picture Library (br). **120 Getty Images:** Print Collector (cl). **Alamy Stock Photo:** Historical Images Archive (clb); Granger Historical Picture Archive (bl). **121 Alamy Stock Photo:** Science History Images (r). **122 Alamy Stock Photo:** CPA Media Pte Ltd (tl); Joaquin Ossorio-Castillo (br). **123 Alamy Stock Photo:** AF Fotografie (cla); Benjamin Phelan (tr). **123 Getty Images:** Leemage (bc). **Alamy Stock Photo:** World History Archive (br). **124 Getty Images:** DEA PICTURE LIBRARY (tc); Print Collector (bl). **124 Getty Images:** ullstein bild Dtl. (cr). **125 Alamy Stock Photo:** Tim Brown (tl); Science History Images (cl). **Getty Images:** Heritage Images (br). **126 Alamy Stock Photo:** UtCon Collection (tl); REUTERS (tr). **Dorling Kindersley:** Dreamstime.com: Daniel Prudek / Prudek (br). **127 akg-images:** (tl). **Alamy Stock Photo:** Artokoloro (crb); Granger Historical Picture Archive (br). **128-129 Alamy Stock Photo:** GL Archive (t). **128 Alamy Stock Photo:** Leonardo Emiliozzi (tl). **Getty Images:** Print Collector (bl). **129 Dorling Kindersley:** Dreamstime.com: Javarman (clb). **Alamy Stock Photo:** PjrStatues (bl); Science History Images (bc1); CPA Media Pte Ltd (bc2). **Getty Images:** Culture Club (br). **130 Alamy Stock Photo:** Ivan Vdovin (tl); Granger Historical Picture Archive (tr); Matteo Omied (bl). **131 Alamy Stock Photo:** Science History Images (tl). **Getty Images:** Stock Montage (clb). **Alamy Stock Photo:** Heritage Image Partnership Ltd (br). **132 Getty Images:** Print Collector (tl). **Alamy Stock Photo:** World History Archive (br). **133 Getty Images:** Heritage Images (t). **Alamy Stock Photo:** PRISMA ARCHIVO (ca). **Getty Images:** Heritage Images (bl). **Alamy Stock Photo:** World History Archive (bc1); CPA Media Pte Ltd (bc2); zhang jiahan (br). **134-135 Getty Images:** Heritage Images (b). **134 Alamy Stock Photo:** Rosemarie Mosteller (tl). **Getty Images:** Buyenlarge (t). **135 Alamy Stock Photo:** Album (tl). **Getty Images:** Universal History Archive (crb). **Alamy Stock Photo:** IanDagnall Computing (br). **136 Alamy Stock Photo:** Album (tl). **Getty Images:** Heritage Images (tr). **Alamy Stock Photo:** Granger Historical Picture Archive (bl). **137 Alamy Stock Photo:** Science History Images (tl); Album (cl). **Dorling Kindersley:** Dreamstime.com: Takepicsforfun (bl). **Shutterstock:** marryframestudio (bc1). **Alamy Stock Photo:** dbtravel (br). **138 Shutterstock:** GTW (tr). **Getty Images:** Print Collector (br). **139 Getty Images:** Heritage Images (tl). **Alamy Stock Photo:** Chris Dorney (tr); The Picture Art Collection (bl). **Shutterstock:** Avigator Fortuner (br). **140-141 Alamy Stock Photo:** Niday Picture Library (t). **140 Alamy Stock Photo:** CPA Media Pte Ltd (br). **Getty Images:** Photo 12 (bc). **141 Getty Images:** MPI / Stringer (tr); Stefano Bianchetti (bl). **Dorling Kindersley:** Gary Ombler / Whipple Museum of History of Science, Cambridge (bc1). **Alamy Stock Photo:** ClassicStock (bc2); dotted zebra (br). **142 Alamy Stock Photo:** Album (tl); Eraza Collection (tr). **Getty Images:** Werner Forman (bl). **Alamy Stock Photo:** PRISMA ARCHIVO (br). **143 Alamy Stock Photo:** Hemis (t). **Shutterstock:** NORTHERN IMAGERY (b). **144-145 Alamy Stock Photo:** Chronicle of World History (c). **144 Getty Images:** Sepia Times (bl1); Sepia Times (bl2); UniversalImagesGroup (bl3). **146-147 Alamy Stock Photo:** IanDagnall Computing (t). **146 Alamy Stock Photo:** INTERFOTO (bl); Album (br). **147 Getty Images:** Science and Society Picture Library (tr). **Alamy Stock Photo:** Art Collection 3 (bl). **Getty Images:** The Print Collector (br). **148 Getty Images:** Photo 12 (tl). **Alamy Stock Photo:** INTERFOTO (br). **149 Alamy Stock Photo:** Art Collection 3 (tr); Heritage Image Partnership Ltd (cl); Magite Historic (b). **150-151 Alamy Stock Photo:** incamerastock (t). **150 Alamy Stock Photo:** GL Archive (bl); CPA Media Pte Ltd (br). **151 Alamy Stock Photo:** Glasshouse Images (tr); CPA Media Pte Ltd (br). **152-153 Alamy Stock Photo:** Chronicle (b). **152 Alamy Stock Photo:** INTERFOTO (tl). **Getty Images:** Heritage Images (c). **153 Alamy Stock Photo:** GL Archive (cl); Photo 12 (tc). **154-155 Alamy Stock Photo:** The History Collection (tc). **154 Alamy Stock Photo:** miscellany (cr). **Getty Images:** Universal History Archive (b). **155 Getty Images:** Science and Society Picture Library (cl). **Alamy Stock Photo:** ephotocorp (cr). **156 Getty Images:** Heritage Images (t). **Alamy Stock Photo:** Album (c); Image Professionals GmbH (bl). **157 Alamy Stock Photo:** Pictures Now (tc); The Natural History Museum (cl). **Getty Images:** Heritage Images (bl). **Alamy Stock Photo:** The Granger Collection (bc1). **Getty Images:** The Print Collector (bc2). **158 Alamy Stock Photo:** Heritage Image Partnership Ltd (tl); IanDagnall Computing (br). **159 Alamy Stock Photo:** AIFA Visuals (cl); The History Collection (tr); Dinodia Photos (b). **160-161 Alamy Stock Photo:** De Luan (tc). **160 Getty Images:** Robert Alexander (bl). **Alamy Stock Photo:** North Wind Picture Archives (br). **161 Alamy Stock Photo:** Heritage Image Partnership Ltd (tr); Paul Nichol (cl); RKive (br). **162 Alamy Stock Photo:** PjrTravel (tl); Granger Historical Picture Archive (bl). **Getty Images:** Universal History Archive (c). **Alamy Stock Photo:** INTERFOTO (cr). **163 Alamy Stock Photo:** Artokoloro (t). **akg-images:** Heritage Images (b). **164-165 Getty Images:** Heritage Images (tc). **164 Bridgeman Images:** Peabody Essex Museum, Salem, Massachusetts, USA (b). **165 Getty Images:** The Print Collector (tr). **Alamy Stock Photo:** BTEU/RKMLGE (cl). **Getty Images:** Science and Society Picture Library (bl). **Alamy Stock Photo:** The Granger Collection (bc). **Getty Images:** Hulton Archive (br). **166 Alamy Stock Photo:** CPA Media Pte Ltd (t). **Getty Images:** Heritage Images (bl); Zhang Peng (br). **167 Alamy Stock Photo:** Science History Images (t). **Getty Images:** Wolfgang Kaehler (bl). **Alamy Stock Photo:** Matteo Omied (br). **168-169 Alamy Stock Photo:** Science History Images (c). **168 Bridgeman Images:** Private Collection (bl1). **Alamy Stock Photo:** INTERFOTO (bl2); Pictorial Press Ltd (bl3). **170 Alamy Stock Photo:** World History Archive (tl). **Getty Images:** UniversalImagesGroup (tr). **Alamy Stock Photo:** GL Archive (bc); World History Archive (cr). **171 Alamy Stock Photo:** robertharding (tr); The Picture Art Collection (bc); Tom Uhlman (br). **172-173 Alamy Stock Photo:** Nick Higham (l). **173 Alamy Stock Photo:** North Wind Picture Archives (cr). **Getty Images:** Mfarr (br). **174-175 Alamy Stock Photo:** Matteo Omied (b). **174 Alamy Stock Photo:** The Granger Collection (tl); The Picture Art Collection (tc); Yakov Oskanov (bl); Historic Collection (br). **175 Alamy Stock Photo:** Science History Images (ca); CPA Media Pte Ltd (tr). **176-177 Getty Images:** Photo 12 (t). **176 Dorling Kindersley:** Richard Leeney / Royal Academy of Music (tl). **Alamy Stock Photo:** AF Fotografie (br). **177 Alamy Stock Photo:** Niday Picture Library (bl). **Getty Images:** Archive Photos / Stringer (br). **178-179 Alamy Stock Photo:** imageBROKER (t). **178 Alamy Stock Photo:** GL Archive (tl). **Getty Images:** Sepia Times (bl). **Alamy Stock Photo:** PS-I (bc). **179 Alamy Stock Photo:** CPA Media Pte Ltd (c). **Metropolitan Museum of Art:** Rogers Fund, 1942 (bl). **Dorling Kindersley:** Dave King / Durham University Oriental Museum (bc1). **Alamy Stock Photo:** World History Archive (bc2). **Metropolitan Museum of Art:** Purchase by subscription, 1879 (br). **180 Getty Images:** Heritage Images (tr). **Alamy Stock Photo:** INTERFOTO (bl). **Getty Images:** Science & Society Picture Library (br). **181 Getty Images:** Sepia Times (tl). **Alamy Stock Photo:** Album (bl); Ian Dagnall (br). **182-183 Alamy Stock Photo:** Photo 12 (r). **182 Getty Images:** DEA / A. DE GREGORIO (clb). **Alamy Stock Photo:** IanDagnall Computing (bl). **184 Getty Images:** Photo 12 (tl); Culture Club (br). **185 Getty Images:** MPI / Stringer (tl). **Alamy Stock Photo:** B Christopher (tr); H.S. Photos (crb). **185 Getty Images:** Heritage Images (bl). **Alamy Stock Photo:** PjrStatues (bc1). **Getty Images:** Nigel Jarvis (bc2); GraphicaArtis (br). **186 Alamy Stock Photo:** INTERFOTO (tr). **Getty Images:** Epics (bl). **187 Alamy Stock Photo:** North Wind Picture Archives (tl). **Bridgeman Images:** The Anson Collection / National Trust Photographic Library / John Hammond (tr). **Alamy Stock Photo:** Chronicle (bl). **Getty Images:** Hulton Archive / Stringer (br). **188 Alamy Stock Photo:** Ian Dagnall (tr); Art Collection 2 (bl); Granger Historical Picture Archive (br). **189 Alamy Stock Photo:** Tim Graham (tr); Science History Images (bl); Universal Art Archive (br). **190 Getty Images:** DE AGOSTINI PICTURE LIBRARY (tl). **Alamy Stock Photo:** Pictorial Press Ltd (tr); imageBROKER (bl). **Getty Images:** Print Collector (bc1); Culture Club (bc2). **Alamy Stock Photo:** Lebrecht Music & Arts (br). **191 Alamy Stock Photo:** Masterpics (tl); Science History Images (bl). **Getty Images:** Stock Montage (br). **192-193 Alamy Stock Photo:** incamerastock (t). **192 Getty Images:** John Stevenson (bl). **Alamy Stock Photo:** Edwin Verin (br). **193 Alamy Stock Photo:** J.R. Bale (tl). **Getty Images:** Hulton Archive / Stringer (tc). **Alamy Stock Photo:** Filip Fuxa (br). **194 Alamy Stock Photo:** Heritage Image Partnership Ltd (tl); The Picture Art Collection (tr). **194 Dorling Kindersley:** 123RF.com: Rolando Da Jose / annika09 (bl); Dreamstime.com: Onur Ersin (bc). **195 Alamy Stock Photo:** Roland Bouvier (tc); Heritage Image Partnership Ltd (tr); The Granger Collection (bl). **196-197 Alamy Stock Photo:** REUTERS (r). **196 Alamy Stock Photo:** Album (cl). **Getty Images:** Heritage Images (bl1). **Alamy Stock Photo:** North Wind Picture Archives (bl2). **198 Alamy Stock Photo:** CPA Media Pte Ltd (tl). **Getty Images:** Photo 12 (br). **199 Alamy Stock Photo:** Niday Picture Library (tl); Balfore Archive Images (cl); Arthur Greenberg (br). **200-201 Getty Images:** Print Collector (t). **200 Alamy Stock Photo:** Alex Segre (tc); Heritage Image Partnership Ltd (bl); Science History Images (bc). **201 Dorling Kindersley:** 123RF.com: F. Javier Espuny / fxegs (bl). **202 Alamy Stock Photo:** FLHC (tl); Album (cr). **202 Dorling Kindersley:** Gary Ombler / Whipple Museum of History of Science, Cambridge (bl); Clive Streeter / The Science Museum, London (bc1). **202 Wikimedia Commons:** Medgyes (bc2). **Getty Images:** Andrei Berezovskii (br). **203 Alamy Stock Photo:** Nigel Reed QEDimages (tl); Chronicle (tr); North Wind Picture Archives (br). **204-205 Alamy Stock Photo:** Granger Historical Picture Archive (cb). **204 Alamy Stock Photo:** GL Archive (tl). **Getty Images:** DEA / G. DAGLI ORTI (cr). **205 Getty Images:** API (tl). **Bridgeman Images:** Private Collection (tr). **Dorling Kindersley:** Geoff Dann / David Edge (br). **206 Alamy Stock Photo:** Niday Picture Library (tc); Lifestyle pictures (bl). **Alamy Stock Photo:** Album (br). **207 Bridgeman Images:** British Museum, London (tr). **Alamy Stock Photo:** Artokoloro (bl). **akg-images:** ART TRADE, VAN HAM (br). **208 Alamy Stock Photo:** North Wind Picture Archives (tl). **Getty Images:** The New York Historical Society (cr). **Alamy Stock Photo:** The Picture Art Collection (bl); Granger Historical Picture Archive (br). **209 Alamy Stock Photo:** Todd Strand (tl). **Getty Images:** Interim Archives (bl). **Alamy Stock Photo:** David Ribeiro (bc1); Colin Waters (bc2); ARCHIVIO GBB (bc3); Pictorial Press Ltd (br). **210-211 Getty Images:** Science & Society Picture Library (c). **210 Getty Images:** Science & Society Picture Library (bl1); UniversalImagesGroup (bl2). **212 Alamy Stock Photo:** INTERFOTO (tl); Niday Picture Library (cr); GL Archive (cl); Ross Jolliffe (bl). **213 Getty Images:** Photo Josse/Leemage (t). **Alamy Stock Photo:** incamerastock (b). **214 Alamy Stock Photo:** INTERFOTO (tl); CPA Media Pte Ltd (tr); Witold Skrypczak (cr); Wahavi (br). **215 Alamy Stock Photo:** The Granger Collection (tl). **Shutterstock:** Everett Collection (tr). **Alamy Stock Photo:** Chronicle (bl). **Shutterstock:** Estragon (bc1). **Alamy Stock Photo:** IanDagnall Computing (bc2); Science Picture Co (br). **216-217 Alamy Stock Photo:** Heritage Image Partnership Ltd (b). **216 Alamy Stock Photo:** CPA Media Pte Ltd (t); World History Archive (bl). **217 Alamy Stock Photo:** MehmetO (tl). **Shutterstock:** Everett Collection (tr). **Alamy Stock Photo:** Art Collection 2 (br). **218 Alamy Stock Photo:** CPA Media Pte Ltd (tl); Everett Collection Inc (br). **219 Alamy Stock Photo:** Lordprice Collection (cl); CPA Media Pte Ltd (tr); Universal Art Archive (bl). **220-221 Alamy Stock Photo:** CPA Media Pte Ltd (c). **220 Alamy Stock Photo:** North Wind Picture Archives (bl1); Hamza Khan (bl2); INTERFOTO (bl3). **222-223 Getty Images:** PHAS (t).**222 Alamy Stock Photo:** Boaz Rottem (tl); 915 collection (b). **223 Alamy Stock Photo:** Joern Sackermann (bl); Granger Historical Picture Archive (br). **224 Getty Images:** Photo 12 (tl). **Alamy Stock Photo:** PjrStatues (cl); IanDagnall Computing (bl). **Getty Images:** Fine Art (bc). **Alamy Stock Photo:** GL Archive (br). **225 Alamy Stock Photo:** GL Archive (tr). **Getty Images:** Buyenlarge (br). **Alamy Stock Photo:** Everett Collection Inc (bc). **226 Alamy Stock Photo:** The History Collection (tl); Austrian National Library/Interfoto (cr); Granger Historical Picture Archive (bl). **227 Alamy Stock Photo:** The Print Collector (tl). **Getty Images:** Universal History Archive (cr). **Alamy Stock Photo:** The History Collection (bl). **Getty Images:** Otto Herschan Collection (br). **228-229 Getty Images:** Geoffrey Clements (bc). **228 Getty Images:** Museum of the City of New York (tl). **229 Getty Images:** Imagno (tl); PHAS (tr). **Alamy Stock Photo:** Everett Collection Historical (cl). **Bridgeman Images:** Wallace Collection, London (br). **230-231 Alamy Stock Photo:** Niday Picture Library (tc). **230 Alamy Stock Photo:** Peter Horree (tl). **Getty Images:** Bettmann (bl); ullstein bild Dtl. (br). **231 Alamy Stock Photo:** GL Archive (tr). **Getty Images:** Heritage Images (bl); Bettmann (bc1); Leemage (bc2); Heritage Images (br). **232-233 Alamy Stock Photo:** North Wind Picture Archives (b). **232 Alamy Stock Photo:** North Wind Picture Archives (tl); INTERFOTO (cr). **Getty Images:** Library of Congress (bl). **233 Bridgeman Images:** Michael Graham-Stewart (tl). **Alamy Stock Photo:** PRISMA ARCHIVO (tr); Chronicle (br). **234 Alamy Stock Photo:** CPA Media Pte Ltd (tl); Pictorial Press Ltd (bl); Photo 12 (cr). **235 Alamy Stock Photo:** The Granger Collection (t); Kayte Deioma (cl). **Getty Images:** George Rinhart (bc). **Alamy Stock Photo:** IanDagnall Computing (br). **236-237 Getty Images:** Keith Lance (tc). **236 akg-images:** akg (tr). **Alamy Stock Photo:** Everett Collection Inc (bl). **237 Alamy Stock Photo:** Heritage Image Partnership Ltd (tr); FLHC26 (bl); Pavel Dudek (br). **238-239 Getty Images:** Bettmann (c). **238 Getty Images:** STR (bl1). **Alamy Stock Photo:** Historic Collection (bl2); RBM Vintage Images (bl3). 240 **Alamy Stock Photo:** The Picture Art Collection (t). **Getty Images:** Universal History Archive (bl); Photo 12 (br). **241 Getty Images:** Hulton Archive (tr); Historical (br). **242 Alamy Stock Photo:** Science History Images (tl). **Getty Images:** Hulton Archive (b). **243 Getty Images:** DEA / A. DAGLI ORTI (t); Marka (bl); Galerie Bilderwelt (bc1). **Alamy Stock Photo:** Sueddeutsche Zeitung Photo (bc2); INTERFOTO (br). **244 Getty Images:** Universal History Archive (tl); Fred Stein Archive (tr). **Alamy Stock Photo:** Heritage Image Partnership Ltd (b). **245 Alamy Stock Photo:** Art Library / © Succession Picasso / DACS, London 2021 (t); Pictorial Press Ltd (bl); INTERFOTO (br). **246 Alamy Stock Photo:** Time Trip (tl); Shawshots (cr); Chronicle (b). **247 Alamy Stock Photo:** Ian Dagnall (tr). **Getty Images:** Bettmann (b). **248 Alamy Stock Photo:** Pictorial Press Ltd (t); Chronicle (bl). **Dorling Kindersley:** Andy Crawford / Imperial War Museum (br). **249 Alamy Stock Photo:** Shawshots (tl); Steve Allen Travel Photography (tr); Science History Images (bl); Shawshots (br). **250 Alamy Stock Photo:** IanDagnall Computing (tl); CPA Media Pte Ltd (bc). **Shutterstock:** Everett Collection (br). **251 Alamy Stock Photo:** Marc Tielemans (tr). **Getty Images:** Paul Popper/Popperfoto (bl). **252-253 Alamy Stock Photo:** Science History Images (c). **252 Getty Images:** Topical Press Agency (tl); Popperfoto (cr); Photo 12 (bl). **253 Alamy Stock Photo:** Entertainment Pictures (bl); Granger Historical Picture Archive (br). **254-255 Alamy Stock Photo:** Sueddeutsche Zeitung Photo (c). **254 Getty Images:** New York Daily News Archive (bl1); Hulton Archive (bl2); Hulton Archive (bl3). **256 Alamy Stock Photo:** Dinodia Photos (tl); CPA Media Pte Ltd (bl). **257 Getty Images:** Hulton Archive (tr); Photo 12 (cl). **258 Alamy Stock Photo:** World History Archive (tl). **Getty Images:** Popperfoto (c); Universal History Archive (br). **259 Getty Images:** ullstein bild Dtl. (tl); Central Press / Stringer (cr). **Alamy Stock Photo:** mccool (cra); Granger Historical Picture Archive (br). **260 Alamy Stock Photo:** Sueddeutsche Zeitung Photo (tl). **Dorling Kindersley:** Dreamstime.com: Gepapix (tr). **Alamy Stock Photo:** Pictorial Press Ltd (bl). **Getty Images:** Fox Photos / Stringer (br). **261 Alamy Stock Photo:** Photo 12 (tr); Andrew Harker (br). **262-263 Getty Images:** Photo 12 (c). **262 Alamy Stock Photo:** Shawshots (tl); CPA Media Pte Ltd (bl); Shawshots (bc1); Granger Historical Picture Archive (bc2). **Getty Images:** Keystone-France (br). **263 Getty Images:** IWM (tr). **Alamy Stock Photo:** mccool (br). **264 Alamy Stock Photo:** Heritage Image Partnership Ltd (tl). **Getty Images:** Picture Post/IPC Magazines (tc). **Alamy Stock Photo:** World History Archive (bl). **265 Alamy Stock Photo:** Pictorial Press Ltd (tl). **Getty Images:** Universal History Archive (br). **266 Getty Images:** Bettmann (tl). **Alamy Stock Photo:** World History Archive (tr). **Getty Images:** Bettmann (bc). **267 Getty Images:** HUGO H. MENDELSOHN (tl). **Alamy Stock Photo:** DBI Studio (br). **268-269 Alamy Stock Photo:** Everett Collection Historical (r). **268 Alamy Stock Photo:** Alexander Perepelitsyn (cl); Science History Images (bl). **270-271 Alamy Stock Photo:** World History Archive (tl). **270 Getty Images:** MARIO TAMA / Stringer (cl). **Dorling Kindersley:** Gary Ombler / Wardrobe Museum, Salisbury (cr). **Alamy Stock Photo:** Everett Collection Inc (br). **271 Alamy Stock Photo:** INTERFOTO (bl). **Getty Images:** Popperfoto (br). **272 Getty Images:** Sovfoto (tl). **Alamy Stock Photo:** Historic Collection (cl); World History Archive (c). **Getty Images:** PAGES Francois (br). **273 Alamy Stock Photo:** World History Archive (tl); INTERFOTO (tr); Stephen Saks Photography (bl); Everett Collection Inc (bc1); Glasshouse Images (bc2); Science History Images (br). **274-275 Alamy Stock Photo:** CPA Media Pte Ltd (b). **274 Getty Images:** Central Press / Stringer (tl). **Alamy Stock Photo:** PhotoStock-Israel (tr). **Getty Images:** Stringer (cb). **275 Alamy Stock Photo:** Mick Sinclair (tr); Dennis Brack (br). **276-277 Getty Images:** New York Daily News Archive (c). **276 Getty Images:** Bettmann (bl1). **Alamy Stock Photo:** CBW (bl2); Granger Historical Picture Archive (bl3). **278 akg-images:** (tr). **Getty Images:** New York Daily News Archive (bl); Science & Society Picture Library (br). **279 Getty Images:** Bettmann (tl); STRINGER / Stringer (tc); Bettmann (br). **280-281 Alamy Stock Photo:** World History Archive (t). **280 Getty Images:** CARL DE SOUZA / Staff (bl); Hulton Archive / Stringer (br). **281 Alamy Stock Photo:** PA Images (bl). **Getty Images:** Handout (br). **282-283 NASA:** (b). **282 Alamy Stock Photo:** REUTERS (tl). **Getty Images:** Bettmann (clb). **282 NASA:** (cb); (crb). **283 Getty Images:** Rolls Press / Popperfoto (tl); Stringer (tr). **284 Alamy Stock Photo:** World History Archive (tl). **Dorling Kindersley:** Gary Ombler / Rob Arnold, Automobilia UK (cr). **Getty Images:** Rolls Press / Popperfoto (br). **285 Getty Images:** Jacques Pavlovsky (tr); Bettmann (bl). **Alamy Stock Photo:** Pictorial Press Ltd (br). **286 Getty Images:** Paolo KOCH (tr). **Alamy Stock Photo:** Newscom (crb). **Getty Images:** Science & Society Picture Library (bl). **Alamy Stock Photo:** betty finney (bc1). **Getty Images:** Karjean Levine (bc2). **Alamy Stock Photo:** REUTERS (br). **287 Alamy Stock Photo:** ITAR-TASS News Agency (tl). **Getty Images:** Universal History Archive (br). **288 Alamy Stock Photo:** FORUM Polska Agencja Fotografów (tc). **Getty Images:** Peter Charlesworth (cra). **Alamy Stock Photo:** Peter Jordan (bl). **289 NASA:** (tl); (c). **289 Shutterstock:** mark reinstein (bl). **Getty Images:** IWM (br). **290-291 Alamy Stock Photo:** BRIAN HARRIS (t). **290 Getty Images:** TASS (c); The Asahi Shimbun (bl); SHONE (br). **291 Alamy Stock Photo:** Hum Images (b). **292-293 Getty Images:** STR (r). **292 Getty Images:** JOEL ROBINE (cl); Chip HIRES (bl). **294 Getty Images:** David Turnley / Corbis / VCG (tl). **Alamy Stock Photo:** Sueddeutsche Zeitung Photo (bl). **295 Alamy Stock Photo:** JAUBERT French Collection (tl); Andia (cr). **Getty Images:** GABRIEL BOUYS / Staff (bl); Tom Stoddart / Reportage (bc1); PAUL J. RICHARDS / Staff (bc2); JOEL ROBINE / Staff (br). **296-297 Getty Images:** AFP / Stringer (b). **296 Getty Images:** Robert NICKELSBERG (ca); Staff (cb). **297 Getty Images:** TASS (tr). **298-299 Getty Images:** NurPhoto (c). **298 Getty Images:** Mint Images (bl1). **Alamy Stock Photo:** Noam Armonn (bl2); Xinhua (bl3). **300 Alamy Stock Photo:** Trinity Mirror / Mirrorpix (tl); World History Archive (bl). **301 NASA:** (t). **Alamy Stock Photo:** Everett Collection Historical (cl); Mark Pearson (br). **302-303 Alamy Stock Photo:** REUTERS (t). **302 Alamy Stock Photo:** UPI (ca); dpa picture alliance archive (bl); REUTERS (br). **303 Shutterstock:** Evan El-Amin (tr). **Alamy Stock Photo:** James Brittain-VIEW (br). **304 Getty Images:** FETHI BELAID (tl). **Alamy Stock Photo:** UPI (tr). **Getty Images:** John van Hasselt - Corbis (bl). **Alamy Stock Photo:** Pool Photo (br). **305 Getty Images:** NurPhoto (tr). **Alamy Stock Photo:** Gelia (cl); ZUMA Press, Inc. (cr). **306-307 Shutterstock:** faboi (tr). **306 Getty Images:** Ulrich Baumgarten (tl). **Alamy Stock Photo:** COP21 (ca); Shoeb Faruquee (bl). **307 Getty Images:** Kiran Ridley (cl); Bill Clark (br).